'In this excellent and authoritative book, N able insights into the troubled waters whe merge in the role of Prime Minister.'

Sir John C—

'A subtle and sophisticated contribution to the debate on the role of the Prime Minister, which also succeeds in being delightfully readable.'

David Lipsey, Labour Peer

'This is a timely attempt at helping us to better understand the role of the British Prime Minister and the challenges of providing effective political leadership. Mark Garnett has developed a thematic study which provides us with a range of new insights: a must-read for students and scholars with an interest in UK politics.'

Timothy Heppell, University of Leeds

'Approachably written, wide-ranging, and both historically aware and bang up to date, Mark Garnett's book helps explain why what has become an almost impossible job – one that offers presidential-style prominence but far less real power than many of us imagine – increasingly seems to attract such improbable politicians. A great read for anyone interested in the past, present and future of British politics.'

Tim Bale, Queen Mary University of London

The British Prime Minister in an Age of Upheaval

In loving memory of Joan Elizabeth 'Betty' Garnett

The British Prime Minister in an Age of Upheaval

Mark Garnett

polity

First published in 2021 by Polity Press

Polity Press
65 Bridge Street
Cambridge CB2 1UR, UK

Polity Press
101 Station Landing
Suite 300
Medford, MA 02155, USA

ISBN-13: 978-1-5095-3935-2
ISBN-13: 978-1-5095-3936-9 (pb)

A catalogue record for this book is available from the British Library.

Library of Congress Cataloging-in-Publication Data

Names: Garnett, Mark, 1963- author.
Title: The British prime minister in an age of upheaval / Mark Garnett.
Description: Medford : Polity Press, 2021. | Includes bibliographical references and index. | Summary: "A timely re-assessment of the role of the British Prime Minister from Thatcher to Johnson"-- Provided by publisher.
Identifiers: LCCN 2020038351 (print) | LCCN 2020038352 (ebook) | ISBN 9781509539352 (Hardback) | ISBN 9781509539369 (Paperback) | ISBN 9781509539376 (ePub)
Subjects: LCSH: Prime ministers--Great Britain. | Prime ministers--Great Britain--History. | Great Britain--Politics and government.
Classification: LCC JN405 .G37 2021 (print) | LCC JN405 (ebook) | DDC 941.086--dc23
LC record available at https://lccn.loc.gov/2020038351
LC ebook record available at https://lccn.loc.gov/2020038352

Typeset in 10.75 on 14 Adobe Janson by
Servis Filmsetting Ltd, Stockport, Cheshire
Printed and bound in Great Britain by 4edge Limited

For further information on Polity, visit our website: politybooks.com

Contents

Preface and acknowledgements

Writing a book is always a memorable experience, and not always in a positive way. An author, perhaps, can be forgiven for recalling the progress of a project from the initial proposal to the submission of a manuscript – and long-suffering publishers might wish that they could forget it. But if any book includes more than a brief reference to the production process it is usually a sure sign that the writer is suffering from an over-inflated ego.

On this occasion, however, a few words about the pre-history of the book seem to be justified. It originated in an invigorating conversation with Louise Knight, beginning with reflections on the political situation of the time and ending with a blurred outline of this book. It was September 2018, when the position of the Prime Minister, Theresa May, had already been the subject of considerable speculation for more than a year. In my innocence, I thought that it might be an appropriate occasion to take stock of developments in the prime ministerial role since 1979. More than once in the intervening months, I have wondered if the old curse should be adapted: to my (probably self-interested) mind, 'May you try to write a book about the Prime Minister in interesting times' seems far more menacing than the original version. Although the research began in 2018, the actual composition of the book has taken place during the 'lockdown' induced by the coronavirus pandemic.

In September 2018 Mrs May had already been the central figure in the most momentous events in British politics since 1945; and since her departure from office in the following summer almost every news bulletin seems to have featured developments which would have deserved inclusion in a study of the prime ministerial role in 'normal' times. Rather than demanding a reconsideration of the whole project, it seemed (to the author, at least) that these happenings, properly understood, confirmed the line of argument in my formal proposal for this book, which was written at a time when the British government felt able to disregard contingency planning for the onset of a viral pandemic. In order to remain true to the original plan (and to stay within the word-limit), developments since May's resignation are outlined in the concluding chapter.

Louise and her colleague Inès Boxman at Polity have exercised considerable patience while I waited (in vain) for a respite from events which were all too likely to have a significant impact on the argument of this book. I am very grateful to both of them; to my colleagues and friends at Lancaster University (especially David Denver and Richard Johnson); to Dick Leonard, who has written with such erudition and eloquence on every one of Britain's Prime Ministers; and to the students who subjected themselves in 2019–20 to my module on this subject. I am particularly sorry that I took so long to finish the book, preventing me from forcing those students to buy it.

Introduction

Speaking outside No. 10 Downing Street on 4 May 1979, Margaret Thatcher declared that being asked to form a government was 'the greatest honour that can come to any citizen in a democracy'. Almost exactly eighteen years later, the incoming Tony Blair referred to 'the huge responsibility that is upon me and the great trust that the British people have placed in me'. When Gordon Brown succeeded Blair in 2007 the new Prime Minister spoke as if he was still being screen-tested for a role he had coveted for so long: 'I have been privileged to have been granted the great opportunity to serve my country. And at all times I will be strong in purpose, steadfast in will, resolute in action.'

Even in an age when political rhetoric is regarded with widespread cynicism it would be difficult to question the sincerity of these sentiments, expressed by three very different politicians. Whether the ascent has been relatively easy and swift, or arduous and prolonged, the individuals who become Prime Minister have reached the summit of their ambitions. As John Major put it in a characteristic statement of the obvious after his party's defeat in the 1997 general election, 'It is a privilege that comes to very few people' (seventy-nine in 300 years). If anything, Prime Ministers tend to be even more effusive on leaving office – notwithstanding any professional or personal setbacks they might have suffered in the duration. In her last speech before her enforced departure from No. 10, Mrs Thatcher chose to overlook the traumatic circumstances of the last few days, assuring her audience that 'It's been a tremendous privilege to serve this country as Prime Minister – wonderfully happy years.' In July 2016 David Cameron said that he was 'very proud and very honoured' to have held the highest office. Three years later, the emotions of the departing Theresa May spilled over soon after her declaration that it had been 'the honour of my life' to serve as Prime Minister.

'Pride', 'honour' and 'privilege': these are the recurring words when British Prime Ministers make their exits and their entrances. In also referring to 'responsibility', Blair was following Thatcher, whose initial reply to questions about her feelings on becoming Prime Minister were 'Very excited, very aware of the responsibilities.' Both Thatcher and Blair occupied the office of Prime Minister for more than a decade and would have served for longer if their parliamentary colleagues had allowed it. Even their warmest admirers would have to acknowledge that the experience left a mark on them. Thatcher's tearful departure from Downing Street was a vivid reminder to the public of the human frailties which lay behind her 'Iron Lady' image. For his part, as leader of the Opposition Blair had been nicknamed 'Bambi' in recognition of his youthful zest; but this sobriquet was rarely heard after the Iraq War, which seemed to affect his health and his physical appearance. The shadow of Iraq even fell over his final appearance at Prime Minister's Question Time (27 July 2007); although his parting performance closed amid applause from many MPs (including Opposition members), Blair began his remarks by honouring three service personnel who had died serving their country, more than four years after his fateful decision to commit British troops to Iraq.

Far from easing into the role of respected elder statespeople, Blair and Thatcher continued to be very divisive figures in retirement. While this is perhaps understandable in those specific cases, far less controversial personalities like John Major and David Cameron are still reviled in some quarters. It would be an exaggeration to say that ex-premiers are without honour in their own country, but since the death of Baroness Thatcher in 2013 there have been no representatives of that exclusive club in the House of Lords, compared to four (Home, Wilson, Callaghan and Thatcher) after the 1992 general election.

Whatever the incumbents might say in public – and however difficult it is to quantify such things – there are good reasons for supposing that the job of British Prime Minister has become more demanding since 1979. For most people, the daily routine of a head of government (or, in presidential systems, heads of state) in any liberal democracy would be distinctly unappealing. When, in 2013, the Mayor of London, Boris Johnson, publicly confirmed that if an unexpected vacancy arose he would rather like to be Prime Minister, he conceded the possibility that it might be 'a very tough job' (Cockerell, 2013). Johnson's career since the 2019 general election serves as salutary testimony to the wisdom of the old adage, 'Be careful what you plot for' (see Conclusion). Leaving aside their extensive formal duties, Prime Ministers are subjected to twenty-four-hour scrutiny from the media; they are like emergency fire-fighters who are expected to rush to the scene of any significant blaze, douse the flames themselves and then give a press conference on the subject. Often they will be dealing with one incident when they are alerted to another. Apart from the unexpected 'events' which Harold Macmillan famously feared, routine matters can suddenly give rise to serious accusations aimed at the Prime Minister in person. As Steve Richards remarks, being leader of a political party in itself brings 'titanic demands' (Richards, 2019, 14). In political systems like Britain's, where electoral politics is conducted on shoestring budgets, the Prime Minister is an obvious fund-raising asset who can never be free from the fear of incipient scandal. Tony Blair's tenure was bookended by the Ecclestone affair (November 1997), which took away much of his initial lustre, and the 'cash for honours' revelations in the months before his enforced departure in 2007, resulting in him giving an exclusive interview to the police. Prime Ministers can expect limited personal privacy even after they have left office, requiring round-the-clock protection. Hounded on their holidays, they are often criticized for taking the temporary breaks which people in stress-free jobs regard as essential. Having a young (and in some recent cases, growing) family might make a Prime Minister look more like a 'normal' human being, but away from the cameras it will tend to have the opposite effect.

Why, then, do so many politicians continue to hanker after the role of Prime Minister? There has certainly been no shortage of aspirants in recent years. After David Cameron's resignation as party leader and Prime Minister in 2016, five Conservatives vied for the vacant positions. Three years later, when Theresa May finally brought an end to her inglorious innings, ten of her parliamentary colleagues volunteered to take her place. If the party had stuck by the rules in place in 1989–90, when Thatcher was challenged first by Sir Anthony Meyer and then by Michael Heseltine, it seems the ballot paper would have been even longer since candidates then required only a proposer and a seconder. However, it would be unwise to take this evidence at face value; more likely, the unusual circumstances of 2019 encouraged people who would normally have hesitated before throwing their hats into the ring to imagine that they might defy the odds (see chapter 2). Despite everything, finding an MP who would refuse to serve as Prime Minister is like looking for a 10-year-old who would turn down the chance to represent their country in a World Cup final.

The excessive personalization of British media commentary too easily gives rise to the notion that recent Prime Ministers have failed because they simply were not equipped for the job. There is no attempt in this book to deny that particular Prime Ministers have made maladroit decisions. However, the main purpose is to explore the possibility that the holders of the office would not have succeeded even if they had been of the very highest calibre. If the position of the Prime Minister has become dysfunctional – or, as New Labour apparatchiks liked to say, 'unfit for purpose' – the implications for British democracy would be profound. Even Prime Ministers who are reputed to be weak are expected to take responsibility for developments and decisions which, for ill or good, affect the present circumstances and future prospects of everyone living in Britain. In addition, whenever questions arise concerning the practices of other institutions, the Prime Minister is usually called upon to take a leading role in reforms. If the office of Prime Minister itself requires radical reform, this would help to explain why recent incumbents have made such a hash of opportunities to improve Britain's system of governance and political culture (e.g. John Major's attempt to clean up Parliament in the wake of 'cash for questions', and David Cameron's selective endorsement of proposals arising from the Leveson Inquiry into the conduct of the press: see chapter 4). From this perspective one can readily understand why Tony Blair blocked attempts to make the House of Lords more accountable, and why David Cameron (again) used his position to prevent even a preliminary step towards a more defensible voting system in the 2011 Alternative Vote referendum. Finally, if it really has become impossible to carry out this job in full conformity with the informal rules and conventions which have prevented the British system of government from becoming an 'elective dictatorship', it would enable us to understand why recent Prime Ministers have tended to act as if these restraints apply to other political actors but not themselves, and why governments now find it necessary to employ so many 'spin doctors' to justify their actions and create the *appearance* of success, often in blatant defiance of practical evidence.

Without anticipating the detail of the argument presented in this book, it is worth noting that while all liberal democracies have been affected by 'spin' in recent decades, arguably Britain is uniquely vulnerable to the contagion. This is because all Prime Ministers since 1945 – with the partial exception of Edward Heath – have felt it necessary to act as 'spin doctors' on behalf of their country, delivering speeches that present Britain as a major power which could (under appropriate leadership) prove even more influential on the global stage than in the days when its empire spanned more than a quarter of the inhabitable world (see chapter 5). It is possible that Margaret Thatcher really accepted this delusional view, although it would be more charitable to suppose that she thought British politicians had exaggerated the extent of the country's relative decline and that it was time for its leaders to err on the opposite side. It is, though, unlikely that any of Thatcher's successors have suffered from serious private illusions about Britain's relative position. Nevertheless, they have all participated, with apparent enthusiasm, in the self-defeating 'spin' operation, declaring that they are 'batting for Britain' (in dealings with the European Union (EU)) and boasting that the country 'punches above its weight' in matters relating to the non-European world. In this respect, at least, Thatcher and her successors have brought an unsustainable tension into their own working lives, forcing them somehow to live up to unrealistic expectations and leading (among other things) to the humiliating departures from office of David Cameron and Theresa May.

The Prime Minister in history and theory

Since its inception (generally associated with the prolonged political dominance of Sir Robert Walpole (1721–42)), the role of British Prime Minister has attracted considerable and understandable attention from a variety of perspectives. The interest has increased in the years since

1979, thanks chiefly to the arrival in office of the most noteworthy individual to hold the office since Churchill was finally chiselled out of Downing Street in 1955. Although the primary subject-matter is the same, and their approaches sometimes overlap, the authors of important studies of the role can be consigned to five camps.

(1) *Contemporary historians*: these focus on individual Prime Ministers – their innate qualities, and their interactions with the broader context of their careers – or a succession of such individuals. Anthony Seldon is a prime example, having published studies of Major, Blair, Brown, Cameron and May, all of which are based on meticulous research including interviews with key participants.

(2) *Practising (or former) politicians*: these include individuals (like Richard Crossman, John Mackintosh and even Dr Gordon Brown) who were academics as well as politicians, but also non-academics (like Tony Benn and Graham Allen) who have tried to reach a critical understanding of the Prime Minister's role rather than merely reflecting on current developments. These observers might seem more authoritative than people whose analyses arise from second-hand knowledge. However, the view from 'the inside' could be misleading for other reasons: certainly the practitioners who have written on this subject are far from unanimous in their conclusions.

(3) *Authors of memoirs and diaries*: these include politicians and important officials who have recounted their experiences and observations without the *primary* purpose of shedding light on the Prime Minister's role. During the Thatcher years it seemed obligatory for Cabinet ministers to write their memoirs. As sources of insights these were of variable quality, but the best (like Nigel Lawson's compendious *The View from No. 11* (1992)) are invaluable. The publication in 1993 of diaries written by the maverick Thatcherite Alan Clark sparked a revival of this genre. Even if original diaries were redacted before publication, their main value for scholars lay in the unwitting revelations – often ones which the authors thought too trivial to leave out. In this respect, Labour politicians and their highly placed supporters have been far more prolific than their Conservative counterparts, so that anyone who was sufficiently interested could compile a voluminous day-to-day record of New Labour's period in office (1997–2010) on the basis of these publications. The main contributor to this avalanche of research-rich material is Alastair Campbell. While his friend Alan Clark

enriched Britain's political literature by recounting the experiences of a narcissist who came close to the inner circles of British government, Campbell's published diaries are the reflections of an incurable, indefatigable reporter, whose diligence as a diarist makes even the prolific Tony Benn look like a dilettante.

(4) *Journalists*: these include authors who have provided day-to-day snapshots for various media outlets, as well as those (like Andrew Rawnsley and Tim Shipman) who have published substantial studies of specific episodes. It seems churlish to deny the most perceptive of these authors honorific membership of the 'contemporary historian' club. They are distinguished here by their different vantage point, as bona fide inhabitants of the 'Westminster village' rather than occasional academic visitors.

(5) Last, but emphatically not least, are *political scientists* whose contributions are outlined in the rest of this section, mainly for the benefit of students of the subject. Readers with non-academic reasons for reading the book can be assured that this part of the literature is not revisited until the concluding chapter; and even then the main purpose of the discussion is to summarize the argument offered here rather than to engage too closely with existing interpretations.

For political scientists who have examined the role since 1945, the key questions have concerned the decision-making *power* of Prime Ministers – 'Can they dominate the policy-making agenda, or are they heavily constrained by the Cabinet and/or other significant actors?' – and an evaluation of the role in relation to institutions in other countries (e.g. 'Is the British Prime Minister becoming more like a US President?'). Before 1979, the most widely discussed contributions came from scholars who argued that the Prime Minister's role was superseding that of the Cabinet, which since the publication in 1867 of Walter Bagehot's *The English Constitution* (1963) had been regarded as the fulcrum of the British system. According to the revised argument, Britain's government was now essentially 'prime ministerial'. Significantly, the best-known proponents of this view – John Mackintosh (1929–78) and Richard Crossman (1907–74) – were both active political practitioners as well as academics.

This new interpretation was not universally accepted, partly because of its troubling implications but also because it seemed at best an over-simplification of the real situation. All systems of government are complex – not least liberal democracies, which are supposed to depend on the voluntary adjustment of interests, mediated by sophisticated bureaucracies as well as political parties which are influential in themselves. Even before the advent of Margaret Thatcher, political scientists had qualified the picture presented by Mackintosh and Crossman (e.g. Jones, 1965, 167–85). They were joined in 1976 by an even more eminent analyst-practitioner, the recently retired Prime Minister Harold Wilson, who tried to demonstrate that Cabinet government was alive and well, thanks not least to his own unswerving fealty to constitutional convention (Wilson, 1976).

In his introduction to a volume devoted to the role of the Prime Minister, Anthony King wrote that, 'With luck, interest in the remarkable premiership of Margaret Thatcher will have the effect of further stimulating interest in the prime ministership' (King, 1985, 10). This was a pretty safe expectation, although the debate became more contentious after Thatcher had left office. Michael Foley's provocative book *The Rise of the British Presidency* (published in 1993) asserted that Thatcher's approach to governance had taken Britain beyond a merely 'prime ministerial' system, and that in important respects she had acted as if she were a President. As an expert in US politics, Foley was able to identify specific examples of 'presidential' tendencies during the Thatcher years. Using terms like 'spatial leadership' and 'leadership stretch', he argued that just like a US President British Prime Ministers can distance themselves from their parties, exploiting the media in particular as a means of reinforcing the idea that their authority arises from a personal connection with the electorate (Foley, 1993).

Foley's book could have appeared at a more propitious time. By 1993 Thatcher's successor, John Major, was projecting a very different style of leadership. Arguably, then, even if a British 'presidency' had risen during the 1980s it had sunk along with Thatcher herself – indeed her downfall could be attributed to a reaction against her domineering style. This course of events seemed to verify the opinion of the former Foreign Secretary Patrick Gordon Walker, who wrote in 1970 that a Prime Minister who 'habitually ignored the cabinet . . . could rapidly come to grief' (Gordon Walker, 1972, 106). Normality seemed to be restored under Major, and for most political scientists 'normality' meant collective government. The membership of the 'collective' did not necessarily coincide exactly with the ministers who formed the Cabinet, but this had never been the case. Rather, the 'core executive' consisted of the Prime Minister and representatives of institutions which enjoyed 'resources' of various kinds – that is, ministers in the most important departments and their senior civil servants (see, for example, Rhodes and Dunleavy, 1993; Smith, 1999). The 'prime ministerial/presidential' approaches depicted politics as a 'zero-sum game', in which an accretion of power for the Prime Minister entailed a corresponding loss for other actors and institutions. The 'core executive model' rejected this picture, presenting the relationship between the Prime Minister and senior colleagues as one of mutual dependence and co-operation. There was room in the core executive model for special advisers, too, but these relative newcomers to the political scene were not regarded as very significant since their 'resources' depended on ministerial favour – that is, if their political employers were unhappy with their services, their influence could be ended abruptly.

By the end of the millennium events had moved on, and in 2000 Foley published a new version of his book with a defiant title (*The British Presidency*) which suggested that his interpretation was now established fact rather than a provocative hypothesis. His argument was based chiefly on the first Blair Government (1997–2001), whose practices seemed in many respects to transcend Thatcher's tentative 'presidential' steps. However, as Foley himself knew very well, any claim that Britain was governed by a President was bound to run into the objections that its head of government was a constitutional monarch, and the Prime Minister (unlike a President) was directly responsible to Parliament. Foley's readers would be aware that he was trying to identify presidential *features* which had crept into a system whose formal constitutional status had not changed. However, his titles (and, often, his style of writing) gave a contrary impression; and others were less equivocal in their equation of New Labour with 'presidential' government. Indeed, the emphatically un-Blairite Labour MP Graham Allen published a very lively tract arguing that it would be much better for Britain if it implemented a formal presidential system of government, rather than suffering from the drawbacks which inevitably arose from a hybrid presidential/parliamentary system (Allen, 2003).

Despite Blair's presidential style the core executive approach was still generally accepted among political scientists at the time of his resignation in 2007 (Diamond, 2014, 193–213). It received timely support from scholars, notably Andrew Blick and George Jones, who found plentiful precedents for contemporary developments, even in the practices of the earliest Prime Ministers like Walpole and Pitt the Younger, who had employed the ancestors of today's 'spin doctors' and special advisers (Blick and Jones, 2010). While invaluable from an historical point of view, this *plus ca change* approach could be countered by the argument that examples drawn from the period before universal adult suffrage (1928) related to a very different political context. Since then, the exigencies of 'total war' would have promoted a lasting enhancement of the Prime Minister's role, even under a premier with none of Churchill's relish for supreme command, or Clement Attlee's eagerness to exploit what remained of the wartime spirit in order to push through a socio-economic revolution.

Since 2003 the debate has continued but in a more subdued and nuanced fashion. While rejecting the 'presidential' thesis, most contributors have accepted that the Prime Minister's role has been strengthened (e.g. Heffernan, 2005; Dowding, 2012). The resulting scholarship has enhanced understanding of British politics in general, but it still reflects the preoccupation of political scientists with definitions, models and institutional comparisons. It is a common refrain in the academic literature that the role of the Prime Minister is still 'under-theorized'. It could be argued to the contrary that much of the work on the Prime Minister emanating from political scientists suffers from an *excess* of theory, being conducted within analytical frameworks which downplay other considerations (in particular, Britain's relative decline as a global power, and the influence of the media; see Rose, 2001)), and draws too heavily on formal interviews tinged (even tainted) by hindsight, rather than contemporary media reports or the published diaries of key participants.

While the core executive approach is a valuable corrective to the notion that the Prime Minister can govern without co-operation of some kind, this is an unavoidable feature even of undemocratic states and thus cannot shed much light on the way in which the role has developed since 1979 (Brown, 2010). The core executive model focuses on the distribution of *power* – that is, in simplistic terms, the ability to get things done, for which co-operation (willing or not) is obviously needed. In Britain, the realization of most policy objectives (better health care, higher standards of education, etc.) cannot possibly be effected by a single person, but depends on co-operation at all levels down to nurses and classroom teachers. The argument presented here is that a more relevant question relating to the Prime Minister is that of *prominence*, particularly in terms of electoral politics. This is much more compatible with a zero-sum game; if the front page of every newspaper features a photograph of the Prime Minister, his or her colleagues are being denied equal publicity, even if they are making more noteworthy contributions to governance.

A book which is more concerned with prominence than power is suggested by other developments in the academic literature. For example, Rod Rhodes and others have investigated developments within the British state, which in their view has been 'hollowed out' in recent decades (e.g. Rhodes, 1994; Campbell and Wilson, 1995). This seems difficult to square with the core executive model, since it implies that ministers and government departments have been losing their ability to effect constructive change and hence have fewer 'resources' at their disposal. On the face of it, this does look like a significant shift in the Whitehall power-game; if ministers have lost status and authority, the same is not true (at least directly) of the Prime Minister, who has no departmental responsibilities. If governmental capacity has weakened, more onus would be placed on the Prime Minister to create the impression of success, for vote-winning purposes. On a related theme, Patrick Diamond has argued persuasively that, having been seriously affected by the hollowing out of the state, civil servants now increasingly find themselves being 'politicized' – that is, working to enhance the popularity of the party in office, rather than pursuing what they conceive to be the national interest (Diamond, 2018). Looking back over the period since 1979, it is difficult not to hanker after the days in which departmental ministers and their civil servants really *did* enjoy 'independent resources'; in terms of the ability to achieve constructive results (and to palm off responsibility when things go wrong) Prime Ministers themselves would be better off if this were still true.

It could be argued that too much of the political science literature on the British Prime Minister has been vitiated by disciplinary perspectives. If we cannot hope for 'joined-up government', we can at least aspire to joined-up thinking, approaching recent developments in the Prime Minister's position without theoretical preconceptions. The changes in the role since Thatcher will become apparent to anyone who reads Harold Wilson's contribution to the debate. In *The Governance of Britain* (1976), Wilson still felt able to describe the role of the British Prime Minister as 'one of the most exciting and certainly one of the best organised' positions in the democratic world (Wilson, 1976, x). If at least one of these claims is no longer true – and 'well organised' is not the term which immediately springs to mind in relation to any aspect of the contemporary British political system – inquiries into the most probable causes must be as broadly based as possible, and as free as humanly possible from any 'mind-forged manacles'.

Rationale and structure of the book

The approach of this book reflects my view that attempts to draw on all of these sources, updated and reassessed at suitable intervals, can themselves serve as useful contributions to the subject, and that these exercises have been too rare. Ideally, books of this kind can be written in a way which informs the general reader as well as offering suggestions for students. The main purpose of this attempt is to provide evidence and analysis which allow all readers to draw their own conclusions about changes in the Prime Minister's role since 1979. In the interests of brevity, and to de-clutter the text, I have tried to confine the references to occasions when particular works really need to be cited. The bibliography would have been much longer if it had included even a representative sample of the publications which have affected my views on this subject.

The remaining chapters of the book deal with various aspects of the Prime Minister's role. The format is thematic, but within each of the themes the treatment is broadly chronological (normally beginning with Thatcher and ending with Theresa May – the early part of the Johnson premiership is discussed in the concluding chapter). There is no attempt to provide an exhaustive list of the Prime Minister's resources, and some aspects of the position (e.g. its reliance in so many ways on prerogative powers, and responsibilities in relation to nuclear weapons) do not figure prominently in the discussion compared to the invaluable works of scholars like Lord (Peter) Hennessy (see, for example, Hennessy, 2000, 102–46). The primary focus of the present study is on the factors which have allowed Prime Ministers to retain so many of the duties and privileges once assigned to the monarchy, despite the subsequent introduction of democratic procedures.

With a structure which is chronological as well as thematic, the book can also serve as a history of UK politics since 1979 – albeit one which is skewed towards the prime ministerial perspective. This explains why devolution within the UK does not feature heavily – British Prime Ministers, including Blair, who oversaw the beginning of the process, have acted as if this constitutional development never happened. The reality, of course, is very different, and the divergencies between the various components of the UK have become increasingly important thanks to the 2016 referendum and the Covid-19 pandemic (which also revealed the centrifugal potential of directly elected Mayors, particularly in the north of England). My only excuse for adopting the prime ministerial perspective is that a separate full-length book would be required to do justice to the subject of devolution.

The composition of the book has coincided with momentous developments; indeed, it could be argued that the British public has been subjected to continuous upheaval since the financial crisis which began in 2007, giving it little chance to pause for reflection. Whatever challenges might come in the future, it is unlikely that the British political system will be capable of meeting them unless the prime ministerial role is reconsidered. H. H Asquith – who was well qualified to pass judgement – famously wrote that 'The office of the prime minister is what its holder chooses and is able to make of it.' The main conclusion of this book is that the one thing a contemporary Prime Minister cannot 'choose' to do is to make a success of the role, which has become increasingly dysfunctional along with the other institutions of Westminster and Whitehall. The only recourse for Prime Ministers who care for 'the verdict of history' is to fall back on a minimalist definition of 'success' – that is, in terms of victory in the next election, even if this is owed primarily to weaknesses or divisions among Opposition parties. For a healthy liberal democracy this would hardly suffice as a measurement of 'success': in particular, it implies that whenever the national interest conflicts with the electoral needs of the Prime Minister's political party, the incumbent of No. 10 is now under overwhelming pressure to prefer the latter. The unsettling signs in recent years that British Prime Ministers have learned to accept this as their over-riding 'performance indicator' is one of the main motivations for this book about their role.

1

Majority leader

Parliament – and more specifically the House of Commons – is a convenient place to start an exploration of the Prime Minister's role. In his great
1867 study of the 'English' constitution, Walter Bagehot depicted the
Commons as a glorified electoral college: its members chose the Cabinet,
which in turn nominated one individual to serve as head of the government (Bagehot, 1963, 150–2). In Bagehot's day, MPs were relatively
free from party discipline, and the requirement that the Prime Minister
should be able to muster a majority in the Commons meant that proven
parliamentary performers (even if they happened to be members of the
House of Lords, in those days before its powers were curtailed) enjoyed a
considerable advantage when the 'electoral college' made its choice.

In the past, Prime Ministers tended to be chosen because they commanded the confidence of the Commons. Now, when Prime Ministers
command the confidence of the Commons they do so *because* they are
Prime Ministers. The purpose of this chapter is to examine the changing relationship between Prime Ministers and the Commons in recent
decades, and the way in which the 'majority leader' is selected today.

The Prime Minister in Parliament since 1979

The fact that Prime Ministers are elected to the House of Commons
on the same territorial basis as other MPs is never forgotten either by

holders of the office or by their constituents. The latter rarely feel that they are inadequately represented, since Prime Ministers always have a well-qualified team to deal with any local or national issues which constituents might raise, and their visits are likely to evoke feelings of pride and gratitude even among residents who voted for one of their opponents. Prime Ministers are usually glad to return the compliments, claiming that the freely expressed views of their constituents help to keep them 'grounded' in public opinion more generally. Yet this commendable attempt to feel the public pulse is not necessarily very informative, since the mere fact of being Prime Minister seems to have a distorting effect on the mindset of one's constituents. Since 1979, in every general election after a Prime Minister has stood down as an MP, the vote for her or his successor as the party's constituency candidate has declined.

Not even the most earnest and perceptive Prime Minister will find it any easier to monitor the mood amongst MPs, which is much more volatile and likely to be concealed from those who seek to gather information on the Prime Minister's behalf. If Prime Ministers conduct their own fact-finding exercises – for example by touring the numerous places of refreshment available to MPs at Westminster – the response is likely to be even less informative. At larger gatherings, like the notorious Conservative 1922 Committee, the banging of desks to greet the Prime Minister could mean almost anything – even, occasionally, sincere support.

In one respect, what Michael Foley called 'leadership stretch' has always been inherent in the role of Prime Minister (Foley, 1993, 120–47). There are unmistakable clues in both of the words of the job title. Being a minister of any kind means that one is a decision-maker, however humble. A Cabinet minister is not only a decision-maker, but also someone who attends meetings where other people's decisions are discussed. People who reach this status are bound to experience a change in perspective which affects their personal relations with backbench MPs. Becoming Prime Minister takes this enforced estrangement to a different level; the people who merely discuss the decisions taken (or proposed) by ministers are far removed from the individual who oversees the whole decision-making process. For politicians who first enter the Commons fired by an ambition to reach the top rung of the ladder, it is natural after they have realized this goal to consign their fellow MPs to three classes: those who would like at some point to succeed them or at least to graduate into the 'decision-making' ranks; a number of embittered politicians whose ministerial careers have already ended; and others who genuinely wish for nothing more than to continue as representatives of the people who gave them the right to sit in Parliament. When contemplating all of these groups, Prime Ministers must find it difficult to repress mingled sentiments of pity, contempt and fear. Thanks to the erection of security gates at the end of Downing Street – one of several relevant developments during the Thatcher years, but this time for very good reasons – the barriers to real collegiality are both physical and psychological. As David Cameron lamented in his memoirs, 'It didn't matter that I took great pains to be accessible and inclusive. Being behind those black iron gates symbolised (and to a certain extent produced) separateness' (Cameron, 2019, 237).

When they answer the first of the weekly Prime Minister's Questions (PMQs: see below), Prime Ministers still have to include 'my duties in this house' as part of their standard reply to an inquiry about their schedule for the day. This is a cleverly worded formula, since there are no prescribed parliamentary 'duties' for any MP, let alone the Prime Minister. If so minded, Prime Ministers can feel that they have discharged their duties merely by turning up for PMQs every week while Parliament is sitting (although when they are unavoidably absent they can supply a deputy). David Cameron might have felt that he 'took great pains' to act like a normal MP, but the days of Winston Churchill, who in his final term of office (1951–5) often turned up to listen to debates even when he had no intention of speaking, are long gone.

Why has this happened? Arguably, a more pertinent question is why an inevitable development was delayed for so long. Until 1979, it might be claimed, the head of government wasted time in the Commons which could always have been used more profitably elsewhere. Even if a particular bill was judged to be very important to the Government's overall purpose, the presence of the Prime Minister on the front bench during debates – unless there was a serious prospect of defeat – could seem superfluous. Indeed, it might suggest a lack of confidence in the Cabinet minister whose department was directly responsible for the proposed legislation. Far better, then, to use the authority of the office more sparingly, saving it for those occasions when the incumbent was really needed.

As so often, the trendsetter in this respect was Margaret Thatcher.

A forensic study of prime ministerial involvement in the House of Commons reports that 'her speech making and her interventions in debates dwindled away to virtually nothing during her long tenure of office . . . Many Tory MPs elected after 1987 claimed almost never to have met her' (Rhodes and Dunleavy, 1993, 288). Thatcher's semi-detachment certainly did not arise from any fears concerning her ability as a Commons performer: her reported concern that she might lose a vote of confidence during the Westland Affair in January 1986 suggests misgivings about the substance of her argument on that occasion, rather than her mode of delivery. Since radio broadcasts of the proceedings of the House began in the year before Thatcher became Prime Minister, voters could hear, as well as read about, her combative debating style. However, until the Falklands War of 1982 her leadership of the Conservative Party was not secure, and many MPs thought that her economic policies were leading the party to electoral disaster. Given the choice, not even the most self-confident individual will spend too long in the company of so-called supporters who either offer insincere encouragement or show active hostility.

In short, the unavoidable institutional considerations which create a distance between the Prime Minister and her or his parliamentary party were reinforced in Thatcher's case by ideological ones. The default position was non-attendance: the Prime Minister would only make the short trip from Downing Street to the Palace of Westminster when there really was no alternative. Displays of Thatcher's parliamentary pugilism were best reserved for occasions when the Government was under attack from the Opposition, and backbenchers were most strongly minded to rally behind their leader, whatever their real feelings. It was perhaps fortunate for Thatcher that her Labour opponents repeatedly called votes of no confidence in her government, providing regular opportunities for her to display her virtuosity. The Opposition even called such a vote on the day when she resigned as Prime Minister in 1990, as if they wanted her to depart in a blaze of glory. After her contribution the Liberal Democrat leader Paddy Ashdown congratulated Thatcher on 'a bravura performance of the sort which she had made her own'; one of her backbenchers, Michael Carttiss, probably spoke for many of his colleagues in the emotionally charged chamber when he exclaimed, 'You can wipe the floor with these people.'[1] Thus Thatcher's infrequent attendance actually augmented her legendary status: it meant that she was never afflicted by the law of diminishing returns.

Thatcher's successor John Major was a much more gregarious individual, with consensual views to match. By the time of his departure from the Commons in 2001 Major had few reasons to thank his immediate predecessor, but he could at least feel some gratitude for her precedent of parliamentary truancy. While Thatcher had been fortunate to face ineffective Opposition leaders, in his second term (1992–7) Major was lumbered with John Smith and Tony Blair, who would have been difficult to master even without the numerous misfortunes which befell Major's government. While Thatcher's relish for verbal confrontation meant that she was at her best when at bay, Major's speaking style reflected a preference for compromise which was increasingly ineffective as Conservative divisions over Europe deepened after 1992. In July 1993, at the height of the parliamentary crisis over the ratification of the Maastricht Treaty, Major famously gave vent to his feelings about critics within his Cabinet. At the time, most media speculation focused on the identity of these disagreeable individuals. Yet Major was talking about the state of his parliamentary party, and the probability that the sacking of Eurosceptic ministers would only make things worse. As the Prime Minister put it, the Conservative benches were already full of 'the dispossessed and the never-possessed . . . We don't want three more of the Bastards out there' (Seldon, 1997, 389–90).

Major's outburst was more understandable because he had just experienced a thirty-six-hour ride on a parliamentary roller-coaster. In a debate on the Social Chapter of the Maastricht Treaty (22 July 1993), Tory Eurosceptics had made it no secret that they were exploiting the issue as their only realistic chance of preventing the ratification of the Treaty. Accordingly, they joined Opposition parties in voting to reject an 'opt-out' which Major had negotiated at Maastricht, in the hope of appeasing potential critics. Major – fresh from a somewhat premature 'end-of-term' party for MPs held at No. 10 – was judged by one of the attendees to have 'opened the debate quite brilliantly. He has never been better. He was simple, direct, passionate . . . When he sat down at the finish, he looked so happy. And we roared our approval and waved our order papers in the air' (Brandreth, 1999, 198–9). A Prime Minister with the ability to command a majority in the Commons, and who had presented a plausible argument with clarity and conviction, ought to have prevailed comfortably. However, the government lost the division by eight votes. Major promptly announced that the government's motion would be brought back on the following day, this time as an issue of confidence which would precipitate a general election if the result was unchanged. When Major spoke in the confidence debate, the same observer thought that he 'was tired and it showed. The speech was workmanlike, but lacklustre.' In contrast, Labour's John Smith was ebullient. In his memoirs, Major himself agreed with these appraisals. However, as Major put it, 'The real action took place outside the Chamber. Conservative constituencies were livid with the rebels for risking the government's survival in defence of a Labour policy' (Brandreth, 1999, 201). MPs duly voted to reverse their decision of the previous day.

If Major had delivered a lame speech on the original motion but followed up with a personal best in the confidence debate, the voting would almost certainly have been the same. He was left to wonder 'Was there something I could have said . . . a speech, a broadcast, an argument which might have begun my party's journey back to sanity?' (Major, 1999, 384–5). On the evidence of July 1993, probably not; certainly, if there was such a verbal formula, Major never found it. It was not surprising that, after the defeat of his party in the 1997 general election, Major immediately sought refuge from politics at the Oval cricket ground, where his beloved Surrey gave the British Universities the kind of pasting which Labour had just administered to the Conservatives.

The Prime Minister versus Parliament

While one senses that Major would have spent more time in the Commons if circumstances had been different, Tony Blair's absenteeism was more in keeping with his character and style of government. Between the elections of 2001 and 2005 he voted in only 7.5 per cent of Commons divisions.[2] These were years in which Labour enjoyed an overwhelming parliamentary majority, so the absence of the Prime Minister was hardly likely to lead to any shock government defeats. Yet the 2001–5 Parliament also saw revolts over the Iraq War which were 'the largest rebellions by MPs of any governing party – Labour, Conservative or Liberal – on any type of policy for over 150 years'

(Cowley, 2005, 5). Iraq, of course, was a highly controversial foreign policy issue – and Blair had not only been present during the crucial debate of 18 March 2003, but had delivered an impassioned speech. However, Labour MPs also rebelled in significant numbers over elements of the government's domestic programme – proposed reforms in education and the health service, and the attempted removal of two chairs of backbench Commons select committees (Gwyneth Dunwoody (Transport) and Donald Anderson (Foreign Affairs)). The latter rebellion, on 16 July 2001, led to government defeats.

The idea that the physical presence – let alone the oratorical powers – of Prime Ministers is unnecessary except on rare occasions of dire need reflects the widespread view that the House of Commons has become a mere 'rubber stamp' thanks largely to the discipline imposed by party business managers ('whips'), enhanced by the increased prevalence of 'career politicians' who realize that their prospects will be impaired by a record of rebellion. However, ample evidence suggests that the House of Commons has become increasingly whip-resistant over recent decades. In this context the votes in favour of Dunwoody and Anderson held particular significance, since these results reflected a desire to curb the power of party whips to interfere with the composition of Commons select committees. The idea of truly independent committee chairs was particularly unpalatable to Tony Blair, who had instituted a parliamentary Liaison Committee before which he would appear for lengthy, twice-yearly discussions. If he could no longer control the membership of this Committee his initiative would no longer look like a bright idea; he might even have to fend off some awkward questions.

The leading authority on parliamentary rebellions, Philip Cowley, has tried hard to dispel the laziest assumptions about the supine nature of MPs. In particular, even before the Iraq votes he stressed that rebellions can be highly significant whether or not the government wins the vote. In the 2001–5 Parliament, despite its crushing majority the Blair Government sometimes had to offer concessions to its critics during the passage of legislation; and even this was not enough to buy off the most determined opponents. While votes leading to government defeats provide great copy for reporters – and moments of high drama even for viewers and listeners with limited interest in political issues – serious students of British politics should pay at least equal attention to the votes which never take place, because the government has accepted the certainty of defeat and retires from the field to rethink its approach.

However, while Cowley's main purpose is to defend MPs from the allegation that the Commons is inhabited by rival flocks of sheep, developments over the last few decades suggest equally interesting conclusions in relation to the executive branch. From this different perspective, it seems that the mistaken view of government MPs as lobby fodder is not restricted to ill-informed commentators. As we have seen, the select few who reach the summit of their political ambitions by 'kissing hands' with the monarch and taking on the role of Prime Minister will find it very difficult to retain their old impressions of the humble parliamentary foot soldiers they have left behind. Even a Prime Minister who originally entered Parliament with limited ambitions – a hypothetical case in the period under review, although John Major might be regarded as a reasonable approximation – will tend to assume that, given the right inducements, a sufficient proportion of the flock can be guided back into the party fold. Ultimately, this thought process is underpinned by the belief that a governing party which indulges in public disagreements is likely to lose the next general election. The prospect of a spell in Opposition is deemed to be an adequate deterrent to all backbenchers: those who seek ministerial office will have to recalculate their planned ascent, those who have abandoned their ambitions will no longer be able to find consolation as awkward players in a winning team, while the MPs who never wanted more than to serve their constituents will become impotent onlookers as their opponents implement distasteful policies. Even worse, MPs who allow their party to fight an election in a state of disunity might lose their own seats.

When evaluating the true significance of parliamentary rebellions, it is necessary to take account of the *subjects* of the votes as well as the scale of non-compliance. Necessarily, contextual factors are impressionistic, whereas votes against a government measure can be counted. However, when contextual factors are taken into account the rebellious propensities of Labour MPs between 2001 and 2005 seem much less impressive than the bare statistics would suggest. Although Thatcher did encounter resistance from 'One Nation' Conservatives – and indeed in April 1986 her government was thwarted by MPs from all wings of the party in its attempt to relax the laws on Sunday trading – her internal critics were effectively hamstrung by the party's refrain that it had always been on the side of 'free enterprise', even during the years when it had accepted the broad outlines of the post-war settlement introduced by Clement Attlee's Labour governments (1945–51). In other words, Thatcher could be seen as a more radical exemplar of a well-worn Conservative theme, and one which had always played very well among grassroots members. For its part, in Opposition after 1979 Labour had accepted many of Thatcher's reforms by gradual steps; but when the party won its landslide majority of 1997 there was a widespread expectation (among the general public, as well as MPs and party members) of at least a modest reaction against 'Thatcherism'. Even Blair's post-election pledge that 'We have been elected as New Labour and we will govern as New Labour' was taken with a pinch of salt; after all, at the beginning of her premiership Thatcher had proposed that 'Where there is discord, may we bring harmony', and even her most ardent admirers would have to admit that these reassuring sentiments were rarely reflected in her subsequent decisions.

From this perspective, whereas Thatcher's most controversial policies were almost invariably attuned to 'core' Conservative voters, many of New Labour's measures represented a direct challenge to the party's grassroots members and MPs who had embarked on political careers in order to preserve (or extend) the Attlee Governments' reforms. The first Blair Government (1997–2001) flew an early quasi-Thatcherite kite by asking MPs to vote for a welfare reform – restricting the benefits available to lone parents – which would not have won support from any Labour member if it had been proposed by a Conservative. As such, the tally of Labour rebels – just forty-seven, plus around twenty abstentions in the vote of 11 December 1997 – was remarkably modest. The impression that the episode had been engineered by the government to smoke out and punish potential troublemakers at an early stage was reinforced by media reports that, although the government easily won the vote, the rebels would be subjected to sanctions of various kinds.

In other words, it could be argued that the most significant rebellions on domestic matters during the Blair years were *provoked* by a government which was working on the assumption that most of its MPs would swallow almost anything which was proposed by the first Labour government in eighteen years. This marked a sharp contrast to the best-remembered parliamentary confrontations during the premiership of John Major, when Tory MPs were the aggressors, even when the government had already met them more than halfway. In fact, shortly after the government's re-election with a reduced majority in April 1992 there had been a departure from this pattern whose significance has been obscured by the vivid memory of the Maastricht debates.

In October 1992 British Coal announced a programme to close thirty-one out of fifty deep mines, leading to the loss of 30,000 jobs. The President of the Board of Trade, Michael Heseltine, promptly unveiled a generous package of redundancy payments and retraining programmes. Although the closures were explained on grounds which the government had used during the 1984–5 miners' strike – namely that the pits were 'uneconomical' – they were denounced by church leaders and Conservative MPs as well as Opposition politicians and trade unionists. Backbenchers on the government side were particularly outraged because the cuts would affect many of the workers who had refused to join the 1984–5 strike. Thus Tory MPs who were already feeling guilty because of the fall of Margaret Thatcher were now being asked to approve a measure which would threaten the livelihoods of people who had played an heroic part in the defeat of the National Union of Mineworkers (NUM). Short of targeting Falklands veterans, the government could not have found a more effective way of alienating its core supporters. The announcement was even less comprehensible because it came just a few weeks after the humiliation of 'Black Wednesday' (16 September 1992), when Britain was forced out of the Exchange Rate Mechanism (ERM) of the European Monetary System (EMS); indeed, the plans had been leaked to the press just two days after that traumatic episode. The government was under attack for its economic management even before that fatal blow to its reputation for competence. Faced with the certainty of defeat over the pit closures, Heseltine cobbled together a package of concessions and was able to win approval for a revised programme once the initial outcry had faded (James, 1997, 186–94).

In his memoirs, John Major claimed that although he had been consulted over the closures and had to accept 'ultimate responsibility', he knew by 'instinct' that the announcement would be 'an absolute political disaster' (Major, 1999, 670). This does not accord with Heseltine's own account, which describes a meeting chaired by Major in the autumn of 1992; at that time, the general view was that the closures 'would not prove that difficult to handle' (Heseltine, 2000, 437). This assumption could only have been based on the experience of the Thatcher years, when the government made numerous grim announcements without suffering sizeable parliamentary rebellions. Yet although the Major Government could claim to have won a clear 'mandate' at the 1992 general election, its overall majority of just twenty-one seats left it vulnerable to just a handful of determined malcontents. The obvious lesson, even before the ERM fiasco, was that the government should consult carefully with potential rebels before taking any controversial decisions. Its failure to do so on this incendiary issue, in those circumstances, meant that for the first time in living memory Conservative rebels who forced a government climbdown were likely to be praised rather than pilloried in the right-wing press. The lesson that there are worse things in politics than a reputation for disunity was not lost on Labour MPs, especially since the fate of the coal mines was particularly important to them.

During the Blair years the parliamentary arithmetic was of a kind which made it difficult for the most maladroit government to bring about its own downfall. As we have seen, however, Blair and his colleagues did not fail for want of trying, starting with the deliberate provocation of the 1997 welfare reforms. After Maastricht, Major had effectively surrendered to his Eurosceptic tormentors. At times it seemed as if Blair's main purpose was to demonstrate that there were no circumstances which could make him equally impotent. Parliament, and the Labour Party in particular, had to be reminded of who was master. As Major had shown, the Prime Minister's ultimate weapon in any serious trial of strength was the threat of dissolving Parliament. Ideally, recalcitrant MPs would be brought back into line by the merest hint that the Prime Minister might make a particular vote into an issue of confidence in the government. Blair's mismanagement of his majority is illustrated by his tendency to make this threat explicit. Thus, for example, at a press conference in December 2003 he staked his personal authority on the passage of legislation which would introduce 'top-up' fees for university students. Over Iraq he had no need to issue a similar warning – if he had lost the vote authorizing action his position would obviously have been untenable – but since then he had made a veiled reference to his 'ultimate weapon' when trying to stave off a rebellion over foundation hospitals (Cowley, 2005, 196–7, 162). Back in 1976, Harold Wilson had written that a Prime Minister who tried 'to bring his colleagues to heel by the unilateral threat of a dissolution . . . would be certifiable' (Wilson, 1976, 40). Whether or not that word was appropriate in Blair's case, his tactics were certainly reminiscent of the Cold War notion of MAD – Mutually Assured Destruction – and invited backbenchers to call his bluff. Usually (as in the case of top-up fees) Blair's confrontational approach was the prelude to a compromise, with rebels winning significant concessions and the Prime Minister staying in office. However, such episodes could only strengthen the feeling that the executive and the legislature were now embroiled in an endemic constitutional struggle, underlying and reinforcing battles over specific policies. This change in Britain's political culture would not be helpful to any successor who lacked Blair's elephantine majority – or, more importantly, the enduring personal prestige arising from his record as an election winner.

The experience of Gordon Brown is particularly instructive in this respect. Philip Cowley and Mark Stuart have charted more than 200 backbench rebellions of varying significance while Brown was Prime Minister, including one which took place less than an hour after he had formally taken office (Cowley and Stuart, 2014, 5). Yet Brown had given every indication that he had learned from the bruising Blair experience, and put forward several proposals to address parliamentary grievances. Whatever his intentions, Brown was soon sidetracked by the first signs of a global banking crisis. In fact, if he had seriously sought a more amicable relationship between the executive and the legislature, he had created a formidable obstacle himself, by announcing in his final budget as Chancellor (March 2007) that the lower (10p) rate of income tax would be abolished from April 2008. In the weeks before that measure was due to take effect, Labour backbenchers launched a concerted campaign to force either a policy reversal, or other concessions which would ensure that no one would be worse off as a result of the change. Faced with the possibility of a catastrophic defeat on a Finance Bill the new Chancellor, Alistair Darling, made a timely commitment to allocate extra money to disadvantaged groups (Cowley and Stuart, 2014, 13–16). The impression that this was a government characterized by genuine errors of judgement rather than a Blairite mission to make enemies is reinforced by its defeat in April 2009 on an Opposition Day motion calling for improved settlement rights for retired Gurkha soldiers. Losing the vote was damaging enough, but the government also suffered a public relations disaster, since the Opposition had been invigorated by the indefatigable campaigning of the actress Joanna Lumley, who was far more popular than any current member of the House of Commons.

Against this background, it was difficult to predict the likely effect of the parliamentary expenses scandal which dominated media coverage of politics for several weeks in 2009. On balance, though, the idea that MPs were greedy as well as ineffectual could be taken as a challenge to prove their value, especially in causes which enjoyed considerable public support. It was not, in short, likely to abate the tendency towards conflict between the Prime Minister and Parliament. This was an unpromising context for the creation of Britain's first peacetime coalition since 1945, as the very fact of joining forces with a political foe was sure to put some strain on Conservative and Liberal Democrat party loyalties during the 2010–15 Parliament. In addition, the coalition was committed to a controversial economic strategy – 'austerity' – which the Liberal Democrats had opposed until David Cameron invited them to help form a government.

However, the period of coalition government is more noteworthy for the instances of conflict *within* rather than *between* the partners. Perhaps the most curious incident was a vote on an increase in the upper limit on higher education tuition fees (9 December 2010), when the Liberal Democrats divided three ways. The largest number (twenty-eight) voted in favour; twenty-one voted against, and eight abstained. In practice the twenty-one 'rebels' were showing their opposition to the leadership by voting in favour of a position which had been a prominent manifesto commitment less than six months earlier. On this occasion, the junior partner in the coalition was issuing its MPs with the most direct of provocations – almost tantamount to a slap in the face – and the relatively low level of outright dissent is surprising. Not to be outdone, the Conservative leadership incited rebellion in its own parliamentary ranks by introducing the Marriage (Same Sex Couples) Bill. On the second reading (5 February 2013), 137 Conservative MPs voted against the measure; 127 supported it. Although this was technically a free vote, Cameron had been a vocal champion of the reform.

By this time, Cameron might have been looking for issues on which he could take a distinctive initiative, because in other respects his agenda was being undermined by unruly MPs on his own side. Anticipating trouble ahead, one of Cameron's first actions as Prime Minister was to propose changes in the procedures of the Conservative backbench 1922 Committee, allowing frontbenchers to retain full membership (including voting rights) when the party was in office. This attempt to stifle dissent was carried in a vote of the Committee, but more than a hundred MPs had opposed it, so Cameron thought it prudent to back down (Cameron, 2019, 239).

In October 2011, eighty-one Conservatives defied a three-line whip to support a motion which called for a referendum on EU membership. A year later, the government was defeated when fifty-three Conservative MPs voted in favour of a cut in the EU budget, rather than the inflation-linked increase which Cameron had suggested. Although the vote was not binding on the government, Conservative Eurosceptics let it be known that they would turn out in even greater numbers if Cameron accepted a budget increase of any kind. This was the type of rebellion – a rejection of a position on Europe which was itself designed to mollify Eurosceptics – which had made Major's life such a misery. In January 2013 Cameron capitulated, offering an in/out referendum on EU membership after the next general election. However, having scented blood Tory rebels wanted to start feasting without delay; on 15 May more than a hundred voted to express 'regret' that the Queen's Speech had not included a government bill paving the way for the referendum.

The most dramatic government defeat occurred on 29 August 2013, on a motion which threatened (but, after a government concession, did not itself authorize) military action against the Syrian Assad regime. The government, which had recalled Parliament in the hope of winning approval for action, lost the vote by 285 to 272. Thirty-nine coalition MPs – thirty Tories and nine Liberal Democrats – joined Labour in opposing the motion. It was an excellent illustration of the executive/legislature split, since many MPs were clearly actuated by memories of Blair's dubious presentation of the case for action in Iraq in 2003.

Whatever its record in other respects, the Cameron coalition was a golden era for connoisseurs of parliamentary rebellions, which took place over a remarkable range of issues and varied widely in their causes and scale. Apart from dissent within Conservative and Liberal Democrat ranks, there was a significant spat which might have caused terminal damage if Cameron and his Liberal Democrat deputy Nick

Clegg had not been fairly laid-back characters who were disinclined to nurse grievances. Again, the trouble arose from the aggression of Conservative backbenchers. On 10 July 2012, ninety-one MPs voted against the second reading of a bill which would have begun a gradual process of House of Lords reform, leading to a mainly elected upper chamber. Although the government won the vote, it was clear that there was sufficient opposition in the Commons to prevent further progress on an issue which had been debated many times and had always seemed likely to end in a compromise. The government decided to withdraw the legislation rather than encounter embarrassing delays and defeats. In retaliation, on 29 January 2013 the Liberal Democrats blocked the implementation of constituency boundary changes which were likely to benefit the Conservatives (partly at the expense of the Lib Dems).

As it turned out, in the 2015 general election the Conservatives were able to pick up plenty of Liberal Democrat seats without the help of boundary changes. The result, for David Cameron, was a blend of Rudyard Kipling's 'twin imposters'; he could take personal satisfaction from the fact that his party had increased its popular vote and secured an overall majority despite its imposition of economic austerity, but the margin (just twelve seats) left him even more vulnerable to pressure from his own backbenchers. As it was, his main problem arose not from rebellious MPs, but from a bill whose second reading (on 9 June 2015, little more than a month after the election) was supported by all parties except the Scottish National Party (SNP) and passed by 544 votes to 53. This was the legislation, introduced by the government itself, to authorize the EU referendum.

This is not the place for a detailed account of the parliamentary chaos which descended in the wake of the 2016 referendum. Theresa May's record of thirty-three defeats – all of which took place *after* the snap election which was called to strengthen her parliamentary position – lacked the rich diversity of the coalition's record, but more than compensated in its crop of parliamentary 'firsts'. Most notably, MPs voted to hold the entire government (rather than an individual minister) in contempt of Parliament, and, on 15 January 2019, inflicted the largest defeat suffered by any government in the democratic era (432–202, on the terms of May's EU withdrawal agreement).

At times during this prolonged and highly complex saga – which continued under May's successor, Boris Johnson, until the general election of December 2019 – it seemed that the battle between Parliament and the Prime Minister would find at least a temporary resolution in favour of the former. Parliament as an institution was widely blamed for the months of political deadlock. However, ultimate responsibility for the mishandling of 'Brexit' lay with the executive, whose initial determination to trigger the process of withdrawal from the EU without parliamentary consent was a remarkable power-grab which was bound to meet resistance somewhere. It was the courts, rather than Parliament, which thwarted May's intentions, by ruling against the government in the case of *R (Miller) v Secretary of State for Exiting the European Union* (January 2017). Despite this reiteration of Parliament's constitutional role, within weeks MPs had complied with the executive's wishes and started the withdrawal process in accordance with Article 50 of the EU's Lisbon Treaty. Even though a majority in the Commons wanted the UK to remain within the EU, the triggering of Article 50 was passed by huge majorities – 498 to 114 on second reading, for example. This was a remarkable contravention of the old Burkean idea that MPs should act as *representatives*, capable of exercising independent judgement, rather than *delegates* who should bow to public opinion. It was eclipsed on 18 April 2017 when the Commons made a mockery of the 2011 Fixed-Term Parliaments Act (which purported to remove the executive's discretion in the timing of elections) and approved May's proposal to dissolve Parliament by 522 votes to 13.

Parliament, in short, was ready to submit to the 'will of the people' as expressed in the narrow victory for 'Leave' in the 2016 referendum. Although the Prime Minister had supported 'Remain', she had contrived to reinterpret the vote into a plebiscite on the power of the executive vis-à-vis the legislature. By calling the referendum when the outcome was at best uncertain, the executive had made a fearful blunder: but some other institution would have to pay the price. However, May botched her opportunistic election, and could only scramble together something which looked like a workable majority thanks to the dearly bought sufferance of the Democratic Unionist Party (DUP). Rather like a series of mishaps in the Grand National, this unexpected result handed the lead back to Parliament; but the divisions which had persuaded May to call an election (in contradiction of previous public pledges) resurfaced whenever Parliament looked set to consolidate its advantage, and by failing to agree on any alternative plan in a series of 'indicative votes' MPs effectively refused at the final fence.

Although Boris Johnson initially looked even less likely to reach the winning line, his decision in September 2019 to remove the Conservative 'whip' from twenty-one MPs who had voted to prevent the executive from regaining control of the Brexit proceedings gave him the necessary momentum. It looked like a throwback to the 1990s, when John Major had withdrawn the party whip from eight MPs (including Michael Carttiss, who in 1990 had told Margaret Thatcher that she could 'wipe the floor' with her opponents) after they had voted against an EU Finance Bill. Major had subsequently allowed the 'whipless wonders' back into the fold; but subsequent changes in the party rules meant that MPs who had been deprived of the whip could not stand for re-election as Conservative candidates. It turned out that the rule change was only a secondary factor in the similar circumstances of 2019; more importantly, Major had been trying to exert discipline over Eurosceptic MPs who cared for their adopted cause more than their party, while the opposite was true of the MPs who incurred Johnson's wrath. In 2019, what might have been taken as a sign of futile vindictiveness by the executive was transformed into a tactical master stroke thanks to the passivity of Johnson's victims; even the ones who had no intention of standing at the next election seemed to think that their punishment for voting in accordance with their personal views was richly deserved, and four of the MPs who subsequently had the whip restored went on to retain their seats in the 2019 general election as endorsed Conservatives. Their submissive attitude was all the more surprising since it coincided with a furore over another executive power-grab – Johnson's attempt to prorogue Parliament, which was subsequently quashed by the courts. Instead of rising like lions to avenge the executive's cynical constitutional ploy, the Commons voted on 29 October to resume their ovine role, authorizing by 438 votes to 20 a general election which the majority of MPs decidedly did not want.

It was never likely that the return of the Conservatives in December 2019, with an overall majority of eighty seats, would put an end to the battle between Parliament and the Prime Minister. However, the lesson of the conflict since 1979 is that even though individual governments might lose the occasional skirmish, through ill luck or mind-boggling incompetence, the executive will always find some way to ensure parliamentary *obedience* (if not *confidence* in the literal sense).

A breakdown of party discipline?

For those who believe that the place of Parliament is to advise rather than to obstruct the executive, the removal of the whip from twenty-one Conservative MPs – who included eight former Cabinet ministers (of whom two had served as Chancellor of the Exchequer and one had recently attracted respectable support in his bid for the party leadership) – probably seemed like a laudable return to resolute leadership after decades in which rebels had been treated too tenderly. Perhaps the best justification for this position is that MPs owe their places in Parliament to party affiliation rather than their personal attributes – a case which gained considerable credence when all of the Brexit rebels who fought the 2019 general election without official Conservative endorsement lost their seats. Yet Edmund Burke's definition of a political party – 'a body of men united for promoting by the joint endeavours the national interest upon some particular principle in which they are all agreed' – was idealistic even at the time it was pronounced, and is now hopelessly outdated, not only because of its gendered language. Political parties – even relatively small ones in parliamentary terms – include people who disagree, often on fundamental issues; some elected representatives, indeed, have at times stuck with their parties even when it has become clear that they have much more in common with their supposed rivals. The job of ensuring that these ill-assorted groups end up in the same voting lobby in the House of Commons has never been easy, which is why it has been entrusted to a team of officials – usually about fourteen strong – known as 'whips'. Especially in the early post-war period, the ability of the whips to crush the spirit of rebellion was the stuff of legend. Allegedly they ran a system of espionage which was far more effective than the Cold War secret services, gathering damaging intelligence on their party colleagues without (unlike MI6) ever divulging their findings to 'the other side'. If the legends were true, MPs were less privileged than other people because the price of entering Parliament was to forfeit the right to cast a truly 'free' vote, even on matters of conscience. The price of integrity could be political and even personal ruin.

However, it is significant that the 'golden age' of party discipline, and the time when party whips were most feared, was the early post-war period when the main parliamentary parties broadly agreed on policy objectives and differed mostly on the means to achieve them. At such a time, most MPs could feel confident that an instruction from their whip to vote either for or against a specific measure was an appeal to tribal, rather than ideological, loyalties; in Parliament, the job of government and Opposition was to magnify small differences, and to oppose or support legislation on which their positions could easily be reversed depending on the benches they occupied.

This situation changed in 1979, when Margaret Thatcher brought a new ideological edge to British politics; and as the Conservative Party moved to the right, Labour lurched to the left. MPs on both sides whose overall loyalty to 'the tribe' had allowed them to over-look misgivings about their respective party's stance on specific issues now began to wonder if they had dedicated their careers to the wrong party. The formation of the Social Democratic Party (SDP) in 1981 gave MPs with loosening tribal loyalties an opportunity to join forces under a new banner; but for understandable reasons the prospect of 'realignment' looked much more tempting to MPs whose party was currently out of office than to disaffected members of the Tory tribe. Had a senior Conservative joined the 'Gang of Four' ex-Labour ministers who launched the SDP, British political history could easily have been very different. As it was, Thatcher's numerous Tory opponents chose to keep their powder dry for future internal battles. It was not until Thatcher's third term (1987–90) that 'One Nation' Conservatives began to mount serious challenges against key elements of the government's agenda; for example, thirty-eight MPs voted for an amendment to the poll tax legislation which would have ensured that the charge was related to the ability to pay. Reluctant to organize concerted parliamentary revolts against their party, discontented moderates focused on the possibility of removing the leader; but it was only when the battle-scarred Thatcherites, Nigel Lawson and Geoffrey Howe, lost their patience with the regime that this 'decapitation' strategy became feasible, and Thatcher's sliding opinion poll ratings did the rest.

Initially, the derogatory nickname 'wet' had been applied to Conservatives who, according to Thatcherites, were unwilling to stand up to the trade unions (and 'socialism' more generally). However, it could easily have arisen from their non-confrontational approach to internal party debates. Once Thatcher had fallen from office the critics of the new Prime Minister, John Major, showed no such inhibitions, particularly on the issue of 'Europe' which, in tandem with the Poll Tax, had precipitated her downfall. If the party whips had played any part in deterring attempts to modify Thatcher's agenda, after the general election of 1992 it became clear that their powers had been exaggerated. The psychology of rebellion had been transformed by the course of events, notably the ERM disaster and Heseltine's pit closure programme. While 'One Nation' Conservatives had voted against her governments in a spirit of semi-apology, Thatcher's avengers regarded Major as a usurper, so that any shame should attach to parliamentary colleagues who continued to support him. Unlike the 'wets', Major's opponents enjoyed the crucial advantage of considerable sympathy from the right-wing press, which in turn ensured invitations from the broadcast media to eloquent Eurosceptics like Teresa Gorman, the hormonally enhanced MP for Billericay. This kind of attention not only gave MPs who opposed the ratification of the 1992 Maastricht Treaty an invaluable opportunity to convey their message to nationwide audiences, but also bolstered their existing feeling that they were heroic figures in a last-ditch battle to save 'conservatism' from traitors to their fallen leader, to their party and to their country. Gorman even published a book whose title (and contents) proclaimed her contempt for the tactics of party managers (Gorman, 1993).

Although Major survived the Maastricht ratification process, his subsequent attempt to relaunch his leadership effectively destroyed his hopes of restoring discipline within the Parliamentary Conservative Party. On the face of it, the response to his appeal at the 1993 party conference for Britain to go 'Back to Basics' showed that the public was still highly moralistic, and that rebellious MPs still had reason to fear the 'dark arts' (sometimes verging on blackmail) which the whips could employ *in extremis*. In reality, when Major's spin doctors wrongly implied that the leader was referring to private morality, they unwittingly transferred part of the remaining power of the whips to the muckraking media. Right-wing tabloid newspapers chose to interpret Major's campaign as a licence to expose the kind of personal peccadillos which whips had presumably known about, but only divulged if all else failed. The tabloid press had no such reservations: if a story had the potential to sell newspapers, it could now be used at the first opportunity, especially if it related to an MP who had not been unswervingly loyal to the cause of Thatcherism. In other words, the information which the whips had kept from public view in the cause of party discipline was now, in the hands of the media, being used to damage the government and make rebellion look sexy. As post-war moral certainties continued to blur into ambiguities after the 1990s, even whips who were tempted to use the old methods of persuasion could no longer be confident that their threats would have any effect. A more 'open-minded' society – partly the product of 'permissive' legislation passed after unwhipped votes in Parliament – certainly added to the complications of party management. One might even consider the role of 'Thatcherite' philosophy in the turbulent years that followed: since dogmatic individualism had wrought radical changes in so many of Britain's institutions, was there any reason why parliamentary parties should be spared from the process of 'creative destruction'?

For Labour MPs and potential candidates enjoying the Tory turmoil between 1992 and 1997, the obvious lesson was that the worst fate for any politician was to belong to an ill-disciplined party. The problem, as we have seen, is that this apparent truism made its greatest impression on a party leadership which had its own reasons for advising MPs to put party before conscience. If Tony Blair pushed loyalty too far, Labour MPs could hardly forget that their Tory counterparts had been celebrated, rather than vilified, in the press during the Major years. The standard disciplinary weapon for whips is the gentle suggestion that dissent, if followed through to a vote, will either delay or destroy any prospect of promotion. Yet recalcitrant MPs who have taken their objections to the party line close to (and even beyond) the point of formal expulsion have occasionally ended up as leaders – Harold Macmillan, Winston Churchill and (early in our period) Michael Foot fall into this category. More recently, Iain Duncan Smith (Conservative leader, 2001–3) and Jeremy Corbyn (Labour leader, 2015–20) have been elevated to the top jobs within the parties because, rather than in spite, of their repeated rebellions (see below). The culmination of this process came in 2019, when Boris Johnson was elected Conservative leader and Prime Minister despite a record of calculated, rather than principled, disobedience.

Looking back on the years since Maastricht, the former Conservative Chief Whip Tim Renton pronounced that 'the ability of whips to maintain unity on the government benches has disappeared' (Renton,

2004, 319). The change since his short stint in the role (1989–90) was symbolized by the removal of the whips' office from No. 12 Downing Street to another location within Whitehall, in order to accommodate government 'spin doctors'. A more poignant piece of evidence – which happened a decade after the publication of Renton's book – was David Cameron's decision to appoint Michael Gove to the position of Chief Whip (2014), despite his glaring unsuitability for the task. Gove's predecessor, the veteran George Young, had been another strange appointment. At least Young knew a good deal about the psychology of rebellion, as a veteran of the battle against Thatcher's poll tax; but he was the kind of person who would help elderly people across the road, whereas most Chief Whips before 1997 would have swerved to knock them over if their superior officers deemed it necessary.

However, the downgrading and semi-humanizing of the whips did not necessarily entail a complete abandonment of parliamentary discipline. If the party's team of corporals could not keep order in the ranks, one could always wheel in the top brass, even including the field marshal. Renton recalled that before the key vote on the poll tax (April 1988) he asked Margaret Thatcher if she would meet 'a handful of rebels to whom I felt she could usefully talk'. However, the poll tax clearly involved Thatcher's personal authority, since she was closely associated with a policy which had been a manifesto commitment. Renton thought that Tony Blair was right to grant interviews to wavering MPs before the vote on Iraq, which was clearly a 'confidence' issue. However, Renton was deeply concerned by the use of the Prime Minister and senior colleagues as means of persuasion on important but less pivotal issues. In particular, he deplored the involvement of Blair, his Chancellor Gordon Brown and even the Secretary of State for Education, Charles Clarke, in attempts to dissuade MPs from voting against the government's policy on variable tuition fees (January 2004; see above). This, after all, had not been a manifesto pledge; indeed, Labour's 2001 programme had ruled out such a change (Renton, 2004, 319, 337, 335–6). The recourse to this kind of tactic suggested that the problem lay with wrong-headed government policy rather than inadequate party management. In effect, key members of the executive were having to use flattery or intimidation to save themselves from the consequences of their own acts of political provocation.

Renton's solution to this growing problem was unsurprising, given his background: to restore some authority to the whips. However, his remedy was based on a confusion of causes and effects. Parliamentary discipline has not broken down because the whipping system no longer works; rather, *no* system of party discipline in a parliamentary democracy can be effective if governments insist on defying their backbench MPs to vote against them on a regular basis. Orderly government is a prerequisite for healthy parliamentary management, not the other way round – just as ministers who are not wholly dependent upon the Prime Minister are essential for rational policy-making (see chapter 3).

A measure of control? Prime Minister's Questions

According to David Cameron – who had helped prepare John Major for Prime Minister's Questions, then witnessed the occasion successively as backbench MP, frontbench Opposition spokesperson, Opposition leader and Prime Minister – the (now) weekly engagement is 'adversarial, noisy, partisan and unpredictable . . . It is as intimidating, demanding, exhausting and downright terrifying as anything you do as prime minister.' However, Cameron's account also emphasizes the potential upsides: it gives the Prime Minister a chance 'to demonstrate that you're the leader of your pack', and 'you always get the last word' (Cameron, 2019, 241–3).

Having the last line in any dramatic performance is not necessarily decisive; otherwise Fortinbras would be regarded as the main character in *Hamlet*. This is not to belittle the advantage of being able to deliver the final riposte – so long as one is furnished by helpful wordsmiths with deadly quips, 'killer facts' or ingenious evasions to meet every occasion. Thanks to their lengthy preparations, Prime Ministers usually are in this happy position when they visit the Commons for PMQs. Nevertheless, these occasions are extremely stressful, and it is little wonder that Tony Blair chose to reduce the ordeals from two quarter-hour sessions per week (Tuesdays and Thursdays) to a single one lasting half an hour on Wednesdays (although this reform came with the beneficial by-product of making attendance at the Commons semi-compulsory on one day rather than two).

The stage fright is understandable. No amount of preparation should be sufficient to save a second-rate performer from humiliation at PMQs, but even really skilful debaters have to be on guard throughout, in case they spoil everything with a single verbal slip. As Cameron noted, 'Weaknesses, failings, uncertainties, lack of knowledge – all these things and more are found out' if the Prime Minister is substandard or below par thanks to fatigue or distractions (Cameron, 2019, 38). The real advantage enjoyed by every Prime Minister is suggested by Cameron's reference to 'leader of your pack'. In normal circumstances, the Prime Minister is at least the nominal chief of the largest 'pack' in the House of Commons. Even if the party is desperate for a change at the top, it has every incentive to use PMQs as an opportunity to engage in outward displays of loyalty by making the loudest semi-articulate noises (the absence of which seemed to affect Boris Johnson's performances during the 2020 coronavirus pandemic).

It is, nevertheless, probably significant that the most notable ovations have been granted to Prime Ministers who have already signalled their intention to depart. Margaret Thatcher's last question time was something of a love-fest – even before she had said a word she was lauded with cries of 'Hear! Hear!' Tony Blair's final utterance (a less eloquent version of Hamlet's 'the rest is silence') was followed by applause from both sides of the House, and although Theresa May's send-off was not unanimous, she was clapped out of the Chamber by the Conservative MPs who had made her premiership so difficult. Yet while the spotlight inevitably falls on the leading members of the cast, backbenchers are more than just 'extras'. Given the media focus on PMQs as opposed to the rest of parliamentary business, even someone who has obeyed the whip in every vote can have their career blighted if they are sufficiently unwise to ask an awkward question of their own 'pack' leader. A backbencher who is caught on camera wearing an unhelpful expression will be deemed to have done more harm to the party than MPs who cast repeated but unpublicized votes against obscure government measures. Thus, while supporters of the British political system continue to praise PMQs as remarkable opportunities for MPs to hold their head of government to account, the weekly show provides the Prime Minister with an excellent opportunity to ensure that the 'accounting' is favourable.

The media focus on PMQs has made the occasion seem both more and less significant than it really is. On the one hand, its guaranteed prominence in news bulletins – and its attractions for users of social media – invites even serious students of British politics to 'bookend' the tenures of Prime Ministers with one-liners. Thus the Blair era seems to begin with his devastating put-down of John Major ('I lead my party. He follows his'), and ends with David Cameron's jibe against a fading Blair ('*He* was the future once'). In reality, far from these brilliant barbs sending their recipients snivelling to Buckingham Palace to submit their resignations, Major remained in office for more than two years after Blair's attack of April 1995, while Blair himself managed to survive the effects of Cameron's sally (December 2005) for eighteen months, before being snuffed out by his own side. The ineffectual nature of PMQs as a means of exposing the ineptitude (or worse) of the incumbent government is also illustrated by the general verdict that William Hague (Conservative leader, 1997–2001) displayed a flair for the occasion which would have matched any previous Opposition leader. Even so, Hague's performances were insufficient to inspire voters – the Conservatives gained just one additional parliamentary seat at the 2001 general election. Indeed, far from rallying his backbenchers through his inspired PMQ performances, Hague presided over a period of continued factional strife within the Parliamentary Conservative Party (Walters, 2001). Perhaps the most profound comment on Hague's 'success' in PMQs is the fact that when Conservative members decided on his successor, they opted for someone (Iain Duncan Smith; see below) whose dour demeanour and plodding delivery made him the worst-equipped leader for PMQs in the media age.

While the preceding evidence relates to the limitations of PMQs as a platform for effective opposition, regardless of the relative qualities of the performers, there is little evidence that Prime Ministers derive any significant benefits, either. Again, John Major provides an instructive example. In June 1995, Major took the remarkable step of resigning from the leadership of his party (but not as Prime Minister) in order to flush out any potential opponents. A challenger emerged in the shape of one of Major's 'bastards' – the Welsh Secretary, John Redwood. At PMQs a week before the ballot (then restricted to MPs), Major was judged to have surpassed himself, thanks at least partly to a rare tactical error by Tony Blair. Two of Major's special advisers remembered that 'Punch followed punch, with Tony Blair cast as Judy' (Hogg and Hill, 1995, 277). Major himself recalled that after one of his cutting retorts, 'the mood of the House changed from that of a Roman circus to Sunday Night at the London Palladium'. According to Major's memoirs, not even Blair could stop himself from grinning when the Prime Minister attributed Redwood's resignation from the Cabinet to the fact that 'he was devastated that I had resigned as leader of the Conservative Party' (Major, 1999, 638). Although a conspiracy theorist might think that Blair had put in a substandard performance at PMQs in order to keep Major in office as an electoral asset for Labour, the Opposition leader had actually regarded the Prime Minister's resignation as a tactical master stoke, and even Blair's director of communications, Alastair Campbell, supressed his personal dislike of Major and congratulated him on this performance (Campbell, 2010, 235). With the wind of victory in their sails, Major's supporters spent the next day 'working the tea rooms' at Westminster, and the weekend press before the ballot suggested that almost all of the party's constituency chairpeople wanted Major to win (Hogg and Hill, 1995, 277–8).

If the importance of PMQs came close to matching its media profile, Major's nonchalant dismissal of Tony Blair's attacks should have allayed any doubts among Tory backbenchers. However, in the vote itself, ninety-nine (out of 339) MPs denied their support to the person who was their party leader as well as the incumbent Prime Minister. The obvious inference was that, as soon as PMQs became a media event rather than a parliamentary ritual, its impact even among MPs would be far less lasting, so that a Prime Minister whose position was vulnerable for other reasons would be condemned to live from one weekly test to the next. Equally, Prime Ministers who were rated as good or even brilliant at PMQs would have to sustain their level; even a superlative performance (evoking cries of 'You can wipe the floor with these people') will tend to be taken for granted once a Prime Minister has established his or her supremacy in that format. As a result, Conservative MPs who disliked David Cameron's policy initiatives on ideological grounds could conspire against his leadership even though he was an excellent performer at PMQs, and Theresa May could never hope to win the confidence of Conservative MPs after the 2017 general election, despite the fact that her attempts to bat back or evade the weekly quota of questions remained reasonably competent through her various trials.

Admirers of the British system of government tend to lay considerable emphasis on PMQs; Harold Wilson even described it as 'the high tribunal of the nation' (Wilson, 1976, 141). Equally, of course, critics bemoan its triviality and the bad manners exhibited by the rival tribes; to them, it can never be more than a hollowed-out sham of democratic accountability, giving Prime Ministers with a decent memory and a talented team of gag writers a clear advantage over MPs who try to develop and sustain a spontaneous and persuasive line of argument. In truth, PMQs is as good, or as bad, as the current Prime Minister and Parliament (led by the Speaker) allow it to be. The only constant factor is that it increases the public prominence of the Prime Minister and the leader of the Opposition.

Choosing a champion

Before the period under review, there were already signs that parliamentary prowess was becoming less important as a qualification for the leadership of Britain's main parties. In 1963, Harold Macmillan manipulated the informal process to choose a Conservative leader in favour of the Foreign Secretary Lord Home, who promptly disclaimed his title and entered the Commons as Prime Minister and plain old Sir Alec Douglas-Home. The latter did have experience of the House, but this had ended in 1951, when he assumed his hereditary title. As such, the returning Home was in a worse position than a parliamentary novice, who might have adjusted to the Commons fairly quickly. In 1951, the Labour leader had been the mild-mannered public school product Clement Attlee, whereas as Prime Minister Sir Alec would have to face up to Harold Wilson, whom even Macmillan (who had served in the Commons almost continuously since 1931) recognized as an unusually artful opponent.

Consciously or not, Macmillan and his co-conspirators were acting on the thoroughly modern assumption that Home's parliamentary performances would not matter: he would be able to command a majority in the Commons *because* he was Prime Minister. If Home's tenure of No. 10 had depended on his ability to match Wilson as a parliamentary performer, the result of the 1964 general election would not have been close; no objective observer could have denied Wilson's superiority. As it was, although the Conservatives lost the election they did well enough to deny Labour a secure majority. Although most of the party had rallied behind Home, after the 1964 election the Conservatives tacitly accepted that Macmillan had made a mistake and did their best to ensure that it could not be repeated. The party rules were changed, so that MPs would be given a formal vote for party leader rather than allowing an individual to 'emerge' (as Home had done) through informal consultations with senior party figures. The first beneficiary was Edward Heath, who was chosen on the ill-founded assumption that he could match Wilson at the dispatch box.

The long-running rivalry between Wilson and Heath was ended by the latter's deposition as Tory leader in 1975; Wilson stepped down as Prime Minister in the following year. Unlike the Conservatives, the Parliamentary Labour Party had always followed a formal procedure for the election of its leader, so the kind of coup engineered by Macmillan on behalf of a personal favourite was not open to Wilson. However, he gave his preferred successor, James Callaghan, advance notice of his intention to resign. Undoubtedly Wilson's choice was influenced to some extent by confidence in Callaghan's ability to cut a suitably 'prime ministerial' figure in Commons debates, despite Labour's failure to win a secure majority in either of the elections of 1974.

By contrast, Heath's refusal to stand down as leader after the general election of October 1974 – his third failure to win a majority in four attempts – provoked a further change in the Conservative Party's rules (overseen, appropriately, by Sir Alec Douglas-Home) which for the first time allowed challenges to incumbent leaders. While other possible challengers flinched, Margaret Thatcher stood against and beat Heath in February 1975. In this case, Thatcher was rewarded for her remarkable chutzpah in standing against the first Conservative leader who had been chosen by an electoral process of any kind. However, she had also shown herself to be a very effective parliamentary debater as part of the Conservative team attacking Labour's economic policy, so her supporters had no reason for apprehension on that score.

Between 1979 and the time of writing (July 2020), the two main parties have been led by sixteen individuals (leaving aside caretaker leaders). Of these, many had qualities which would have made them respectable candidates in the days when parliamentary performance was a crucial consideration for aspiring leaders. However, at least two (one from each side) would certainly not have been chosen if parliamentary performance had been more than the marginal factor which it must have been for Macmillan in 1963; indeed, before 1979 any leadership aspirations they had shown would have been taken as signs of eccentricity.

The individuals in question only rose to the leadership of their respective parties because of further rule changes, which took the final choice of leader away from those who were really qualified to judge their performances in the Commons – that is, Bagehot's 'electoral college', the MPs. By 1997, both Labour and the Conservatives had tried to appease their grassroots members by giving them an important role in leadership elections. In the Conservative case, the new system at least permitted MPs to reduce the field of contestants to two over a series of ballots before handing the final verdict to party members. But in 2001 this parliamentary safety net proved to consist of over-cooked spaghetti, when the anticipated run-off between candidates from the left and the right of the party (Kenneth Clarke and Michael Portillo respectively) failed to materialize, since Portillo's underwhelming campaign had been further damaged by rumours concerning his personal history. Almost by default, the candidate previously designated as the 'honourable runner-up' by the Conservative right wing, Iain Duncan Smith, took Portillo's place as the challenger to Clarke, who had narrowly won the third and final ballot among MPs and had all the necessary attributes for leadership except antipathy towards the European Union. This single disadvantage was enough to secure victory for Duncan Smith (Bale et al., 2019, 135–6). Thus, the leadership of a great political party passed to an individual whose only claim to prominence had been his persistent record of rebellion against its European policy during the 1990s – something of which he openly boasted during the 2001 leadership battle.[3] The MPs who voted for Duncan Smith in preference to Portillo did so in the full knowledge that there could be no serious comparison between these two individuals as parliamentary performers (Denham and O'Hara, 2008, 59–62).

If the parliamentary perspective really mattered, the choice of Duncan Smith looks even more maladroit than Michael Foot's elevation to the Labour leadership in 1980. Presenting Foot as a potential Prime Minister was widely seen as a hopeless instance of miscasting, not least (and significantly) because he had been badly injured in a car accident in 1963 and thus looked older than his years in television appearances. However, Foot was a Rolls-Royce compared to Duncan Smith's Reliant Robin in terms of parliamentary skills. Although the House of Commons is irredeemably partisan, the acid test for a good leader in that environment must still be the hypothetical case in which the final outcome of key votes depends on the eloquence of rival speakers. More realistically, a party leader with a gift for oratory is better equipped to enthuse the party faithful than someone whose speeches, in terms of delivery and content, would only appeal to those whose minds are closed to any alternative position. Although he was seen as a disastrous leader, Foot always received (and deserved) a respectful hearing in the House; Duncan Smith was not even very good at preaching to the converted (as he demonstrated at his party's conferences). A less sentimental party than Labour would have dispensed with Foot's services before the 1983 general election; a less ideological party than the Conservatives would not have allowed Duncan Smith anywhere near the leadership in the first place.

Labour took more than a decade to emulate the Tories in this respect. But in 2010 it showed distinct symptoms of plumping for leadership candidates who pleased the party as a whole regardless of their parliamentary prowess, when the preference of MPs for David, rather than Ed, Miliband was over-ridden by other elements of the party. In terms of parliamentary stature, David was the better qualified Miliband; but he had enjoyed more opportunities than Ed to shine in set-piece debates, so this could be rationalized as an occasion when the extra-parliamentary party decided to go for potential rather than proven ability.

However, no such excuse was available to the Labour Party when in 2015 it anointed Jeremy Corbyn as Ed Miliband's successor. In terms of nominations by the Parliamentary Labour Party, Corbyn came fourth of the four candidates who progressed to the final round of voting. Corbyn resembled Duncan Smith in having built his reputation on principled disloyalty; although Corbyn cast far more votes against his party than Duncan Smith, the latter compensated for his infrequent disobedience by voting against the official Conservative line on the issue (Europe) which was calculated to cause maximum damage. More importantly in the present context, in both instances the voting records of Corbyn and Duncan Smith spoke more eloquently to the extra-parliamentary selectorate than any words that either had ever uttered in Parliament. Unlike leftist predecessors who had either won or aspired to the Labour leadership (e.g. Foot and Tony Benn), Corbyn was not regarded as a good parliamentary orator except by those who shared his views. As in the case of Duncan Smith, the votes of ordinary party members in 2015 saddled a potential party of government with a leader who palpably lacked the confidence even of his own cohort of MPs.

The decision of Conservative MPs to select Boris Johnson as one of the two candidates to proceed to the final round of voting in 2019 falls into a different category. Any parliamentary reputation (deserved or not) enjoyed by Corbyn or Duncan Smith prior to their election as leaders arose from their dogged perseverance in the face of hostility from loyal MPs within their own parties. They might never have come close to commanding a majority in the House of Commons in their rebellious days, but at least they had never shown signs of treating the Chamber as a means to a personal end. In his first parliamentary stint as MP for Henley (2001–8) before he decided to put himself forward for London's elected Mayoralty, Johnson's speeches made no favourable impression. This remained the case between his return to the Commons in 2015 and his promotion to Foreign Secretary after the Brexit referendum in 2016. Johnson's attempt to identify (and, by implication, to compare) himself with Winston Churchill was self-evidently improbable. However, by 2019 a considerable number of grassroots Tories had convinced themselves that membership of the European Union presented an existential threat to the UK. Cometh the hour, cometh the Churchill impersonator. Tory MPs were acutely aware of the enthusiasm for 'Boris' among their constituency members, and feared the grassroots reaction if they kept Johnson out of the final ballot. As a result, in the general election of 2019 the two main British political parties were led by individuals who would not have been serious contenders for their positions if parliamentary considerations had been an important (let alone crucial) factor.

It is possible to regard the broadening of the choice of party leaders to grassroots members as an inevitable development for a variety of reasons. But whatever the precise triggers for the procedural changes in both of the main UK parties, the effects were likely to strengthen the position of incumbent leaders. The ultimate arbiters of their fate would no longer be the parliamentary colleagues who could evaluate their qualities at first hand; rather, it would be people who were unlikely to have met them in the flesh. The Conservative Party's rules, as modified in 1997, were designed to evade the real nightmare scenario, in which a leader who has been defeated in a vote of confidence among his or her MPs is reinstated by the votes of the extra-parliamentary party.

No doubt recalling the situation in 1975, when, given the chance of a party-wide ballot, a majority of constituency members would have supported Heath rather than Thatcher, the Conservatives stipulated that a leader who had been beaten in a vote of confidence among MPs would be excluded from the ensuing contest. However, the 2019 Conservative leadership election suggested that this precaution was either unnecessary or futile. A leader who was deemed incapable by the parliamentary party, but still commanded the affection of grassroots members, would be most unlikely to face a confidence vote in the first place, let alone lose it. Conservative MPs were only able to get rid of Duncan Smith because grassroots members had woken up to their mistake after two years of maladroit leadership. The indefatigable but ineffective attempts of Labour MPs to dethrone Jeremy Corbyn confirmed this impression; unlike Duncan Smith, who never had the chance to test his popularity in a general election, Corbyn was rendered invulnerable to defenestration by the result of the 2017 general election, and given a licence to exhaust the faith of his supporters in the ensuing 2019 contest.

In 1975, when Heath was toppled by Thatcher, the resentment of ordinary party members against 'disloyal' MPs was informed by a mixture of attitudes which now seem quaint and outdated. With hindsight, the mid-1970s can be seen as the end of a brief post-war interlude in which elitists and meritocrats (especially, but not exclusively, those who supported the Conservative Party) could feel that deference was automatically due to the leader whose appointment had been based on the free choice of MPs. This feeling allowed the Conservatives, when permitting the existing leader to be challenged, to place a very low threshold on the necessary level of initial backing; only two MPs (who could remain anonymous) were needed to nominate a challenger. It was assumed that an involuntary change at the top would only take place if there was overwhelming evidence that this was unavoidable, so that even if grassroots members continued to support the supplanted leader they would gradually reconcile themselves to the new regime (as happened in Thatcher's case).

By 2019, the balance of deference had been reversed, and many MPs felt compelled to surrender their personal views whenever these conflicted with the perceived preferences of grassroots members. The last vestige of Walter Bagehot's 'electoral college' had been removed. The only lingering residue of the old ways is the reluctance of individuals who hope to be candidates in any party-wide ballot to betray their hopes of a change of leader too openly. Thus as soon as Theresa May began to look like a 'lame duck' leader after the 2017 general election, Boris Johnson's prominent antenna of self-advancement started twitching, but he had to curb his enthusiasm, no doubt remembering the fate of another former MP for Henley, Michael Heseltine, who explained his failure to succeed Margaret Thatcher in 1990 by saying that 'In our party, the man who wields the dagger never picks up the crown.' This dictum had already been disproved (albeit in 1975 the assassin who had been rewarded was a woman rather than a man).[4] Indeed, if in 1990 the Conservatives had already given the final say over the choice of leader to the party as a whole rather than restricting it to MPs, Heseltine's chances of picking up the crown would have been much better than under the prevailing rules, which entrusted the decision to guilt-wracked Tory MPs rather than the constituency members whose support Heseltine had been cultivating carefully since his resignation from the Cabinet in 1986.

There is, of course, a perfectly respectable case to be made for parties choosing leaders who reflect the views of their most radical supporters. If such individuals prove capable of generating country-wide enthusiasm, the choice will have been vindicated. If not, the results will become apparent at the next general election, if not before; and party members can decide for themselves whether they want to repeat the mistake. However, the effects of the first-past-the-post electoral system – and the advantages enjoyed by the two main UK parties in terms of media support, financial resources, 'brand recognition', etc. – mean that even if leaders have become a crucial element in voters' choices (see chapter 6) a party which makes a bad decision is unlikely to suffer the full consequences. A more serious situation arises when both of the major parties choose leaders who are viewed negatively by a majority of voters. Thanks to the distortions of the electoral system, this means that Britain can be left with a Prime Minister who is distrusted (even despised) by a majority of his or her own parliamentary colleagues. If, as we have argued, Prime Ministers are 'majority leaders' because of the position they hold, the individual whose party prevails in this unpopularity contest will stand a good chance of serving a full term in office.

Conclusion

Between 1979 and the 2016 EU referendum, the 'received wisdom' was that MPs provided governments with 'lobby fodder', and that even those who expressed reservations about specific government policies would come round in the end. This assumption explains at least some of the odium visited upon MPs during the expenses scandal of 2009; indeed, if MPs had been regarded as conscientious servants of the public the 'scandal' would probably have been restricted to one or two egregious examples, rather than affecting very trivial offenders like the then Prime Minister Gordon Brown and the Opposition leader David Cameron.

As we have seen, whatever the justice of other complaints levelled at Parliament, in recent decades MPs have certainly not been guilty of excessive obedience to their party whips. Rebellions have become far more frequent, and the roll call of dissidents in the two main parties has grown. During the Thatcher years many Conservative MPs (even senior ministers) felt compelled to support government policy against their private convictions. But under her successor, John Major, rebel leaders became heroes rather than pariahs. These individuals were fully fledged rebels, in that they were trying to change the party's established policy of reluctant engagement with 'Europe' into one of outright opposition. Under Tony Blair the balance changed, since almost every Labour MP who decided to enter the government lobby on issues like welfare, health and education had to do so in defiance of private convictions, and/or previous public pledges. Back in 1956, an American political scientist wrote that a key constraint on the position of Prime Minister was 'the necessity of not taking action which is clearly unpalatable to large numbers of their party supporters' (Carter, 1956, 262). Blair was untroubled by this consideration, further entrenching the resolve and credibility of serial rebels but consoling himself with the thought that, as in PMQs, the executive would always have the last laugh.

On the face of it Brexit was a game-changer which suddenly handed all of the cards to MPs. David Cameron had been forced to call a referendum because of a breakdown of discipline amongst Conservative MPs under the combined weight of developments within both major parties since 1979. Theresa May, who inherited Cameron's dilemma along with his position, tried to solve this problem by excluding Parliament from the Brexit process. Thwarted by the courts, she exposed the absurdity of the Fixed-Term Parliaments Act (for which she herself had voted) by engineering a general election in the expectation that this would provide her with a more compliant Parliament. Although May's power-grab failed, for students of the prime ministerial role the most significant thing is that she made the attempt. Her successor, Boris Johnson, fared better. Although some elements of his story were those of an archetypal 'insider', other aspects – his appearances in quiz shows, but also (ironically) his failure to shine in the Commons before becoming a populist Mayor of London – fitted him for the role of champion of the people against Parliament (and the courts). For the first time in nearly a decade, after the general election of December 2019 Britain had a Prime Minister who was unquestionably Majority Leader; but it remained to be seen how long he could retain even its nominal confidence.

2

Cabinet-maker

In many respects, the patronage at the direct disposal of a Prime Minister has declined sharply in recent decades. But there is one area in which he or she is still the key decision-maker. The choice of ministers is, of course, always constrained to some extent: some colleagues might be judged too dangerous to leave out, while others might refuse the jobs they are offered. But the final team sheet, and the positions allocated to each member, are the result of the Prime Minister's reflections on the available personnel in the political context of the time.

This consideration might seem obvious, but it needs to be noted in order to point out the absurdity of comparing the position of real Prime Ministers when nominating colleagues for the first time, or conducting subsequent reshuffles, with an 'ideal' scenario in which the choices are entirely free. In that situation, the number of qualified people would exactly match the available positions, and every prospective applicant would either have a proven aptitude for the jobs they are given or at least have shown obvious potential to do them well. They would also be fervent supporters of the incumbent, with no inclination to take the top position themselves until the inevitable, but much regretted, moment when the beloved leader decides to step down. In addition, the people who miss out on selection would gladly concede that, on this occasion at least, they did not deserve to be included. This situation is deeply improbable even in dictatorial regimes. In reality, all Prime Ministers, to some extent, have to offer jobs to ministers in the knowledge that alternative choices would have been more helpful, or (more rarely) to accept that the candidates whom they would like to include in their team cannot be persuaded to accept the position. They know that, in the 'real' world of politics, for every appointment there will be several unsuccessful aspirants who are likely to bear grudges.

Since (albeit to varying degrees) they all exhibit human characteristics, most Prime Ministers find Cabinet-making very difficult. In particular, having to dismiss a minister in a reshuffle, or, on first taking office, to disappoint someone who has proved effective in a 'shadow' capacity, is something which Prime Ministers anticipate with even less relish than their weekly session of PMQs. It must be equally trying to see the satisfied smiles of semi-secret (or even undisguised) personal enemies who, for one reason or another, are impossible to exclude.

Nevertheless, it is unlikely that any British Prime Minister has ever lacked some emotional compensation for the difficult decisions. If the ideal scenario is vanishingly unlikely, the 'total nightmare' – one in which no friends can be rewarded, and the whole ministerial team has to be made up of disagreeable individuals – is no more probable. A Prime Minister whose appointments are *all* enforced would almost certainly resign rather than suffering that indignity.

In practice, the choice of ministers at any time is partly free and partly constrained, depending on circumstances but also on the temperament of the Prime Minister. The obvious expectation is that a Prime Minister whose party enjoys a vulnerable parliamentary position will feel under considerable constraint, and will have to ensure that the full range of opinion within the party is represented within the Cabinet. By contrast, a Prime Minister with a healthy parliamentary majority will feel much less constrained, but this does not mean that he or she will always try to appoint a ministerial team of nodding dogs. Even a Prime Minister who seems to exercise total command of the parliamentary party will feel tempted to offer places to people who have put up some resistance in the past. The obvious ploy is to cajole a few token dissidents into positions where they are unlikely to cause serious embarrassment – where, in fact, they can do less damage to the Prime Minister than if they were left outside the government. But a more bullish Prime Minister could think of offering a fairly senior Cabinet place to a feared opponent, in the expectation that exposure to the very different pressures of ministerial life will make them rethink their previous record of backbench recalcitrance, and that even if they continue to make trouble 'inside the tent' their inclusion will detach them from their parliamentary allies, as well as making the Prime Minister look magnanimous.

This chapter examines several of the ministerial reshuffles since 1979, contrasting the instances where the Prime Minister seemed relatively free from constraints with those in which many appointments were unavoidable. While it would be a mistake to place too much reliance on a handful of case studies, it is noteworthy that the Prime Ministers who seek control over their Cabinets, and are apparently in a position to realize that objective, seem the most accident-prone in their use of political patronage.

'Near-ideal' scenarios: Thatcher (1987) and Blair (2001)

Although no Prime Minister has ever come close to the 'ideal' scenario, the years since 1979 offer at least two examples when the constraints on prime ministerial Cabinet-making *should* have been unusually light. Both Margaret Thatcher and Tony Blair enjoyed considerable parliamentary majorities throughout their spells at No. 10, so the formation of ministerial teams in the aftermath of any their election victories could have been chosen as case studies. However, in Thatcher's case there are good reasons to suppose that her freedom of action was greater after the general election of 1987 than those of 1979 and 1983. In 1979, Thatcher was essentially 'on probation'. Her party had achieved a clear majority (forty-three seats), but there were many doubters in her ranks and the party had fought against a deeply discredited Labour government which had been forced from office by a parliamentary vote of no confidence. In 1983 the Conservative overall majority soared to 144 seats, but between 1979 and 1983 Thatcher's personal approval ratings had varied dramatically (reaching a low, according to Mori, of just 25 per cent 'satisfied' against 66 per 'dissatisfied' in December 1981). Although by the time of the 1983 election Thatcher's popularity had received a considerable boost from the 'Falklands Factor', the contest itself was unusual thanks to the various weaknesses of the Labour Opposition and the emergence of a serious alternative for non-Thatcherite voters in the shape of the alliance between the Social Democratic Party (SDP) and the Liberals.[5]

The 1987 election is a better example, since after that Thatcher and her admirers could claim that the Conservative majority, though reduced from 1983, was no fluke. Having reminded his readers that 'British electoral contests are parliamentary, not presidential', Thatcher's authorized biographer nevertheless claimed that in the 1987 election 'The force of her personality – and the sense that she and her policies were essential for national recovery – had won the Conservatives an overall majority of 102' (Moore, 2019, 4; see chapter 6). In interviews at the time Thatcher stressed (with justification) that securing such a wide margin of victory at the third time of asking was a remarkable achievement. She dismissed any suggestion that she might stand down at some point before the next election, and even refused to rule out the possibility of staying in office until the year 2000 (Campbell, 2003, 527).

In Blair's case, the 1997 general election, which gave his party an overall majority of 179 seats, might be regarded as the high point of his authority in terms of Cabinet-making. Certainly, if Blair had been an incoming Conservative Prime Minister he would have enjoyed an enviable position. But he was constrained by his party's rules, which dictated that politicians who had been elected to the Shadow Cabinet (by an annual ballot of the party's MPs) should be given positions in the full Cabinet when the party took office. Thus, although after the Labour landslide of May 1997 Blair could place favoured colleagues in the most important Cabinet positions, he was not free to range beyond his existing frontbench team. After the initial appointments the institutional shackles were off – in theory, Blair could have appointed the full roster of shadow ministers on 2 May 1997, and replaced all of them with more congenial colleagues on the following day – but in practice he would require a further electoral endorsement before attempting a wholesale ministerial reconstruction. The opportunity arose when Labour's gargantuan majority of 1997 was reduced only slightly in the 2001 contest.

The Thatcher reshuffle of June 1987

In Thatcher's terse account of the 1987 post-election reshuffle, she identified her 'first priority' as the need 'to see that I had the right team of ministers to implement the reforms set out in our manifesto'. These chiefly concerned key domestic policy areas such as education, local government and health. In the first two positions the serving Cabinet ministers (Kenneth Baker and Nicholas Ridley, respectively) were retained. Health, then covered by the sprawling Department of Health and Social Security, was entrusted to a rising young 'Thatcherite', John Moore. Significantly, Thatcher's retrospective account does not mention the promotion to Cabinet (as Chief Secretary to the Treasury) of another, even younger, MP – John Major (Thatcher, 1993, 589).

Thatcher's memoirs also ignore the fact that her reshuffle left in place several key ministers whom, with hindsight, she might have wished to move. The three 'great officers of state' – the Home Secretary (Douglas Hurd), Foreign Secretary (Sir Geoffrey Howe) and Chancellor of the Exchequer (Nigel Lawson) – were retained. However, none of these colleagues were ideal from the Prime Minister's perspective. Hurd had risen through the Cabinet ranks because of his obvious competence, but was suspected as a former associate of Edward Heath. Howe and Lawson had played central roles in the establishment and consolidation of the Thatcherite approach to economic policy; but long before 1987 Thatcher had lost respect for Howe (who had been moved from the Treasury to the Foreign & Commonwealth Office (FCO) in 1983), and had begun to distrust Lawson (who had become Chancellor in Howe's place).

Thus while Thatcher could feel confident that the government's specific manifesto pledges would be implemented by approved individuals, she had good reasons for displeasure with the overall 'team' – hence the reticence in her memoirs. Even some of the people entrusted with the manifesto commitments failed to live up to expectations, for different reasons; John Moore proved unequal to his responsibilities, and left the Cabinet in 1989, while Ridley was deficient in tact and (through his maladroit handling of the poll tax) would almost certainly have been forced out long before his fall in the dying days of the Thatcher administration, had it not been for his unwavering devotion to Thatcherite ideas and to his leader (Ridley, 1991). Kenneth Baker, for his part, was Ridley's antithesis – personally ingratiating and good on television, but another former 'Heathite' whose adherence to the Thatcherite cause always seemed provisional at best.

In short, even after what she herself regarded as an historic and very personal vindication, Thatcher was left with a Cabinet which lacked her ideological drive and/or presentational aplomb. She had, at least, been able to recall her close friend Cecil Parkinson to the Cabinet as Energy Secretary after he had served a period in purgatory following his enforced resignation from the government in October 1983. But Parkinson was suave, and Ridley combined radical fervour and acerbic wit with aristocratic languor. What Thatcher needed to complement these true believers was a street fighter; and in the days before the election the man who had excelled in this role, the Party Chairman Norman Tebbit, notified Thatcher of his intention to step down, due to domestic commitments arising from the grievous injuries which his wife had suffered in the Irish Republican Army's (IRA's) attempt to assassinate Thatcher and senior ministers at the 1984 Conservative conference.

Although Tebbit's reasons for resignation should have been beyond suspicion, he had also been bruised during the 1987 election campaign when his strategy was challenged (and at least partially subverted) by the Secretary of State for Employment, David Young. Young's chances of winning this particular battle were increased by his advocacy of a more prominent role for Thatcher herself in the campaign. As a special adviser (or 'SPAD', as special advisers are often abbreviated), Young had been a key figure in the government's privatization programme and received a peerage along with a Cabinet position in 1984. However, he had never been elected to Parliament, and as such was not in a strong position to question Norman Tebbit's plan for the 1987 general election. In pondering his own position, Tebbit was well aware that Young had raised himself even further in Thatcher's estimation and could expect a significant promotion. In fact, Young had aspirations to succeed Tebbit as Party Chairman, and would have been appointed after the election if Thatcher had felt that she enjoyed an entirely free hand. Instead, he became Secretary of State at the Department of Trade and Industry – a position which Tebbit had held from 1983 until 1985, when Thatcher made him Party Chairman.

Overall, one might conclude that in 1987 Margaret Thatcher flunked the chance of exploiting her personal dominance of the political scene, and instead of creating a team in her own image created a Cabinet of the uncommitted. Indeed, on the basis of Charles Moore's authorized biography one could identify her failure to make a clean sweep of the faint hearts as the original basis of an establishment plot to unseat her before she had the chance to win an historic fourth election victory. Thus, for example, Young's hopes of succeeding Tebbit as Party Chairman were undoubtedly baulked by the moderate Lord (Willie) Whitelaw, who 'told her firmly that the party would not wear it' (Campbell, 2003, 535). This was just one illustration of the tactics used to restrain Thatcher's radical urges. As Charles Moore shows, the people who advised her about the reshuffle had all at one time been elected politicians, in keeping with the previous trend of Cabinet-making consultations (Wilson, 1976, 28–33). Whitelaw – now in the House of Lords, but a veteran of numerous general election campaigns – was present partly in his capacity of Deputy Prime Minister, which had no constitutional status but when embodied by Whitelaw could hardly be ignored. Tebbit also attended, despite his determination to resign as Party Chairman. The ad hoc appointing committee also included the new Chief Whip, David Waddington. However, Waddington's predecessor, John Wakeham, was present in spirit if not in person, since before the election he had submitted a lengthy memorandum concerning Cabinet appointments. Wakeham – who himself would move up to a full Cabinet position in the reshuffle – intimated that no major changes were needed, at least in the top jobs. However, he openly suggested that Thatcher should be thinking about her eventual successor when conducting the post-election reshuffle – an idea which, as we have seen, Thatcher herself had no wish to contemplate at least until after another election (Moore, 2019, 6–12).

Thus, in the immediate aftermath of what she took to be her greatest triumph, Margaret Thatcher acquiesced in the appointment of a Cabinet which, whatever the merits of individual members, was more likely to watch her fall from office without intervening on her behalf than to fight to keep her in Downing Street. Rather than resorting to the facile Thatcherite conspiracy theories, there are two explanations for the Prime Minister's decisions in June 1987.

First, Thatcher was heavily constrained by a lack of suitable candidates. Although the Conservative Party was undergoing a process of 'Thatcherization', this could not happen overnight. Even where constituency parties had swung in her ideological direction, there was too much affection for long-serving MPs to allow the kind of 'purge' which would have given Thatcher a parliamentary squad in her own image. Even the hated Heath hung on to his seat at Old Bexley and Sidcup, despite occasional attempts to displace him, until his retirement in

2001 at the age of eighty-four. Thatcher was reduced to scouring the backbenches for any promising newcomers who might be showing symptoms of neo-liberal fervour, and the results were predictably mixed. For example, in the 1987 reshuffle Thatcher promoted Michael Forsyth (born 1954, elected MP for Stirling in 1983) to a junior position in the Scottish Office. His Thatcherite zeal – inflicted on a country which was increasingly alienated by Conservative governance – could not endear him to the moderate Secretary of State, Malcolm Rifkind. Conflict within the party in Scotland soon increased the difficulty of persuading the Scottish people to accept the poll tax, which was introduced north of the border a year before its extension to England and Wales.

Although it was hardly Thatcher's fault that the pool of believers remained shallow during her time in office – it deepened considerably after her departure, as a kind of belated revenge on the moderate John Major – she had partially drained it herself by making it difficult for Norman Tebbit to stay in office regardless of his domestic circumstances. Her evident preference for Lord Young as an electoral supremo suggests another reason for the limited and unhelpful reshuffle. Young had come to Thatcher's attention as a special adviser. In hindsight, the conflict between Tebbit and Young can thus be seen as the first instalment in a long-running battle for favour between elected politicians and aides who were accountable only to their employer. The fact that in 1987 the unelected individual bested the politician, in an encounter where all the experience (and previous record of success) lay with the latter, was not a good augury.

In fact, Thatcher's penchant for unelected advisers had already been causing friction within the government. Charles Powell, who was seconded from the FCO to serve as Thatcher's Private Secretary in 1983, was far more influential over the Prime Minister's thinking than any of his old Foreign Office colleagues or their Secretary of State, Geoffrey Howe. Powell's influence largely arose from his tendency to agree with Thatcher's own thoughts, encouraging her to believe that, except for routine matters, she could (and should) act as her own Foreign Secretary. After 1987 Thatcher's growing misgivings about the policy of her Chancellor, Lawson, encouraged her to entice back to Whitehall the monetarist economist Sir Alan Walters. In fact, Walters had continued to proffer his wisdom to Thatcher after an earlier stint as economic adviser (1981–3). By the time that his reappointment was announced in July 1988, he was well known as a vitriolic critic of Lawson. The only rational explanation for Thatcher's move was a willingness to undermine her own senior colleague, even at a time when Lawson was extremely popular among Conservative backbenchers (Campbell, 2003, 587). In effect, after 1987 Thatcher was beginning to assemble a personal, unelected 'shadow' team in the hope of bypassing the Cabinet she had appointed.

Blair in 2001

Tony Blair's personal reaction to his second electoral victory was similar to Thatcher's feelings after her hat-trick. His press adviser, Alastair Campbell, thought that he 'felt this was more his mandate in a way' (Campbell, 2011, 635). That was not the end of the similarities. According to Anthony Seldon, 'Blair was confident that, at last, he had affairs more or less as he wanted them' (Seldon, 2004, 469). But in retirement Blair remembered things differently, complaining that 'Around me, at the top, were people who for one reason or another were lukewarm' about the New Labour project, while he 'had now become militant for radical change'. Actually, Blair mentions several elected politicians who were bound to him heart and soul – John Reid, David Blunkett, Tessa Jowell, Charles Clarke, Alan Milburn, Hilary Armstrong and John Hutton. Compared to the swollen ranks of the Parliamentary Labour Party they were not very numerous, but this gave Blair more scope for the promotion of kindred spirits than Thatcher had enjoyed in 1987 (Blair, 2010, 335). One fellow-traveller in the first-class compartment of 'Blairism' who had put himself beyond the pale of promotion was Peter Mandelson – a central figure in the creation of New Labour who had been forced to resign from the first Blair Government on two occasions, due to personal matters rather than principled disagreements.

The 'top' people listed by Blair as deficient in reforming zeal were the Deputy Prime Minister (John Prescott), the Chancellor (Gordon Brown), the Foreign Secretary (Robin Cook) and the Home Secretary (Jack Straw) (Blair, 2010, 335). Prescott had long outlived his usefulness as a conduit between Blair and 'Old Labour' backbenchers, and during the election campaign he had embarrassed the leadership by punching a demonstrator who had thrown an egg at him from close range. However, as Blair's elected deputy he was invulnerable to a similar assault from No. 10. Instead, his ministerial role (centring on local government) was sharply curtailed; his compensation was the creation of an Office of the Deputy Prime Minister (as Andrew Rawnsley put it, 'a shiny doorplate designed to soothe that sensitive ego with the impression that his power was not really being shrunk' (Rawnsley, 2000, 507)).

Blair was able to reduce the roll call of recalcitrants by one, demoting Cook from the FCO to Leader of the House of Commons and replacing him with another person on the naughty list, Jack Straw. This left a vacancy at the Home Office which could be filled by a true believer, David Blunkett. In his memoirs Blair conceded that Cook had 'done well', which was a generous assessment since Cook had incurred criticism for apparently departing from his own promise to follow a foreign policy with a strong 'ethical dimension', and there had been lurid coverage of his marital problems (Blair, 2010, 340). Cook considered resignation, despite a pep talk from Alastair Campbell in which neither man, apparently, talked about the possibility that Cook could use his new job to make Parliament more effective. This consoling thought only seems to have dawned on Cook when he talked through the situation with his new wife, Gaynor (Campbell, 2011, 637; Cook, 2003, 2).

This left Blair with the painful problem of his Chancellor. The Prime Minister had come under pressure from his allies to seize this (probably unique) opportunity either to sack Brown, or, even better, deftly to transfer the balance of guilt by offering him the FCO (which Brown would have refused). Blair decided that he couldn't – perhaps even shouldn't – bring the unstable partnership to an end. Had he known what Brown had been thinking he might have reconsidered. According to Blair's account, 'when I tried to say to him [that] the second term must be different from the first and you must cooperate, he immediately said he knew I wanted to get rid of him' (Blair, 2010, 340). So instead of using the reshuffle to give himself a more congenial Chancellor, Blair ended up with Gordon Brown Mark II; outwardly the same person, but likely to be even more obstructive, glowering and vengeful.

Thus, like Thatcher in 1987, Blair in 2001 was mainly concerned with an agenda of domestic reform whose success seemed to depend on a reliable team of second-tier ministers. Also like Thatcher, he was hampered by an apparent lack of faith among his most senior colleagues – particularly those who occupied 'the great offices of state'. While Thatcher had made no changes at this level, Blair did at least thin the ranks of unbelievers by sacking Cook. But in 1987 Thatcher's relationship with her Chancellor (Lawson) had yet to break down completely, and although she had developed the habit of humiliating Geoffrey Howe in Cabinet meetings she could only do so because, unlike Gordon Brown, Howe was not blessed with a volcanic temperament (indeed, if Howe had put up some resistance Thatcher would have treated him with greater respect).

In 1999 Blair had complained to his natural supporters at a meeting of the British Venture Capital Association that his attempts to reform the public sector had left him with 'scars on my back'. After the 2001 election he took steps to ensure that any future wounds would be inflicted on his inadequate ministers. Before long Downing Street seemed to be equipped with more 'units' than an over-stocked branch of IKEA. In addition to the long-established Downing Street Policy Unit, there was now a Strategy Unit and a Delivery Unit. The last named was particularly ominous for the ministers who survived or benefited from the post-election reshuffle. It was headed by a Chief Adviser on Delivery, who answered directly to the Prime Minister. Obviously Downing Street had always marked ministerial homework to some extent, but now the Prime Minister could rely on a small army of apparatchiks (some, inevitably, recruited from the private sector) who had a vested interest in concluding that ministers 'could do better', resulting in a summons to the headmaster's study.

Considerable academic angst was generated by the idea that Blair was creating a separate department of state – a Prime Minister's Department – in all but name. Andrew Rawnsley, a seasoned observer of Westminster and Whitehall, had no doubts on the matter (Rawnsley, 2000, 507–8). We will return to this question (see chapter 3), but for now the main point is that the creation of these units – staffed as they were by unelected people with a licence to run the slide rule over the 'delivery record' of elected politicians – illustrates the sharpest contrast between the 1987 and 2001 reshuffles. After her third election victory, as we have seen, Thatcher took counsel from politicians who had devoted most of their adult lives to democratic politics. According to Alastair Campbell, before the 2001 election Blair told him that 'he alone would decide the cabinet' (Campbell, 2011, 632). What this meant, in practice, was that he would choose the Cabinet without any input from elected colleagues. It seems that the list of appointments was rejigged very slightly after representations from Gordon Brown, but Robin Cook learned that 'the Cabinet reshuffle had been settled on the afternoon of polling day in Sedgefield between Tony and his travelling entourage of Anji [Hunter] and Alastair Campbell'. Although the timetable recorded by Campbell in his own diary is different, the essential message is the same; Cook was told that not even Jonathan Powell, Blair's grandly named 'Chief of Staff' and thus a likely participant in such personnel matters, was involved in the deliberations of 'a very tight little cabal' (Cook, 2003, 7). If true, this would provide a piece of prime ministerial trivia which connects the reshuffles – on both occasions the Prime Minister employed an unelected person from the Powell family who was more influential than most Cabinet colleagues, but nevertheless took no direct part in Cabinet-making.

While both Powells are shadowy figures in accounts of the two reshuffles, it is the name 'Anji Hunter' which catches the eye when comparing 1987 with 2001. It can hardly fail to do so, since it features so regularly in the published diaries, the autobiographies and even the serious histories. For example, Anthony Seldon devoted a (brief) chapter of his biography of Blair to a person whom hardly anyone – even those with a keen interest in political developments under Blair – will have heard of. In Campbell's diary, the Hunter affair extends over several pages, which can be explained because his partner, Fiona Millar, was closely involved. In his exasperation, Campbell compared the saga to the American television soap opera *Peyton Place*, but maybe he had confused this with the British comedy *Upstairs, Downstairs*, which dramatized conflicts between the servants in an Edwardian stately home. In any event, the episode was more evocative of indecorous rivalry between Mrs Masham and the Duchess of Marlborough at the real-life court of Queen Anne than of orderly proceedings within a healthy liberal democracy.

Anji Hunter and Tony Blair had established a close friendship when they were both teenagers. Having worked for Blair in the early years of his career, Hunter left for domestic reasons before rejoining the Labour Party machine in 1992. In 1997 she was given the role of 'Director of Government Relations'. In reality, her job description was less relevant than the role she played – that of Blair's female, unaccountable alter ego, using her attractive personality to win friends and influence people in places where even Blair feared to go in person. Her location close to the centre of British decision-making was usually summed up in the claim that she gave Blair an insight into the thinking of 'Middle England', though he had plenty of people doing that already through the medium of carefully choreographed 'focus groups'.

By the time of the 2001 general election, Hunter was ready to move on and had a job offer from the oil company BP. But while Blair was unsentimental in his treatment of elected colleagues with less lucrative prospects, he would move heaven and earth to retain the services of Anji Hunter. He duly persuaded her to stay with an enhanced but still ill-defined role, even though this caused considerable tension within his own family (his wife Cherie was understandably perplexed by his reliance on Hunter) and strained relations between Campbell and his partner Fiona Millar, who worked for Cherie (Blair, 2010, 336–7; Campbell, 2011, 637–9). Hunter eventually left Downing Street in the following year, and contrary to Blair's fears in 2001 the sky did not fall in on him and his administration.

To reinforce the impression that special advisers and spin doctors were now in the ascendant, it was in the aftermath of Blair's second victory that the government's whips were turfed out of No. 12 Downing Street and moved to No. 9. The convenient access previously enjoyed by elected party officials was now appropriated by appointees (see chapter 1).

To look in detail at the reshuffles of 1987 and 2001 – just fourteen years apart, which is hardly a heartbeat in the existence of the British premiership – is like entering two different worlds. Yet in the Thatcher reshuffle one can detect that the world of Tony Blair was struggling to be born. In 1987, there were already signs that the Prime Minister was becoming dependent on unelected individuals who happened to agree with her. Margaret Thatcher was a constitutional innovator by temperament and deed, rather than by conviction and theory. As such, she probably did not realize the true significance of her decisions after 1983, when she began to show a preference for the company and counsel of special advisers. Thatcher loved an argument, but for policy-making purposes she wanted to surround herself with people who told her that her views were correct. Blair, by contrast, wanted to keep hold of people who were allowed to disagree with him from time to time, so long as they gave the impression of liking him as a person. This might have been a change for the better compared to the Thatcher years, had it not been for the fact that under Blair there were far more special advisers, each of whom apparently enjoyed a licence to bark instructions to elected ministers.

Suboptimal scenarios: 2010 and 2015

Having considered examples of Cabinet-making when the Prime Minister was in a strong position thanks to a comfortable parliamentary cushion, the obvious points of comparison are occasions when the overall majority was thin, even non-existent. These conditions applied in three consecutive elections from 2010. However, in the first two cases the Prime Minister (David Cameron) could be said to have come out of the general elections well. In 2010 he had led his party back to office after thirteen years in the wilderness, and five years later the Conservatives achieved a majority of twelve seats despite having presided over a period of economic 'austerity'. Knowledge of subsequent events did not prevent Cameron from giving the title 'The Sweetest Victory' to the chapter of his memoirs which covers the 2015 election.

As we have seen, in 1987 and 2001 Prime Ministers with large majorities were still far from free (not least in respect of senior appointments), but also placed constraints on themselves while privately cursing the lack of talent at their disposal. The main problem was that Thatcher and Blair were divisive figures within their parties. While Cameron had made much of his Blair-style drive for Conservative 'modernization', in practice before 2010 this had chiefly taken the form of encouraging a more diverse cast of parliamentary candidates. 'Modernization' stalled completely with the advent of a global financial crisis in late 2007, after which the party was preoccupied by economic issues and could unite behind the 'austerity' programme.

Cameron would still have faced some very tough decisions in 2010 if his party had fared well enough to govern alone. As it was, in terms of Cabinet-making the context of 2015 was still suboptimal, but one in which Cameron could turn his lack of freedom to advantage. There were two Cabinet-makers, not one; and since his Liberal Democrat partner, Nick Clegg, broadly shared his views Cameron could feel fairly relaxed about any appointments suggested from that quarter. Indeed, he quickly agreed to award five Cabinet positions to the Liberal Democrats – a more generous allocation than their parliamentary strength would have justified.

Unlike Thatcher in 1987 and Blair in 2005, Cameron had few doubts about his three most senior colleagues. The new Chancellor, George Osborne, was his closest political ally (and a personal friend). William Hague, the Foreign Secretary, was also regarded as wholly reliable (and capable) by Cameron. In sharp contrast to the toxic Blair–Brown relationship, Cameron and Osborne had agreed that the former (who was more than four years older) should serve as leader while Osborne waited for his own chance; Hague had already thrown the dice (1997–2001) and, although he would have been an ideal 'caretaker' in a crisis, he showed no sign of hoping for this eventuality. The ambitions of Theresa May, who became Home Secretary after serving as Shadow Leader of the House and covering Work and Pensions, were less clear. However, even if she and Cameron were unlikely to become soulmates the Prime Minister could be confident that she would approach her demanding departmental duties with steely-eyed efficiency, under-pinned by a pronounced sense of public duty.

As a pragmatist with no taste for theological debates about Britain's membership of the European Union, Cameron could never have satis-fied the ambitions of the party's ever-growing army of 'Eurosceptics'. However, the limited stock of Cabinet posts at his disposal gave him a ready-made excuse for restricting their numbers. For example, his main rival for the party leadership in 2005, David Davis, had resigned three years later as Shadow Home Secretary and triggered a parliamentary by-election in a quixotic gesture of protest against Labour's policy on identity cards. Although Davis won the by-election, he was not reappointed to the front bench. If the Conservatives had won the 2010 general election, Davis could not have been denied a Cabinet role. As it was, he could be told to keep waiting until a suitable vacancy arose. With Davis out of the frame, Cameron was able to balance the appointment of Kenneth Clarke – viewed by the sceptics as an incur-able 'Eurofanatic' – as Justice Secretary by offering Iain Duncan Smith his first ever Cabinet post as Secretary of State for Work and Pensions. Since Duncan Smith had been forced out of the party leadership in 2003 he had co-founded a think tank, the Centre for Social Justice, to address the most pressing issues facing his new department. Thus while Duncan Smith was an unlikely associate for any group of 'modern-izers', he seemed well qualified for a position which had nothing to do with his other hobby horse – hatred of the EU – so that his inclusion seemed justifiable in itself, as well as keeping him out of mischief on the backbenches.

Cameron also had complete confidence in the team of advisers he brought with him to Downing Street. There were two controversial members of his encourage – his Director of Communications, the former *News of the World* editor Andy Coulson, who lasted only a few months before resigning over his involvement in the 'phone hacking' scandal (see chapter 5), and the Director of Strategy Steve Hilton, a long-standing friend of Cameron's and a radical thinker whose frustra-tion at the cool reception for his ideas led to his own departure in 2012. While Hilton was an advocate of reform (and reduction) of the civil service, Cameron was much more at ease with senior figures like Gus O'Donnell, the Cabinet Secretary until the end of 2011, and his successor Jeremy Heywood. Cameron hoped to reduce the number of special advisers at Downing Street, against the advice of Tony Blair and others (Seldon and Snowdon, 2015, 29). There would be no return to the days when unelected people like Alastair Campbell and Jonathan Powell could give orders to civil servants (Cameron's Chief of Staff, Ed Llewellyn, was an amiable, conciliatory figure rather than an 'enforcer'). Cameron also signalled his desire for a less hyperactive centre by dismantling Blair's Delivery Unit.

In an important sense, though, the partial downsizing of Downing Street missed the point. Both Cameron and Osborne had been spe-cial advisers themselves, albeit unusual ones since they always had a taste for democratic politics rather than hoping to spend their careers influencing decision-makers without taking the trouble to get elected. Almost certainly this explains their sober assessment of the value of 'SPADs', compared to the unbridled enthusiasm of their supposed role model, Tony Blair. This view was vindicated by the lack of really seri-ous trouble caused by Cameron's personal team (Coulson resigned because of his actions prior to working for the Conservatives, and although Hilton made considerable waves this was because of what he was *prevented* from doing). The problems were caused by other people's 'SPADs'. Liam Fox resigned as Defence Secretary in October

2011 due to a scandal involving his special adviser, and the tenure of the Education Secretary, Michael Gove, was truncated because of his abrasive attitude towards the teaching profession and members of the education 'establishment', in which he was warmly seconded by his own 'Chief of Staff', Dominic Cummings.

When Cameron set about the task of forming a 'Conservatives Only' Cabinet after his 'sweetest victory' in 2015, he must have started to detect an unpleasant aftertaste. Since he had pledged to hold an in/out referendum on Britain's membership of the EU, it was obvious that his ministerial appointments would be constrained by the need to provide something which at least approximated to a balance between likely 'Leavers' and 'Remainers'. In reality if not in name, Britain had been governed by coalitions since the arrival of 'New Labour' in 1997 introduced the toxic feud between 'Blairites' and 'Brownites'. In hindsight, the brief 2010–15 interlude, when the government was called a coalition but was generally characterized by goodwill interspersed with occasional unavoidable rows, looked anomalous. When he formed his Cabinet after the 2015 general election, the 'Heir to Blair' was back in the position which confronted John Major after 'Black Wednesday' in 1992; and this time the 'Bastards' were emboldened by Cameron's weakness.

Nevertheless, among Cameron's 2015 Cabinet the overwhelming majority were 'Remainers'. Only five full members – Chris Grayling, Theresa Villiers, John Whittingdale, Duncan Smith and Gove – wanted Britain to leave the EU. Cameron had shown his limited enthusiasm for the first two individuals by omitting them from the 2010 Cabinet, even though they had held frontbench positions before the election (Grayling, indeed, could have expected appointment as Home Secretary). Cameron regretted missing more than one opportunity to dismiss Duncan Smith, whose plans for welfare reform had incurred Osborne's displeasure and had begun to look like a policy disaster in waiting. If Duncan Smith had been a 'Remainer' rather than a memento mori of heroic resistance to Major's Maastricht Treaty (see chapter 1), he would have been swatted away after the 2015 election without hesitation or regret. Although Whittingdale's private life was somewhat colourful, his position was presumably safe because he was considered an appropriate person to appease his party's hatred of the BBC without carrying any influence on policies outside his remit.

As for Gove, at the time of his appointment as Justice Secretary in 2015 his position on the referendum was ambiguous, something which Cameron regarded with anxiety. After asking for Gove's resignation as Education Secretary in 2014, Cameron had looked with increasing desperation for things his one-time friend might do to justify his continuation in the Cabinet; it was difficult to decide whether Gove was more badly miscast as Justice Secretary than he had been in his previous non-starring role as Chief Whip (2014–15). When Gove snubbed Cameron's overtures and declared for 'Leave', the Prime Minister was badly hurt. He should have been less surprised by the similar decision of the former Mayor of London, Boris Johnson. Cameron had been doubtful about the role he should give to Johnson after his contemporary at Eton and Oxford had decided to return to the Commons in 2015. Since Johnson was officially still London's Mayor, the Prime Minister had a valid excuse to deny him any official position. However, he could not avoid extending a degree of recognition (and enhanced status) to an individual who was now better known for his ambitions than for any services he had rendered to London, and allowed Johnson to attend 'political' meetings of the Cabinet.

Compared to his electoral prospects back in 2013, when he had made his fateful referendum pledge, the 2015 result allowed Cameron to think that his hand would be strengthened in forthcoming negotiations for revised terms of EU membership. Although the unwaveringly pro-EU Liberal Democrats had (rather recklessly) argued for an in/out referendum in the past, a general election in 2015 which left Cameron with no alternative but to re-establish his coalition with Clegg et al. would have been horribly difficult to manage, given the state of his own party and the increasing popularity of the United Kingdom Independence Party (UKIP) (Bale, 2016, 400). Free from the coalition, Cameron could 'bat for Britain' in the forthcoming talks without worrying about Lib Dem disapproval of his tactics, before presenting the inevitable EU concessions to the public (and, more importantly, his party) as a triumph for Britain.

If this scenario had been realized, and the case for 'Remain' had secured the comfortable (though not overwhelming) victory which David Cameron had good reason to expect after his party had won the 'sweetest victory', his Cabinet appointments would have looked quite sound. The post-election reshuffle left the three senior offices of state in the same hands – Osborne at the Treasury, May at the Home Office, and Philip Hammond (who had succeeded Hague in 2014) at the FCO. All three were 'Remainers', but to differing degrees; more accurately, they could all say with honesty that they had no great liking for the EU, but (like the Prime Minister himself) they based their approach to the referendum on a careful calculation of Britain's national interest. If the referendum went as expected, few changes would be required at 'second-tier' levels (the Duncan Smith problem having been solved by his resignation in March 2016). On the assumption that Gove and Johnson would come on board (after compulsory shows of reluctance, to save face with unreconstructible Leavers), both could be rewarded in one way or another to give them a platform to face off against Osborne when the time came to choose Cameron's successor (according to the latter's plan, shortly before the next election).

The May reshuffles

The failure of Cameron's referendum gamble made his position untenable, and his resignation was followed by a leadership battle which offered unattractive insights into the state of the Conservative Party. As it was, the public was too distracted by the post-referendum emotions of elation, recrimination and bewilderment to register the true significance of the unseemly scrap. Thus when Theresa May emerged as the new leader and Prime Minister in July 2016 – well ahead of the expected timetable, since the other leading contenders had sabotaged either each other or (in the case of Andrea Leadsom) themselves – even non-Conservatives who had watched the fiasco with amazement and concern could breathe a sigh of relief. May's elevation was widely approved, and on paper it seemed like the best solution to the country's dilemma, since she was regarded as a cool pragmatist who had supported 'Remain' even though (unlike most of her colleagues) she was receptive to both sides of the argument.

Yet little was known about Theresa May beyond a presumed capacity to take hard-headed decisions in the national interest. Very few members of the public knew that she exemplified, to an almost surreal degree, one of the tendencies we have already noticed in this chapter – the psychological dependence of elected politicians upon unelected special advisers. The reconstruction of Cameron's shattered government was conducted by May in close consultation with her long-standing favourites, Nicholas Timothy and Fiona Hill, who had worked for May during her long and difficult years at the Home Office. They had, however, made themselves less than popular, and by 2015 both had left government service. Now that May was Prime Minister they were back, with personal scores to settle and (in Timothy's case) an ideological agenda to pursue.

With her psychological props back in place, and emboldened by the favourable public reception of her ascent to the premiership, May now acted as if she had already secured a resounding electoral mandate. Osborne, who had been hailed as one of the heroes of 2015, had made himself the top target on the 'Leaver' hit list through his (understand-able but counterproductive) tendency to present worst-case scenarios as if they were very likely results of a Leave vote. To say the least, May had not been Osborne's favourite minister, and now she had the chance of revenge. Typically, though, the negative briefing about Osborne was left to her advisers. According to Osborne's account, the most insulting feature of their face-to-face encounter was her attempt to patronize him, suggesting that he should 'get to know the Conservative Party better' (Seldon and Newell, 2019, 77). Tacitly, May was suggesting that Osborne – despite more than two decades of service – knew less about his party than the unelected hired hands, Timothy and Hill (nicknamed 'the Chiefs'), who had advised her on Cabinet appointments.

There were other peremptory sackings – those of Oliver Letwin, who had been a key figure in the formation of Cameron's coalition government, and Nicky Morgan, who in her capacity of Education Secretary had apparently clashed with May in Cameron's Cabinet. Since May was unencumbered by Cameron's complex cocktail of feel-ings towards Morgan's predecessor at Education, Michael Gove, she used the pretext of the latter's dismal showing in the leadership contest to halt his peregrination through inappropriate governmental roles, and return him to the backbenches.

Apart from its usefulness as an example of a Prime Minister's *real* political weakness being changed by contextual factors into an apparent position of strength, this reshuffle is also noteworthy as an illustration of the incumbent's ability to reshape the institutional archi-tecture of Whitehall. Theresa May showed that she meant business – and that her business was to 'deliver Brexit' – by creating two new government departments: the Department for Exiting the European Union (DExEU), and the Department for International Trade (DIT). The first was highly unusual in that its success would lead to its rapid disappearance. The second, by contrast, could achieve no concrete results while DExEU existed, since under the terms of the Lisbon Treaty (2007) a state which had decided to leave the EU could not sign any trade deals until it had completed the formal process of withdrawal. Having created these bodies, May bestowed upon them Secretaries of State with impeccable 'Leave' credentials, but rather tarnished histories in the eyes of more objective observers. As we have seen, Liam Fox (DIT) had been forced to resign from the coalition Cabinet thanks to a scandal involving a special adviser, while David Davis (DExEU) had resigned as Shadow Home Secretary in 2008 in a way which raised questions about his political judgement. Having dared to dispense with Gove, May could hardly exclude Boris Johnson, another leading 'Leaver' with a blemished reputation. The offer of the Foreign Office was a clever move, since Johnson was unlikely to refuse such a prestigious post even if he suspected that it would keep him away from the key decisions. He would at least have the chance to work alongside Priti Patel (International Development), who had raised her public profile considerably during the referendum campaign. Another Leaver, Chris Grayling (Transport), was retained despite a patchy performance in previous ministerial roles.

May's new team was generally presented as a new attempt to balance 'Leavers' and 'Remainers'. However, in terms of the Cabinet, at least, this terminology was unhelpful. The Leavers had always been a miscellaneous bunch, likely to respond in different ways (on the basis of contrasting calculations) to unfolding events. The Remainers, by contrast, had decided to work on the basis that the referendum result could not be overturned, and were now better understood as supporters of a 'soft Brexit' (or even 'BRINO' – 'Brexit In Name Only') – that is, one that embodied the closest possible relationship with the EU which was compatible with the referendum result. These ministers included the new Chancellor, Philip Hammond; the Home Secretary, Amber Rudd; and the Secretary of State for Health, Jeremy Hunt. The Secretary of State for Work and Pensions, Damian Green, also fell into this category; and as a long-standing friend of May who had worked with her at the Home Office he was more influential than his official role suggested.

Given these circumstances, a realistic option for Britain's second woman Prime Minister was to emulate the initial tactics of the first one, by ensuring that the key decisions were taken by the ministers who shared her outlook even if they were a minority within the full Cabinet. If that had been her intention, the reshuffle would have left her in an even stronger position than Thatcher's in 1979, since there was good reason to suppose that, given a lead, the former Remainers would have acted as a more cohesive group than their opponents. However, having constructed a Cabinet which could have been mobilized behind a compromise settlement with the EU, May allowed herself to be persuaded that a 'hard' Brexit was the only viable solution. Thus, at a stroke, she risked isolation within the Cabinet (with the exception of the ultra-loyal Green); she had cut the ground from under the feet of ministers who had accepted the referendum result on the (logical) assumption that it would have to end in a compromise; while the hard-line Leavers (and their backbench sponsors) would never throw their full weight behind someone who had campaigned on the losing side.

When May called a 'snap' general election to exploit her protracted 'honeymoon' with the voters (if not with her Cabinet colleagues) her main objective was to use the ballot box to over-ride the resistance of the other branches of government – Parliament and the judiciary. However, the anticipated personal 'mandate' would also give her the chance to appoint a Cabinet much more to her liking. An overwhelming victory would elevate May into the 'near ideal' position for Cabinet-makers – perhaps making her even stronger than Thatcher and Blair had been in 1987 and 2001. A Blair-style landslide, following an even more 'presidential' campaign, might even allow her to contemplate the removal of under-performing Brexiteers like Johnson, Davis and Fox. Her prime target, however, was her Chancellor, Philip Hammond, who (in accordance with a familiar script) was seen to have 'gone native' at the Treasury even though he had merely persisted with the view (i.e. that Brexit would have detrimental economic effects) which May herself had expressed before the referendum.

After the election, having performed what she chose to interpret as her duty to country and party by cutting an expensive deal with the Democratic Unionist Party (DUP), May was forced to recognize that her position vis-à-vis the existing Cabinet was not so much sub-optimal as supplicatory. Far from sacking Johnson – who had quickly recognized that his immediate personal interest lay in offering May ostentatious support – she had to accede to his demands for concessions to the FCO. She also felt compelled to bring back Michael Gove, exposing him at the Department for Environment, Food and Rural Affairs (DEFRA) to a different tribe of the 'experts' he had derided during the referendum campaign. But the most significant change of the reshuffle was the enforced departure of the 'Chiefs', who were convenient (and very apposite) scapegoats for the election fiasco. May was left to find compensations in the promotions of two Europragmatists, Damian Green (who was briefly First Secretary of State and effectively Deputy Prime Minister) and David Gauke (moved from Chief Secretary of the Treasury to Work and Pensions, and thence to Justice Secretary).

As we have seen, even at the best of times ministerial reshuffles can be very difficult for Prime Ministers, who will have to convey unwelcome tidings to lachrymose or combustible colleagues. However, sacking someone who has outlived his or her usefulness is probably less of a strain than feeling forced either to promote or leave in place a person that you hate, despise or both. Even then, the pain will probably fade after a while. But when ministers refuse point-blank to recognize your authority to make such decisions, the wounds are fatal. You have, effectively, ceased to be Prime Minister.

This is the lesson which Theresa May should have heeded when she tried to reconstruct her Cabinet six months after the general election, in January 2018. By that time, her less-than-dreamy team of June 2017 had been denuded by four departures (including Green), due to illness or scandals of varying kinds. At least none of the resignations were directly connected to Brexit; but this was not a source of satisfaction for May, who had to try to give the appearance of balance within her incohesive Cabinet even though she had handed the political initiative to hard-line Brexiteers. In terms of political influence, by this time the effective 'Cabinet' was the backbench European Research Group (ERG) of Tory MPs, whose voting strength in the House of Commons effectively blocked the way to a compromise Brexit. The sense that 'Leaver' ministers felt that they could now write their own rules was best exemplified by the conduct of Priti Patel, who embarked on an inappropriate 'fact-finding' visit to Israel without official sanction. May followed the rule book by sacking Patel in November 2017; but other, equally reckless, Brexiteer ministers knew that they were effectively immune from dismissal or reprimand.

Tragicomically, there were attempts to choreograph May's misguided reshuffle of January 2018 as if the centre was still in control of ministerial movements. In a belated flash of common sense, May had appointed a new Chief of Staff (Gavin Barwell, MP for Croydon Central from 2010 to 2017) with experience of the democratic process, rather than a special adviser. According to Anthony Seldon, Barwell was a key figure in the reshuffle, along with the Chief Whip, Julian Smith, but with support from the Cabinet Secretary Jeremy Heywood. The illusion of 'business as usual' was sustained by an attempt to plot the proposed changes on a whiteboard (Seldon and Newell, 2019, 370).

The proposed reshuffle might as well have been scribbled in invisible ink. It was not especially surprising that the main troublemakers in January 2018 were people who, like May, had been 'Remainers' in the 2016 referendum: the Cabinet's Brexiteers had no reason (as yet) to make May's life even harder. Jeremy Hunt, the Health Secretary, who had been relocated on the whiteboard to Business, Energy and Industrial Strategy (BEIS), refused to budge. Justine Greening, the Education Secretary, was offered a similar move, to Work and Pensions, but demurred due to her commitment to education and, more pertinently, her belief that 'the government [was] falling apart and I didn't want to be part of it any more'. Even the presentation of events, which had been unpleasantly efficient under the iron grip of Alastair Campbell in the Blair years, was becoming farcical, thanks at least in part to social media. The rumour mill was churning out unfounded stories about ministerial appointments even as the supposed beneficiaries were walking up Downing Street (Seldon and Newell, 2019, 371).

Conclusion

No series of case studies of the Prime Minister as Cabinet-constructor can yield the kind of 'models', let alone 'laws', which appeal to political scientists. It would be nice, for example, if one could say on the basis of the foregoing discussion that Prime Ministers who seem to enjoy a free hand in making appointments will always create their own constraints and immediately resent them, while those who embark on the process fully (even painfully) aware of their constraints soon learn to work within them, and thus do a much better job.

The first generalization seems applicable to the Thatcher and Blair examples. Blair was constrained by a single individual – Gordon Brown – but he was chiefly responsible for that problem, having mishandled the relationship since the latter allowed him a free run at the Labour leadership in 1994. After 1997, Blair's allies chose to attribute Brown's understandable resentment to 'psychological flaws' – not a very reassuring assessment of the custodian of the nation's finances. It is not surprising that Brown made the most of the institutional resources at the Treasury, which Blair could not deny to him given greater seniority, knowledge and experience. However, in 1987 Thatcher had no need to create her own constraints, since she really *was* hampered by the inevitable time lag between the establishment of her ascendancy (1982 and the Falklands) and the emergence of a mainly Thatcherized parliamentary party (post-1992).

The idea that Prime Ministers actually benefit from unavoidable constraints fares no better on close inspection, since it merely underlines the crucial interaction between context and character. In future years it might even seem that Prime Ministers whose parties have fallen short of an overall majority, and are forced to lead a formal coalition, are in the most fortunate position. However, in 2010 the context and the main characters were near-perfect for a sensible accommodation, and there can be no guarantee that such a happy conjunction will recur.

Picking the members is not, of course, the limit of prime ministerial influence over the Cabinet. She or he also controls the agenda, and can sum up the discussion in a way which (if necessary) gives undue weight to one side. However, this part of the Prime Minister's role is less important than it used to be, since it is unlikely that worthwhile discussion takes place, even when the full Cabinet actually meets. Since 1997 Prime Ministers have been attracted to the idea of holding Cabinet meetings outside London, suggesting that these meetings should now be regarded (to adapt Bagehot's terminology) as an 'undignified' part of the British political process – a photo opportunity, rather than a crucial decision-making forum.

The death of Cabinet government in Britain has been announced on so many occasions that one can understand why some observers still clutch at any evidence of continued vitality – hence, for example, the persistent view, even in academic circles, that Margaret Thatcher was brought down by a handful of ministers rather than a much more widespread feeling in the parliamentary party that she had become an electoral liability, a mood to which almost all of Thatcher's colleagues responded with timidity rather than 'treachery'. In truth, for a contemporary Prime Minister the time spent in Cabinet meetings is scarcely more profitable than attendance at the House of Commons (see chapter 1). Although under the Ministerial and Other Salaries Act of 1975 the number of Secretaries of State is limited to twenty-one, this still makes Cabinet an inconvenient body for decision-making (and several other ministers are usually given the right to attend when relevant). On many of the topics under discussion, a majority of attendees will have limited interest or knowledge. It would be far more efficient to take decisions either at formal gatherings of relevant individuals in Cabinet subcommittees, or in ad hoc meetings which are basically conversations between the Prime Minister and a handful of those chiefly concerned. Yet, as Tony Blair found, the latter method is dysfunctional when the attendees are regarded as cyphers, lacking respect from within their parties or from officials within their departments. These considerations involve the Prime Minister's role in policymaking, which will be discussed in the next chapter.

3

Policy-maker

On the traditional model of policy-making in the UK, the Prime Minister oversees a process in which the key actors are ministers and Whitehall departments (see Dorey, 2014, 70–132). When necessary and after consultation with interested parties, the latter generate proposals for reform which are offered for consultation (in the form of Green Papers) before being enshrined in pre-legislative White Papers. The proposals are discussed in a relevant Cabinet subcommittee before consideration (and, almost invariably, endorsement) by the full body. The Prime Minister can be involved in various stages of this process, by recommending policy changes to ministerial colleagues, commenting on any developing plans and offering personal support if the proposals encounter resistance. With no departmental responsibilities of their own, 'activist' Prime Ministers can inject dynamism into the government as a whole, influencing and encouraging reform in several policy areas at once. Equally, of course, Prime Ministers can stand back from the policy-making process, leaving ministers to get on with the jobs to which they were appointed.

It is not impossible that this orderly approach to policy-making will ever return, but there are good reasons for thinking it unlikely. Before 1979, the general rule was that ministers and their senior civil servants were the chief instigators of policy changes within their departmental remits. Now the expectation is that the initiative for the most significant reforms will come from No. 10, and the litmus test for any important policy proposal will be its likely effects on the popularity of the party in office. This chapter traces the key developments which have, since 1979, resulted in the 'hollowing out' of the British policy-making process, focusing in particular on the misfortunes of the Home Office.

The impact of Thatcher

The 'hollowing out' of Whitehall departments has been a protracted process, but the key trends were set under Margaret Thatcher. Her personal impact was registered in several ways – some reflecting her initial vulnerability as Prime Minister, others resulting from her overall mission to reverse a decline in Britain's fortunes which she attributed to decades of 'consensus' politics, in which successive governments and their senior civil servants had tacitly accepted that their role was to cushion voters from the effects of their country's reduced global status and relative economic decline.

The relegation of Cabinet

Thatcher's first step was to subvert the spirit of the traditional policy-making model. Previously the general rule had been that policy proposals were discussed by a relevant Cabinet subcommittee, attended by a range of suitably qualified ministers who could be expected to detect any glaring practical or political problems. This meant that colleagues who were not directly involved in a policy initiative were usually ready to endorse the proposals without more than a cursory discussion when they came up before the full Cabinet. However, Thatcher knew at the outset of her premiership that her political approach, and her analysis of Britain's post-war experience more generally, were opposed by a majority of her Cabinet colleagues. She had signalled in advance of the 1979 general election that she wanted to avoid lengthy Cabinet discussions, by which she meant that she had no taste for debates which would expose the level of dissent. Her best chance of stifling open disagreement was to ensure that her key (economic) policies had already been approved by subcommittees packed with 'Thatcherites', and to hope that her opponents would not dare to reopen these questions when they came up for endorsement by the full Cabinet.

This approach had the desired effect until July 1981, when ministers from a variety of departments rebelled against proposed cuts to government spending, on the grounds that these would further damage an economy which had already suffered as a result of earlier decisions. Among other effects whose full significance was not recognized until much later – including the 'downsizing' of Britain's manufacturing sector in the face of punitive interest rates, despite the unique potential for government investment offered by North Sea oil – the feeling of national malaise had been registered in a series of urban riots in the weeks leading up to the July discussions.

The enforced retreat over spending cuts was a serious setback for the Prime Minister, who had advertised her inflexibility at the previous year's Conservative Party conference (see chapter 4). But if the Cabinet could not by bypassed, she could start to change its composition. In September 1981 she sacked three dissident ministers. The veteran Party Chairman, Peter Thorneycroft, was edged out and replaced by Thatcher's close ally Cecil Parkinson. Other adherents, like Nigel Lawson and Norman Tebbit, were promoted to the Cabinet. In her main speech at the 1981 conference Thatcher told her party that 'Nothing is beyond this nation. Decline is not inevitable . . . I remember what our country used to be like and I know what we can become again.' Away from the cameras, at an overflow meeting of supporters, she delivered a new version of her 'You turn' speech of the year before: 'We don't say back to the centre ground; we say, stand on your principles like a rock.'[6]

Personnel changes at the top, however necessary, were only part of Thatcher's plan to revitalize British government. Well before the Falklands conflict which transformed her political fortunes, Thatcher had fostered a series of developments whose effects would be felt long after the early battles of her premiership had been forgotten. These changes originated from outside Westminster and Whitehall, and the key agents were not ministers or officials.

The obsession with the private sector

Searching for plausible explanations of Britain's relative decline compared to other European nations like West Germany, Thatcher concluded that successive governments of both main parties – infected as they were by 'socialist' attitudes and practices – had lost touch with the 'wealth-creating' private sector. Now that 'the party of free enterprise' was back in office, it should hasten to correct this historic mistake. As the dutiful daughter of a small businessman, Thatcher's personal sympathies lay with plucky entrepreneurial 'underdogs' (like the pioneer of low-cost airlines, Sir Freddie Laker). But she also felt considerable respect for the representatives of big businesses. Having survived the long years of socialist onslaught, they must have many invaluable lessons to teach the government and its servants.

In 1979, Thatcher established an Efficiency Unit under Sir Derek Rayner, a senior executive within Marks & Spencer.[7] Before his return to the company as chairman in 1982, Rayner had reviewed Whitehall's functions and recommended a variety of reforms to improve performance and cut costs. Apart from his genuinely impressive business career, Rayner had also been a government adviser in the early 1970s (albeit in the specialized field of defence procurement). However, his reforming efforts under Thatcher marked the beginning of an obsession with targets, performance management, etc., which received a very cool reception from government employees.

The 'Rayner reforms' coincided with Thatcher's spending cuts which fell heavily on the civil service – 16,000 posts were culled before Rayner's return to Marks & Spencer – and also with a vogue for 'macho' management in the Anglo-American private sector, which meant that 'businesslike' attitudes were being forced on Britain's bureaucrats at the very time when private sector practices were more alien from the civil service ethos than ever before. Although recruits to the civil service were attracted for the usual range of reasons, the very best of them (able individuals who really wanted to serve the public) were the ones who were *most* likely to feel that their world had changed unpleasantly and irretrievably. If civil servants were being asked to improve efficiency in a less ominous context, morale and performance might not have been affected so badly. As it was, a basic grasp of human nature would have anticipated that government employees would take whatever action was required to give the appearance of working harder (to save their jobs) while taking far less pride in their tasks and finding their only pleasures in the workplace in the delightful release which came from 'clocking off'.

Thatcher's relentless propaganda in favour of 'wealth-creators' had a wider, cultural effect. When meeting someone socially for the first time, public servants at the middle rank and below were now under a compulsion either to conceal their place of employment, or to apologize for it. This mood, of course, was not conjured by the Thatcherites out of thin air; Britain's relative post-war decline, and the fading of the initial idealism associated with the domestic policies of the Attlee Governments (1945–51), had made the civil service a particular target for 'anti-establishment' propaganda from the left as well as the right since the 1960s. However, for hostile (and even quite well-informed) observers the civil service was the easiest target for satire in the broadcast media. In this context, most commentators cite the brilliant BBC series *Yes Minister*, which appeared just as the Thatcher Government was attempting to remould the spirit of the civil service but which (in the person of Sir Humphrey Appleby) presented a caricature of its practices when it was at the height of its prestige. Unsurprisingly, despite her general distaste for the BBC, Thatcher herself was an ardent admirer of *Yes Minister*. Nevertheless, this fertile field for ill-informed public merriment had been ploughed many times before in less sophisticated fashion. Even Charles Dickens had invited his readers to laugh at the futility of bureaucracy, and more recently a *Monty Python* sketch of 1970 had lampooned a 'Ministry of Silly Walks'. The effect, though, was far more acute in the early 1980s when civil servants were afflicted by so many simultaneous detrimental trends.

The other damaging cultural change of the 1980s was the new feeling, authorized by government pronouncements as well as virtually all media outlets, that individual worth could and should be gauged by earnings (or lifestyle, whether or not it was 'earned'). Again, this attitude was not the exclusive product of 'Thatcherism', but in the 1980s it received an official stamp of approval (Garnett, 2007, 214–65). On this score, civil servants were hammered by the zeitgeist whichever way they turned – while clerks were treated with contempt because of their relative poverty, tabloid newspapers publicized the affluence of the best-rewarded bureaucrats in a manner which implied that civil servants as a whole were overpaid. In time, as private sector pensions were raided by 'entrepreneurs' for their personal use, hostility turned towards the supposedly 'gilt-edged' provision enjoyed by public servants, even if they had been paid a pittance before their retirement.

Margaret Thatcher did not regard herself as a constitutional innovator; rather, she thought that in various ways she had injected new life into the existing system. However, she could only persist in this misapprehension because she had never understood, let alone sympathized with, the role of the British civil service. It was the duty of senior officials to preserve the distinction between the interests of the state and those of the political party which happened to be in office. In a ramshackle, uncodified system the civil service had begun to act as a brake on elected ministers who, for various reasons, were impatient to implement change without necessarily thinking through the consequences. Since the Attlee Government had introduced further restrictions on the House of Lords, making it little more than a source of reflection on measures passed by the Commons, the need for such constitutional retardants (which, of course, could be bypassed during genuine national emergencies) had become more evident. Thus, if the civil service really *had* become more obstructive since 1945, this could be justified as an example of a flexible constitution creating informal 'checks and balances' when they were needed to guard against executive dominance. The need for strengthening such barriers to 'elective dictatorship' had been identified in 1976 by Lord Hailsham, who in 1979 became Thatcher's Lord Chancellor (Hailsham, 1976). Yet from the start of her premiership, Thatcher's attitude towards the civil service betrayed an ignorance of such contextual factors, presumably owing to her unhappy experience as Secretary of State for Education (1970–4) when she had been unable to arrest her Department's established policy of replacing selective grammar schools (of which she herself was a product) with comprehensives, which she regarded as seminaries of socialism.

'Hiving off'

Before Rayner's departure, Thatcher had removed a barrier to reform by abolishing the independent Civil Service Department and dividing its functions between the Treasury and the Cabinet Office. Rayner was succeeded as Thatcher's adviser on efficiency by Robin Ibbs, a director of Imperial Chemical Industries (ICI). Under Ibbs, the Efficiency Unit produced a report (*Improving Management in Government: The Next Steps*) which congratulated the government on its initial changes, while warning that 'there is still a long way to go'. The report called for 'sustained pressure' to change 'the cultural attitudes and behaviour of

government' (Efficiency Unit, 1987, 1). The most radical recommendation was that, wherever possible, government functions should be taken
from the direct control of departments and entrusted to 'agencies'
which enjoyed varying degrees of autonomy. This could be interpreted
as a recognition that civil servants would cling to their lamentable 'cultural attitudes and behaviour' so long as they were allowed to remain
within their institutional silos. If they could be prised out of Whitehall,
however, it would be much easier to subject them to the new manage-
rial culture. Instead of dragging the private sector into Whitehall, the
government should push Whitehall into the private sector (or the nearest realistic approximation).

By the mid-1990s, more than three-quarters of civil servants had
been transferred to these agencies, and the first scandals associated
with the change had emerged (the notorious Child Support Agency was
established in 1993 and quickly won recognition for inhumanity and
maladministration). An obvious effect was to reduce ministerial accountability to Parliament. Ministers would now set the policy framework, so
that any shortcomings in 'delivery' of services could be blamed on the
agency. But poor delivery could easily arise from ill-advised policy decisions or the failure of government to provide adequate funding. Even in
these instances, the creation of agencies offered ministers an invaluable
first line of defence; whether or not the 'delivery' had been inadequate
because of government decisions, the agency was bound to be the initial
(and hopefully the only) focus of the media outcry.

The other foreseeable (and, presumably, desired) development
arising from *Next Steps* was a significant shift in the balance between
ministers and their civil servants in terms of policy-making. When
departments were directly responsible for service delivery, senior civil
servants could gather intelligence regarding serious deficiencies and
recommend necessary reforms to their ministers. Now, ministers were
more likely to learn about problems within their remit from media
reports – and their civil servants would be in the same position. Stripped
of this essential early warning mechanism and caught on the hop as a
result, ministers were much more likely to blame their civil servants for
failing to perform a duty which, thanks to political decisions, was no
longer within the competence of even the most eagle-eyed Permanent
Secretary. In their panic-stricken realization that legislation might be
needed, ministers would be much more likely to exclude civil servants

from the process and rely instead on special advisers, whose knowledge of the field covered by the department was unlikely to be more profound than that of their minister, and whose priority would be essentially the same – that is, the avoidance of negative media headlines in the short term, whatever the ultimate implications for the policy area covered by the department.

This is not to say that *Next Steps* freed ministers entirely from the shadow of accountability. But even before Thatcher's enforced departure in 1990 there was a noticeable trend for ministers to resign because of mishaps in their private lives (or verbal indiscretions) rather than for proven professional incompetence. In this instance (as in so many others), Thatcher's legacy visited itself mainly on John Major, her chosen successor, although Tony Blair's government did not escape unscathed. In large part, this was because Thatcher's attempt to make the civil service more businesslike had only succeeded in demoralizing staff at all levels, and making it much harder to convict ministers of avoidable *political* mistakes. When personal scandals were exposed, and the paparazzi arrived on ministerial doorsteps, the dependence of ministers on prime ministerial support became all too evident: misbehaviour was much more likely to be condoned by No. 10 when the culprit was in favour for other reasons.

Pragmatism versus ideology

In the early 1980s, the best way to incur displeasure was to show less than wholehearted commitment to 'Thatcherism'. This was well known to the government's Conservative critics, who tended to express themselves in coded messages rather than spelling out their misgivings. They might have saved themselves the trouble; Lord Thorneycroft, for example, sealed his fate by joking with journalists that he was neither a 'wet' nor a 'dry' (in the terminology of the time), but was afflicted by 'rising damp'. Thorneycroft's age (seventy-two) could be used as a cover story for his dismissal in 1981. But others who were removed or reshuffled were in their political prime, had proven their ministerial competence and seemed to have unblemished private lives.

In 1979, Thatcher had been unable to avoid the appointment of a Conservative moderate, James Prior, as Secretary of State for Employment, despite the entreaties of her allies who regarded Prior as a spineless appeaser of trade unions. Prior's chief antagonist was another member of Thatcher's unpaid army of entrepreneurs, John Hoskyns, who argued for a radical assault on the privileged position which trade unions had established under successive post-war governments. However, in the years before *Next Steps* and the hollowing out of Whitehall, Prior was able to stand his ground against Hoskyns. Prior's preference for gradual reform was based on the experience of the Heath Government, which had tried to address the problem in a single piece of legislation and had encountered overwhelming resistance. The 1980 Employment Act focused on 'secondary picketing' – the weapon which unions had deployed most effectively in the disputes of the previous decade. While unions responded by organizing a 'day of action', their extra-parliamentary protests were unlikely to work this time since they had lost public support through their actions during the 'Winter of Discontent' (1978–9). Feeling that his 'step-by-step' approach had been vindicated, Prior had begun to consult on new legislation when, shortly after the Cabinet rebellion of July 1981, he was removed from his position.

Prior's successor, Tebbit, was widely regarded as a political thug – 'a semi-house-trained polecat', as he had been described by the Labour leader, Michael Foot. Officials in his new department soon discovered that his private manner belied his unsmiling public persona. However, it was probably more helpful that Tebbit tacitly accepted the wisdom of Prior's strategy, using the latter's plan as the basis for his own Employment Act of 1982. The main target of this legislation was compulsory union membership in the workplace. Abolition of this so-called 'closed shop' was a key objective among right-wing Conservative backbenchers, but Tebbit decided not to go that far at this stage. As he put it, 'I was determined first to form public opinion, and then to be always just a little behind rather than ahead of it as I legislated' (Tebbit, 1988, 182–5). It was the sort of pragmatic, non-confrontational approach which drove John Hoskyns to doubt Margaret Thatcher's radical credentials. Having failed to convince the Prime Minister of the need for revolutionary change, replacing senior civil servants with political appointees and massively increasing the policy-making capacity of No. 10, Hoskyns resigned as head of the Downing Street Policy Unit before the 1983 election (Hoskyns, 2000).

The transformation was never going to happen overnight, but

Hoskyns and his ilk had achieved far more than they thought. Nowhere was the subsequent change more evident than in the Department of Employment. After the 1983 general election Tebbit moved to Trade and Industry, where once again he established excellent relations with officials (including a young Andrew Lansley (see below)), as he threw his energies behind the government's fledgling privatization programme. In his absence, the Department of Employment, which until recently had been a significant policy-making actor, was essentially reduced to two functions – finding inventive ways of reducing the official unemployment count, to spare the government's embarrassment, and trying to please the Prime Minister by proposing new legislation to shift the balance of the workplace in favour of employers.

Hollowing out the Home Office

One department which apparently changed very little during the Thatcher years was the Home Office. Despite being classed as one of the 'three great offices of state', it was also seen as a slaughterhouse of political reputations due to its ill-defined and unpredictable remit. Security, crime, the justice system and immigration were all policy areas in which disasters could strike with minimal notice. As a result, the Home Secretary was rarely a magnet for positive publicity.

The first three Home Secretaries to serve under Margaret Thatcher – William Whitelaw (1979–83), Leon Brittan (1983–5) and Douglas Hurd (1985–9) – all encountered problems. But these reflected the usual hazards of the job, compounded by new challenges arising from socio-economic change. For example, Whitelaw had to contend with the 1981 inner city riots, and within weeks of taking office Douglas Hurd was attending the funeral of PC Keith Blakelock, who had been murdered during a disturbance on Tottenham's Broadwater Farm estate. Yet Hurd – a very experienced observer of officialdom whose natural metier was the Foreign Office – was impressed with the calibre of his colleagues. As he put it, 'There was no question in those days of special advisers dictating policy', and he saw no requirement for more than one personal aide (Hurd, 2003, 317).

The self-inflicted problems began in 1989, when Thatcher appointed the former Chief Whip, David Waddington, as Hurd's successor. Waddington knew the Home Office well (he had been a junior minister there from 1983 to 1987). However, his return as Secretary of State was a surprise to many, and it seemed to owe something to the fact that, unlike his predecessors, Waddington supported the restoration of the death penalty. Yet this did not guarantee favourable treatment from the right-wing press. Waddington was not reappointed when John Major replaced Thatcher in 1990, and he felt that his career had been truncated by negative publicity following a riot at Strangeways Prison, Manchester (now Manchester Prison). The fallen minister was most aggrieved by the fact that during the early stages of the riot his best sources of information were national newspapers; even in these days before the Prison Service was awarded formal agency status, Waddington was given the impression that the department's political head should not be involved in such 'operational' matters (Clarke, 2016, 284; Marsh et al., 2000, 318). In short, there were already signs that the government's policy of 'hiving off' would be particularly damaging to the Home Office, raising serious questions about accountability.

Waddington's successor, Kenneth Baker, was determined not to fall foul of the right-wing press. His presentational flair had been exhibited as Thatcher's last Party Chairman (1989–90), and his well-developed sense of impending trouble was activated soon after his appointment, as a series of attacks on humans by dogs in spring 1991 generated lurid newspaper headlines. Baker was surprised to encounter considerable resistance from officials who evidently thought that new legislation would be a bad idea. Even after he had left government Baker continued to 'spin' on behalf of the Dangerous Dogs Act, but it was recognized within Whitehall as over-hasty and poorly drafted, raising 'all sorts of ghastly administrative problems'. As the historians of political disasters put it, 'Enacting the measure was overwhelmingly a symbolic act, intended to symbolize the government's determination to deal with an issue, not really to achieve anything in particular' (King and Crewe, 2013, 295; Marsh et al., 2000, 318–19). As such, far from being an aberration it provided a model for future policy-makers throughout Whitehall.

After the 1992 general election Kenneth Clarke took Baker's place. Already well accustomed to the ways of Whitehall, Clarke was impressed by the quality of his officials but felt that the Home Office had 'the most distinctive – and old fashioned – culture of any government department in which I had ever served' (Clarke, 2016, 286). In other words, the

Home Office had not yet succumbed to Thatcherite managerialism. Contrary to his image as a 'One Nation' Conservative, Clarke was the ideal person to effect the desired transformation. However, there was little he could achieve in just over a year (he moved to the Treasury in June 1993); true to his usual form, his energies were devoted to fights with vested interests (in this case the Police Federation).

During Clarke's brief stint, the Shadow Home Secretary, Tony Blair, pledged that a future Labour government would be 'tough on crime, tough on the causes of crime'. Although Clarke recognized the vacuity of this 'brilliantly meaningless slogan', it presented a considerable challenge to a Conservative Party which assumed 'ownership' of law and order issues (Clarke, 2016, 291). Clarke's successor, Michael Howard, duly sought to re-establish his party's reputation with his own highly questionable sound bite, 'Prison works' – a position which conflicted very sharply with Clarke's liberal approach to sentencing policy. Howard had been complicit in Thatcherism's most notorious legislative felonies – the poll tax, and Section 28 of the 1989 Local Government Act, which was both homophobic and unenforceable. At the Home Office he continued to work on the assumption that doing things very visibly was preferable to doing the necessary things quietly and well. A blizzard of legislation emanated from Howard's Home Office, imposing a considerable burden on the House of Lords, which was left with the job of detecting and correcting the legal defects. While Clarke had taken on the Police Federation, Howard declared war on judges who were well aware that prison did not work, since they had to preside over so many cases involving unreformed ex-inmates.

Under Clarke the prison service had finally been given agency status, and its first Director-General, the businessman Derek Lewis, received the impression that the main priority was to improve conditions in the prisons, not least by reducing overcrowding. However, this ambition was in direct contradiction of the 'prison works' approach; and when stories of escapes and riots hit the headlines, Howard could not respond in the approved knee-jerk fashion because (unlike Clarke, who had benefited from Waddington's warnings and insisted on an active role) on operational matters the Home Secretary now had to defer to the Director-General. Frustrated beyond endurance, Howard sacked Lewis, leading to a notorious *Newsnight* interview in which Howard repeatedly refused to answer questions about his dealings with the agency.[8]

Thus Howard's hyper-sensitivity to negative headlines had led to the passage of flawed legislation, and a prison service torn between the conflicting priorities of retribution and rehabilitation. In fact, far from proving that the Home Office was a political graveyard, Howard did eventually rise from the dead, becoming Conservative leader in 2003 (but only after a humiliating bid for the position in 1997 which was overshadowed by continuing controversy over Derek Lewis and the *Newsnight* interview). Clarke himself showed that it was possible to go on to better things, being widely praised for his ensuing service as Chancellor (and only missing out on his party's leadership because of his refusal to bow to the rising Tory tide of Euroscepticism). The chief victim of Howard's regime was the Home Office itself.

When Blair became Prime Minister in 1997 it was obvious that he would take a keen interest in Home Office matters. His first Home Secretary, Jack Straw, was in some ways a reversion to the Hurd model. Thanks to Labour's long years in the wilderness Straw had no previous ministerial experience, but as a long-serving frontbench politician who had been a special adviser in the 1970s he was unlikely to be discomposed by dysfunctionality within Whitehall. Instead of disclosing endless battles with obstructive officials, Straw's memoirs record an unusual degree of job satisfaction and genuine regret when, after the 2001 general election, he was moved to the FCO (Straw, 2012, 323).

Even so, Straw's tenure was far from trouble-free, including the fuel protests of September 2000 which demonstrated the difference between a government's ability to shape the news cycle and its capacity to influence events in the 'real world'. Other problems he faced were significant straws in the wind for his successor. In the summer of 1999 a media storm was aroused by delays in the processing of thousands of passports. In part, the problem was created by a new computer system – a familiar theme in stories of recent government disasters. But Straw discovered that, ironically, the Passport Service was a victim of its own apparent success. Having previously been spared from the negative publicity which had affected so many areas covered by the Home Office, it had become complacent.

Straw's other serious problem had very similar features. A sharp increase in the number of applications by asylum seekers overwhelmed the Immigration and Nationality Directorate, which had also been struggling with computerization. To make matters worse for the Home

Office, it still had direct responsibility for this Directorate which was based more than ten miles from Whitehall, in a grim 1970s tower block in Croydon. Challenged in the House of Commons, Straw accepted overall responsibility and paid tribute to the staff of the Directorate, but also apologized for the backlogs and promised that measures would be taken to improve the service. It was a parliamentary tightrope walk but the wily Straw just about managed to keep his balance.[9]

Before Tony Blair left office, both the Passport Service and the Immigration Directorate had been turned into Executive Agencies (the latter having been branded 'unfit for purpose' by another Home Secretary, John Reid). With commendable understatement, in his memoir Straw notes that although there might have been some merit in the thinking behind such bodies, this was 'nothing like as much as the enthusiasts thought . . . Even from Opposition I had profound concerns that the way they operated was leading to a lack of accountability and ministerial grip' (Straw, 2012, 297). By 2013 immigration became so politically embarrassing to the then Home Secretary, Theresa May, that she had to establish a new UK Visas and Immigration Service, back under Home Office control. But the Thatcherite autopilot which had been trying to steer British government since the early 1980s could not be switched off, and the agency concept persisted despite unanswerable evidence that it was a menace to crew and passengers alike.

After the 2001 general election Blair replaced Straw with a more fervent supporter, David Blunkett (Campbell, 2011, 343). Between 1997 and 2001 Blunkett had been entrusted with another of Blair's favourite policy areas, Education (which since 1995 had been yoked together with Employment (see above)). Here Blunkett had been forced to exercise unaccustomed tact on a number of occasions when Blair himself, or No. 10 officials, offered impractical suggestions. Thus, for example, in September 1997 Blair asked Blunkett to develop a strategy which would include an informal target of providing child care for everyone under the age of sixteen. Blunkett had to point out that this was completely unrealistic (Blunkett, 2006, 42–3). He could expect similar suggestions at the Home Office; Straw remembered being instructed by Blair, out of the blue, to reduce car crime and burglary by 30 per cent, and replying by asking 'would you like me to produce a new plan for pushing water uphill?'[10]

Despite some irritations – including having to deal with a

Director-General of Schools who 'knew very little about schools' – Blunkett recorded few serious complaints in his diary during his time at Education and Employment and clearly found that job very fulfilling (Blunkett, 2006, 32). His attitude towards the civil service in general was transformed by his encounter with the Home Office. At a Cabinet meeting just a few months into his new role, he responded to a proposal which would clarify the relationship between special advisers and civil servants by asking, 'can we build into it legislation that protects the government from the civil service? . . . The civil service are very lucky that we can't sack them' (Blunkett, 2006, 354).

It is dangerous to attach too much significance to the testimony of a single witness. But Blunkett has unusual credibility, not least because he was outspoken and honest (often, as he concedes, to his own disadvantage), entered government with a genuine desire to make a positive difference to people's lives, and was a very keen student of politics who had remained on close terms with one of his tutors, Bernard Crick, a prolific writer on the British system of government. In addition, the published version of Blunkett's diary includes reflections after the events he describes, as well as his contemporary observations.

In the record he made after his outburst in Cabinet, Blunkett elaborated on his grievances against his civil servants: 'Every time I want to do something, the Department argues with it. Everything I've done of any worth on immigration and nationality has been in spite of the Department rather than with their support.' In the following year he noted that 'One of the problems in the Home Office is that even the better people are reactive rather than looking for solutions and getting ahead of the situation as fast as they can' (Blunkett, 2006, 355, 485).

In part, the problem illustrated the way in which New Labour's much-vaunted 'joined-up government' actually worked, following on from the 2000 fuel protests which had been caused by Treasury taxation policy and left to the hapless Home Office to sort out. At Education and Employment, Blunkett had eagerly promoted the government's view that immigration (especially of skilled workers) should be encouraged to meet the challenges of the new 'knowledge economy' (Consterdine, 2018, 185–7). But almost since its inception the Home Office had been geared towards the *exclusion* (or deportation) of 'aliens'. In other words, at Education and Employment Blunkett, with strong backing from No. 10, had been allowed to muse over the abstract advantages of unlimited immigration. As Home Secretary, he found himself among people whose whole working lives had been overshadowed by the *practical* results of wrong-headed government decisions. The predictable result was a butting of heads rather than a meeting of minds, not least because Blunkett brought with him a battalion of special advisers who were equally estranged from practical considerations.

Blunkett should not have been surprised that his officials tended to be 'reactive', since the Home Office was essentially the Department for Unpredictable Happenings and was likely to remain so, even after some of its functions had been transferred to other departments. His failure to understand the reluctance to take legislative initiatives is even more perplexing, since his published diary provides ample evidence that this was the fault of his own Prime Minister. After his first week in the post, he followed a lengthy tirade about the ineptitude of officials by noting that 'they jumped every time No. 10 spoke. If No. 10 said they thought priority should be given to something (No. 10 being [Blair's Principal Private Secretary] Jeremy Heywood and the advisers around him, or even any junior spokesman ringing across), they panicked. They had obviously been completely programmed by, and under the control of, No. 10, including on legislation and press work' (Blunkett, 2006, 271–2). The comedic value of such comments is tinged by tragedy, not just for the officials who had to work with such a minister but also for Blunkett himself. As the leader of Sheffield Council during the heyday of Thatcherism (1980–7), he had generated considerable respect through media appearances in which his integrity and passion shone through. As soon as he became a minister, however, he acted as if he owed everything to 'Tony', and 'jumped every time No. 10 spoke' without any of the excuses available to Home Office staff.

While it is doubtful that Blunkett's officials had been 'completely programmed' by No. 10 as the Home Secretary asserted – they just had no means of resisting its unrealistic instructions – his own thought process as recorded in his diary was imbued with Orwellian doublethink. For example, when pondering the root causes of the Department's dysfunctionality he suggests that his Conservative predecessors had failed to 'use their special advisers effectively' – thus proposing a key source of Home Office problems as their most promising solution (Blunkett, 2006, 355). He did not, though, criticize the Conservatives for a far more serious blow to Home Office performance and morale

– the *Next Steps* programme. Instead, Blunkett deplored the fact that the department had 'so many advisory groups, special and service agencies, so many bodies that nobody has any control over – and virtually accountable to nobody at all', as if this was the fault of the Home Office itself (Blunkett, 2006, 282).

Thus Blunkett had adapted Blair's sound bite: he had identified the causes of the problem (and, implicitly, the culprits), but chose to be tough on the victims. His expressions of sympathy were reserved for political colleagues, and for himself. In April 2004, Beverley Hughes, the Immigration minister, was forced to resign after the appearance of critical media reports about the awarding of visas to migrants from Eastern Europe. Given the approach to immigration which he had absorbed in Education and Employment and carried into the Home Office, Blunkett thought that laxity in such matters was a cause for congratulation rather than censure. In his diary, he asked if 'there [is] anywhere else in the world where a minister would have lost his or her job not because of their own policy decision, not because of incompetence, but because of the failures of others' (Blunkett, 2006, 631). Thus in Blunkett's parallel universe Hughes had been brought down by civil servants, rather than by the media which had identified her (instead of the Home Secretary himself, who held overall ministerial responsibility) as a scapegoat. The episode did nothing to deter Blunkett in his courtship of the right-wing press, even after it brought about his own departure from the Home Office (in December 2004) amid allegations over his private life. After being recalled to the Cabinet in 2005, Blunkett was forced out again, this time by a financial scandal. Almost immediately, he agreed to write a regular column for the *Sun* newspaper – the most prominent of the media outlets which had blighted his career.

As if to underline the changes which were taking place, in September 2004 Blunkett was asked to account for an apparent security breach at Buckingham Palace. In his diary account he protested that 'I am becoming tired now of apologising for the failures of others' (Blunkett, 2006, 688). There was, at least, no question of resignation over this issue, unlike a similar situation in July 1982 when an intruder had managed to get into the Queen's bedroom and the Home Secretary, William Whitelaw, offered to leave the government. Also, for once, Blunkett recognized that the 'failures' had not arisen within the Home Office. However, the Metropolitan Police, which for quaint historical reasons had been placed under the direct purview of the Home Office, was not entirely to blame. The 2004 intruder had been protesting against the decisions of another agency – the one ostensibly devoted to Child Support, and whose chronic and crass mismanagement was well known to the New Labour government. In such instances, 'joined-up government' was exposed as yet another New Labour sound bite, which (if it meant anything at all in practice) summed up the way in which mistakes in one policy area could be palmed off on one department after another until the media's appetite was exhausted.

With the greater clarity of thought which accompanies semi-detached status, during the Iraq crisis Clare Short noted in her own diary that the civil service was 'working very badly because all power has been sucked into No. 10' (Short, 2004, 197). However, her identification of Downing Street as the location of all 'power' can be questioned. In his early days at Education and Employment, David Blunkett recorded a conversation with Tony Blair over the government's Education Standards Agenda. Blunkett guessed that Blair had persuaded Gordon Brown to provide adequate funding for the initiative, because Blair knew that implementing the Agenda without the necessary resources would be 'a public relations disaster' (Blunkett, 2006, 28). In other words, while Blair's pre-election mantra had been 'education, education, education', to be more accurate it should have been 'good publicity, good publicity, good publicity'. In this context, control over policy-making had to move from departments to the centre, just as the Downing Street machine determined ministerial media appearances. But it seems a misnomer to describe this as an exercise of 'power', if this is taken to mean an ability to achieve desired policy outcomes. At most it could be seen as an attempt to use power over one group of people (ministers and civil servants) in the hope of exerting some influence over another (newspaper owners, editors and headline writers) who might in turn affect the choices of British voters; the real-world effect on the nation's children was in danger of being overlooked.

Prime Ministers and policy-making

Despite the carnage being wrought elsewhere in Whitehall, there was one department – the Treasury – which continued to escape the 'hollowing out' process. As a result, interactions between No. 10 and the

Treasury fall into a separate category. For different reasons, the Foreign & Commonwealth Office (FCO) will be examined elsewhere (see chapter 5). But in terms of departments charged with 'delivering' a government's domestic agenda, it is reasonable to argue that the traditional model of policy-making no longer applies. If Downing Street so chooses, it can become the primary policy actor across the whole range of responsibilities covered by these departments; and it is usually ready to make that choice when key electoral considerations appear to be at stake.

For understandable reasons, most students of this subject have focused on Downing Street's *capacity* for intervention. Measuring this in numerical terms – that is, the number of advisers working for the Prime Minister – scholars have found, evidently to their satisfaction, that compared to the White House Staff they were relatively few even under Blair. As a result, Britain could not have entered a period of 'presidential' government after all.

However, if one examines policy-making in Britain from the perspective of ministers and departments, a different hypothesis is suggested. If departments have been deprived of independent policy-making capacity – if they have come to see themselves, essentially, as vehicles for the delivery of a government's electoral pledges, rather than custodians of the long-term national interest, and if their ministers, for various reasons, are motivated primarily by a quest for positive media coverage which will please the Prime Minister and improve their prospects for promotion – the 'numbers game' becomes far less important. Even the most hyperactive, sleep-deprived Prime Minister will find it difficult to exert policy-making dominance across the whole range of policy issues. But, other things being equal, a small body of advisers authorized by the Prime Minister can make departments feel unable to take any policy initiative without approval or prompting from No. 10. Special advisers, of course, will tend to do the job very badly: with no understanding of the department in question, or the associated problems of implementation, they will tend to order the impossible, then wait for the department to take the consequences. They will do so with greater confidence since departmental ministers, to varying degrees, are influenced by their own special advisers, who share their mindset and have personal ambitions which make the dreams of civil service 'empire builders' look very modest.

If the basic element of our hypothesis seems plausible – that is, that most departments of British government have been 'hollowed out' since 1979, handing the initiative to the Prime Minister and his or her unelected aides should they choose to exploit this situation – we can evaluate the records of each incumbent from this perspective, without reference to an academic debate which has been preoccupied in recent decades by a comparison between the British executive and the American presidency. While the analysis is inevitably impressionistic to some extent, it can be conducted on the assumption that Prime Ministers now face far fewer constraints in terms of policy-making than has ever been the case since the step change in government activity resulting from the election of the Attlee Government in 1945. Contrary to the assumption that the ideal situation for highly interventionist Prime Ministers is the ability to pick up the phone in person and bark orders, this method of control is less convenient than the feeling that one has appointed a wholly reliable minister who will carry out one's wishes without even asking for instructions – a system of 'remote control'. For Prime Ministers. the nearest approximation to perfection is a scenario in which, thanks to like-minded Cabinet colleagues, they only feel compelled to intervene in those policy areas which interest them the most.

Margaret Thatcher

As we have seen (chapter 2), Margaret Thatcher was unable to appoint a Cabinet to her liking in 1979. Key policy areas, particularly relating to the trade unions, were under unfriendly control. Having to admit (temporary) defeats in these fields, she concentrated on economic policy, where the relevant ministers would work on her behalf without having to be prompted. Since economic policy was the key battleground in Thatcher's early years, this ability to exert control through support rather than dictation proved decisive, and her ability to marginalize her 'wet' critics was consolidated by the Falklands factor.

However, not even the substantial Conservative majorities of 1983 and 1987 provided a guarantee that Thatcher could govern by 'remote control', since the talent pool of 'true believers' was somewhat shallow (see chapter 2). In this context, the Westland crisis of 1985–6 is particularly instructive. While Thatcher was an ideologue, who from an early age had taken the view that government interference in economic activity was likely to prove counterproductive, her Defence Secretary, Michael Heseltine, believed that carefully targeted intervention (especially in declining urban areas) could be highly beneficial. Heseltine was also a charismatic politician, with obvious leadership potential (and an undisguised ambition to succeed Thatcher at some point). As Defence Secretary since 1983 Heseltine had performed according to script, being particularly robust in seconding Thatcher's argument that the basing of American nuclear weapons in Britain would guarantee the country's security rather than making it a more likely target for the Soviet Union.

Despite Heseltine's energetic compliance with Thatcher's main priority on defence issues – thus fulfilling the desired outcome of influence by 'remote control' – it was always possible that conflict between these incompatible individualists would arise at some point. As Secretary of State for the Environment (1979–83), Heseltine had appreciated that no government decision could be taken on purely economic grounds, and had paid particular attention to the plight of areas (like Merseyside) whose situation, at least to some extent, reflected previous government decisions rather than pure 'market forces'. In addition Heseltine, in the sharpest possible contrast to Thatcher, was unafraid of deeper integration within 'Europe'. Indeed, by the time of the Westland crisis he was in a unique position to understand the irrelevance to contemporary politics of nineteenth-century assumptions about Britain's 'sovereignty', since it was impossible to square such notions with the acceptance of American nuclear weapons on British soil unless (as Thatcher herself seemed to do) one took the view that the 'special relationship' with the US could never entail a diminution of sovereignty.

From Thatcher's point of view, the Westland Affair was a rude reminder that, despite her personal role in the 1983 Conservative election victory, control over policy could not be taken for granted. Heseltine's argument that the ailing Westland helicopter company should be rescued by a European-dominated consortium was contested by the Secretary of State for Trade and Industry (DTI), Leon Brittan, who (supported by Thatcher and key members of the Westland board) preferred an American-led bid. It was natural for Thatcher to think that Heseltine would be persuaded to desist once the relevant Cabinet committee had ruled in favour of the American consortium. But Heseltine persevered, even after the full Cabinet had endorsed Thatcher's approach. Although the Prime Minister was tempted to sack Heseltine, she was advised that this would be too dangerous. Instead, she decided to use more devious tactics to make him back down (and, hopefully, resign). The Solicitor-General, Sir Patrick Mayhew, was invited to give a private opinion on a public letter in which Heseltine had developed his case. Mayhew's view was that Heseltine's letter contained 'material inaccuracies'; although his response was addressed to Heseltine and marked 'confidential', its contents were leaked to the Press Association by a DTI official acting with the encouragement of No. 10.

Heseltine and his allies could now take the high constitutional ground, arguing that Thatcher had broken both the letter and the spirit of the normal rules of Cabinet government. However, these 'rules' were conventions which were amenable to adaptation; and Thatcher herself had shown considerable skill in using them to her advantage during her initial struggles with her Cabinet. In January 1986 Heseltine lost his battle, resigning during a Cabinet meeting when Thatcher announced that all future statements on Westland would have to be cleared in advance by the Cabinet Office. She still had reason to fear that the affair had given the Opposition an opportunity to damage her premiership, perhaps even irreparably; but the Labour leader, Neil Kinnock, delivered a poor speech in the ensuing vote of confidence and Heseltine decided to refrain from further controversy in return for a partial public apology from the Prime Minister (Heseltine, 2000, 313).

Whatever his motivations, Heseltine had provided a test case of Cabinet government in the mid-1980s. If an argument over policy could be presented as a clash between two middle-ranking Cabinet ministers, the winner would be the minister who enjoyed the Prime Minister's support. This was not surprising, but Thatcher had been prepared to fight dirty to make sure that Brittan 'won' the argument, and although many voters would have followed the drama with interest their pre-vailing response to the constitutional imbroglio was probably one of bemusement. Certainly few would have comprehended why a Prime Minister who had emerged defiant and unbowed from the Falklands War, the IRA assassination attempt at Brighton in October 1984 and the 1984–5 miners' strike could possibly be removed from office because a minister (however popular) had challenged her policy-making authority.

This lesson could hardly be lost on ministers of Heseltine's rank whenever they felt tempted to challenge Thatcher's decisions in future.

The more rational reaction, after Westland, was for such ministers to anticipate Thatcher's likely reception of any policy choice and take this as their guide. Some had been working on these lines since the 1983 election. Thus the Community Charge or poll tax, which had been rejected as unworkable when Heseltine was the responsible minister (at Environment), was brought back into play after the 1983 election by politicians who had limited sympathy for 'Thatcherism'. Eventually it was implemented by an Environment Secretary (Chris Patten) who, left to himself, would have disagreed with the Prime Minister on almost every important policy issue. Non-Thatcherite ministers in other departments rushed forward with 'radical' ideas of their own. Norman Fowler, who became Secretary of State for Employment after the 1987 general election, championed legislation to end restrictive practices among dock workers, whom Thatcher had been reluctant to confront due to their ability to disrupt trade. After 1987, further resistance by dockers was self-evidently futile, and the moderate Fowler was delighted to have been given this chance to establish some Thatcherite credentials. Kenneth Baker, who had been spurned initially by Thatcher because of an old association with Edward Heath, won his own ideological spurs as Education Secretary (1986–9) by introducing a raft of reforms which, among other things, further undermined the independent policy-making scope of local authorities (Jenkins, 2006, 116–20).

After Westland, and her party's victory in the general election of 1987, Thatcher could feel confident that her personal agenda would be advanced by most of her ministers (see chapter 2). Between 1987 and 1990 domestic policy-making resembled an auction in which career-minded ministers took turns to bid for Thatcher's favour. However, there was one ministry, at least, which was not prepared to adopt Thatcher's presumed policy preferences on autopilot. The steadfast, and heartfelt, support of Treasury ministers (headed by the Chancellor, Sir Geoffrey Howe) had been essential to Thatcher's survival during the recession-blighted years of 1979–81. The merest suggestion of dissent from Howe would almost certainly have forced a humiliating policy reversal, and possibly even a change of leader given Thatcher's personal commitment to a doctrinaire 'monetarist' approach. But once that 'heroic' struggle was over, Thatcher seems to have taken Treasury support for granted, not least because she had replaced the mild-mannered

Howe with a more radical 'Thatcherite' (Nigel Lawson) after the 1983 general election.

Although Lawson was widely regarded as a major contributor to the Conservative Party's political dominance between 1983 and 1987, his appointment proved to be a fateful mistake. Lawson, who saw the Treasury as the summit of his ambitions rather than a stepping stone to the premiership, was far less tractable than Howe had been; he would much rather have resigned than accepted direction from his neighbour at No. 10. His concentration on stewardship of the economy meant that his influence over policy more generally consisted of close supervision of departmental spending (an approach which cost the government dearly since he made no serious attempt to dissuade Thatcher from introducing the poll tax). Equally, though, Lawson was guarded in his discussions with Thatcher on the direction of his economic policy. This became a source of considerable tension when, by the mid-1980s, Lawson had to accept that the original strategy of exerting influence over the rate of price inflation through control of the money supply was not working. Lawson believed that membership of the Exchange Rate Mechanism (ERM) of the European Monetary System (EMS) would be a workable alternative to 'pure' monetarism. Under the terms of ERM membership, the value of the pound would be allowed to fluctuate only slightly in relation to other European currencies. In essence, Lawson was arguing that currency stability was an essential safeguard against inflation, since the discipline of the ERM was a disincentive to governments who tried to escape from economic difficulties through the inflationary route of currency devaluation. While the record of most European countries was no better than Britain's in this respect, membership of the ERM would link the UK economy with that of West Germany, with its enviable post-war combination of low inflation and healthy economic growth. In preparation for an application for full ERM membership, even before the 1987 general election Lawson, in co-ordination with the Bank of England, had been 'shadowing' the West German Deutschmark, ensuring as far as possible that British interest rates moved in tandem with those set by the Bundesbank.

Lawson's problem was that Thatcher was deeply antipathetic towards Germany, East or West; and although as Prime Minister she never came close to advocating withdrawal from the European Community (EC), her attitude fell a long way short of enthusiasm for European integration. Although she had conceded early in her premiership that Britain would join the ERM 'when the time is ripe' – and before the 1979 general election the Conservatives had criticized the Callaghan Government for its hesitant approach – it was always clear that in her eyes the ripening process would be excessively prolonged. Since 1979, three consecutive election victories had convinced Thatcher that her instinctive views were correct – that governments should accept the 'natural' operation of market forces, and that the value of national currencies could not be stabilized by artificial devices like the ERM. Lawson was certainly no admirer of the EC, but his notion that the ERM could serve British interests by providing a useful weapon against inflation placed him a galaxy apart from Thatcher, whose worldview was freighted with second-hand memories of World War II.

Although most Britons were probably even less aware of the full implications of the disagreement this time than they had been during the Westland Affair, this challenge to the Prime Minister's policy-making role was of a different order of magnitude. In the case of Westland, Thatcher had disagreed with a middle-ranking minister, and furthermore she had been able to engage another minister (as well as the unwitting Solicitor-General) as champions in her cause. But the conflict over the ERM was no 'proxy war'. In his bid to persuade the Prime Minister, Lawson joined forces with Foreign Secretary Howe. To an objective observer, this should have strengthened his hand considerably since Howe had served in two of the 'great ministries of state' and could therefore bring more than one perspective to the table. However, Thatcher's dislike for Germans was (nearly) matched by her contempt for Geoffrey Howe, so that Lawson would probably have been better advised to act on his own.

Nevertheless, whatever her private feelings about her antagonists Thatcher was in a difficult spot, which was not helped by the fact that the other 'great minister of state', the Home Secretary Douglas Hurd, was a moderate 'Europhile'. The Lawson–Howe combination seemed to have stormed the Thatcherite citadel at last during an EC summit at Madrid in June 1989. The Prime Minister agreed to apply for ERM membership when five economic conditions (relating to Britain as well as its European partners) had been satisfied. For Howe and Lawson, the key point was that Thatcher could be held to concrete criteria, rather than being able to fall back on the opaque 'time is ripe' formula.

It is hardly surprising that Thatcher's allies refer to a 'Madrid Ambush', as if the Prime Minister had been the unsuspecting victim of a dastardly plot. Yet she was certainly not without her suspicions, and lost no time in organizing the fightback. A few weeks after the Madrid summit it was announced that her former economic adviser, Alan Walters, would be recalled to the colours (see chapter 3). Walters had already written a newspaper article in which he described the ERM as a 'half-baked' concept and credited himself with having persuaded Thatcher to keep out of it. After his return to Thatcher's service the piece was reprinted in more than one serious British newspaper (Campbell, 2003, 687). Lawson responded by telling the Prime Minister that Walters was making his position untenable, undermining his authority as Chancellor. The only solution was for Walters to resume his academic career in America, after an interlude to spare any embarrassment. According to Lawson, Thatcher replied that 'If Alan were to go, that would destroy *my* authority' (Lawson, 1992, 960–1: italics in original).

Even more than thirty years after the event, it is difficult to assess this episode with critical detachment – all the more so since Britain's membership of the ERM proved to be short-lived and miserable, causing long-term damage to the Conservative Party. Since Britain's ignominious exit in September 1992, Thatcher's avengers have been able to present the story as an epic struggle, in which the Prime Minister's eventual defeat revealed the sort of treachery she had always been up against. Lawson's own memoir (written before the ERM fiasco but published just a few weeks afterwards) was a treasure trove for serious students of economic policy-making during the Thatcher years, as well as being an attempt to vindicate his record in the eyes of well-qualified observers. But general readers were bound to be daunted by more than a thousand pages of text which were not characterized by a profusion of insider gossip. Given the sensational circumstances of his departure from office, Lawson might have been wiser to postpone his exhaustive apologia and publish a short, snappy book about the ERM controversy at the first opportunity.

As it is, in Lawson's published account the two key episodes in the ERM affair are separated by nearly 500 pages. The first was an ad hoc meeting of ministers which took place on 13 November 1985. Over the previous months the possibility of ERM membership had been discussed in similar meetings and seminars. During that time, Lawson had gradually warmed to membership while Thatcher had become more hostile. The Prime Minister had prepared for the discussion in the manner which had served her so well during her first term, doing her best to ensure that the general mood of the meeting would, at worst, reaffirm the previous 'wait and see' position. Thus she allowed Geoffrey Howe, who was known to support an immediate application, into the meeting but balanced him with the Party Chairman, Norman Tebbit (normally a reliable supporter), Leon Brittan (DTI), whom she probably expected to blow with the prevailing wind from No. 10, and John Biffen, who had no reason to be there in his capacity of Leader of the House of Commons and was evidently asked to attend only because of his well-known enthusiasm for the free market. Willie Whitelaw, the Deputy Prime Minister, was recruited in the expectation that, once he had summed up the discussion in Thatcher's favour, his jovial personality would dissipate any ill-feelings. The party's Chief Whip, John Wakeham, was lined up to report that the parliamentary party would feel equally delighted to uphold the existing position. The views of non-ministerial attendees – special advisers, civil servants and the governor of the Bank of England – would of course not be canvassed, which for Thatcher was a blessing since the Bank's governor, Robin Leigh-Pemberton, supported Lawson.

The meeting did not proceed according to Thatcher's plan. Only the superfluous Biffen opposed Lawson's preferred option of an immediate application (Biffen, 2013, 388). Whitelaw – apparently oblivious to the storm which was brewing – summed up the meeting accurately. Senior members of the government were in favour of Lawson's policy, and not least because they had considerable confidence in his economic judgement. In an instant, Thatcher could see that her strategy of running economic policy by remote control, through the appointment of a fellow-travelling Chancellor and clever manipulation of Cabinet committees, had rebounded against her. The best she could do was to threaten resignation if Lawson's opinion prevailed, before stomping out of the room. None of this drama was suggested by the terse paragraph allotted to the occasion in Thatcher's memoirs, which included the masterly understatement that it 'did not advance us any further than the earlier meetings' (Thatcher, 1993, 697).

Although Lawson's colleagues assured him that Thatcher would come round in the end, he could only remember that the Prime Minister had just expressed doubts about his ministerial competence in front of senior colleagues. She had also shown contempt for the considered opinion of key figures within her party. Significantly, when she chided Whitelaw and Wakeham later for their failure to back her, instead of truthfully telling her that they had been convinced by Lawson's case, they protested that they had not been fully briefed about her attitude in advance (Moore, 2016, 421). Thatcher's official biographer Charles Moore includes this story as part of an account which (as usual) is heavily slanted in Thatcher's favour; but he leaves the distinct impression that the party's most experienced power-brokers were sufficiently worried about the possible implications for Thatcher's position – at a time when the rotor-blades of Westland were about to chop at the government – that they decided to rally behind the Prime Minister in defiance of the honest opinions which they had just delivered on the subject of ERM membership. As in her first term, Thatcher had found a way to prevail on a crucial policy issue thanks to her vulnerability rather than her strength.

Ironically, although six of the seven ministers who attended the meeting had left Thatcher's government before her own departure, only one of them was sacked – Biffen, her sole defender at the 1985 meeting (Thatcher, 1993, 589). Despite his long-standing economic liberalism, Biffen was disinclined to play the sycophant even when he agreed with the Prime Minister. Indeed, he had earned a reprimand in 1984 when his dissatisfaction with the quality of Cabinet meetings was reported in the press.[11] In a memoir filled with one-line put-downs, Thatcher allowed her ghostwriters to attribute Biffen's dismissal after the 1987 election to the fact that 'he had come to prefer commentary over collective responsibility' (Thatcher, 1993, 589). In reality, Biffen's 'commentary' chiefly reflected his view that collective Cabinet government was no longer working under Thatcher.

When the crisis over Lawson's position finally came to a head in 1989, Thatcher declared (first in a televised interview, then later in Parliament) that 'Advisers advise, ministers decide!' This sound bite tends to be used by Thatcher's admirers to absolve her from any accusation that she transgressed against constitutional proprieties. However, Thatcher's words are an open invitation to more inquisitive observers. Whom did she mean by 'ministers'? She cannot have meant her Chancellor as an individual, because she disagreed with him and wanted to prevent him from acting on his decisions. Obviously she did not have in mind the ministers who sat in judgement on Lawson's proposal for immediate ERM entry in November 1985, because they had decided against her and she over-ruled them.

Then there is the implication in Thatcher's remark that advisers have a secondary role because they only offer advice. The message of the ERM saga is that their political importance depends upon the person they are advising. If, like Alan Walters, they bolster the Prime Minister of the day in his or her resistance to the long-pondered policy of a senior minister – and if, as in this case, they are appointed to carry out this specific role – then their influence over decision-making is arguably more weighty than that of the democratically elected minister.

In other words, 'Advisers advise, ministers decide!' should be trans-lated as 'Ministers decide, but their decisions will not take effect if *my* advisers advise me to over-rule them.' This imperious outlook explains (and perhaps partially excuses) the attitude of ministers who served in Thatcher's governments after 1983 and played along with the Prime Minister's ideological project because they could not draw upon the institutional resources enjoyed by the Treasury. It also explains why after Lawson's resignation Thatcher appointed a person (Major) who seemed properly subservient. Yet the 'Iron Lady', whose mindset had been forged during the second instalment of Britain's war with Germany, had inadvertently passed the torch to a representative of a new generation which was more interested in accommodation than conflict.

John Major

The decision of Conservative MPs in November 1990 to select John Major, rather than Michael Heseltine, suggested a revulsion against Thatcher and her style of government, not an ideological counter-revolution. Heseltine's policy disagreements with Thatcher went beyond Europe and the poll tax – the issues he highlighted during the leadership election campaign – and his approach to politics sug-gested that he would merely offer a different kind of radical upheaval. John Major exhibited no such symptoms, and as Thatcher's evident preference he was the obvious choice for MPs who craved a period of 'consolidation'. Major was understandably nonplussed by Thatcher's threat to act as a 'back-seat driver', because she had become an electoral liability and he would have preferred to stick her out of sight in the boot. But whether Thatcher was visible or not, the Conservative satnav would remain on the course she had set; Major would just be more observant of speed bumps and hazard warnings.

The change of style was apparent from the outset, and was reflected in an entirely different approach to policy-making. The 1990 leadership contest had begun in circumstances reminiscent of *Macbeth*, but seemed to have found its denouement in *All's Well that Ends Well*. Major was happy to offer Cabinet places to both his leadership rivals, and soon established good working relationships with Heseltine and Douglas Hurd (who had also stood but without evident enthusiasm). Having agreed to return to Environment and take responsibility for reform of the poll tax, Heseltine was encouraged to find his own solution. Although Major had no alternative but to become the public face of Britain's contribution to the war to end Iraq's occupation of Kuwait (see chapter 5), his approach to conflict was in marked contrast to Thatcher's. Far from attempting to trespass on the territory of his Foreign Secretary, he treated Hurd as a personal friend as well as according him the professional respect which was due to his expertise (Hurd, 2003, 414). Ironically, Major's relations with his 1990 rivals were much easier than his dealings with Norman Lamont, who had been appointed Chancellor chiefly because of his prominent role in Major's leadership campaign.

The appointment of Lamont to the Treasury proved to be a mistake, not because he had a personal policy agenda which would bring him into conflict with No. 10, but rather because it made him the frontman and potential fall guy for a decision which had already been taken, thanks largely to the new Prime Minister. When Major succeeded Lawson as Chancellor in October 1989, he continued to press for British membership of the ERM, and a year later he finally overcame Thatcher's resistance. Having to admit defeat on this issue had only made the Prime Minister more anxious to assert overall control of government policy on 'Europe', triggering Geoffrey Howe's resignation and the series of events which ended in her downfall.

In later years, Lamont became an outspoken Eurosceptic. But back in 1990 he accepted Major's offer of promotion from Chief Secretary of the Treasury to Chancellor even though it was obvious that Britain's membership of the ERM would form a substantial part of his remit. For his part, Major did not hesitate to identify himself with the policy, declaring on 10 September, as the UK's membership came under pressure, that leaving the ERM would be 'The soft option, the devaluer's option, the inflationary option.' Significantly, before Major issued that defiant message, he consulted his special adviser, Sarah Hogg, rather than his Chancellor (Major, 1999, 326).

On 'Black Wednesday' – 16 September 1992 – economic forces beyond the government's control forced Britain to suspend ERM membership (indefinitely, as it turned out). In the preceding hours Major had held a series of meetings whose attendees included Kenneth Clarke, Heseltine, Hurd and the Chief Whip Richard Ryder, as well as senior civil servants and special advisers. According to Hurd, Clarke compared their role to that of 'additional doctors brought in at the last moment simply to witness the death of the patient' (Hurd, 2003, 426). Major's own explanation for his failure to convene a meeting of the full Cabinet in the critical hours – namely, that 'decisions were needed speedily' – is not very convincing, since he did manage to summon the ministers in whom he had invested the greatest trust. For Major, this had the added advantage that responsibility for the emergency measures of 16 September – notably two dramatic hikes in interest rates – was shared. But these were not decisions which a Prime Minister could possibly take without at least some consultation beyond the obvious dialogue between Nos. 10 and 11. In fact, in a situation which resembled an impromptu war Cabinet Major's colleagues were certainly not passive, and there were some robust discussions about the most appropriate steps the government might take if its position unravelled and Britain was ejected from the ERM (Major, 1999, 333–4).

It could be argued that, in the few months straddling the decline and fall of Thatcher and the installation of Major in her place, the position of Chancellor was passed from one over-promoted minister (Major) to another (Lamont). However, when Major forced his old campaign manager to leave the Treasury in June 1993, Lamont certainly proved the equal of his predecessors Howe and Lawson in the art of the resignation statement. Indeed, in his ability to identify the real problems afflicting the British policy-making process, Lamont's speech is possibly the best of the three. Early in the speech, he noted his astonishment that 'when things go wrong, often it is the civil servants who are blamed when it is we politicians who make the decisions and it is we politicians who should carry the blame'. In his peroration he broadened and sharpened his critique:

> There is something wrong with the way in which we make our decisions. The government listens too much to the pollsters and the party managers. The trouble is that they are not even very good at politics, and they are entering too much into policy decisions. As a result, there is too much short-termism, too much reacting to events, and not enough shaping of events. We give the impression of being in office but not in power. Far too many important decisions are made for 36 hours' publicity. Yes, we are politicians as well as policy-makers; but we are also the trustees of the nation. I believe that in politics one should decide what is right and then decide the presentation, not the other way round. Unless this approach is changed, the Government will not survive, and will not deserve to survive. (Lamont, 1999, 524)

The key phrase – 'in office but not in power' – was particularly wounding for Major because it suggested that his style of government, which initially seemed a refreshing contrast to the previous eleven years, was becoming a liability. However, a superficial reading of Lamont's message could be met with a plausible response; Thatcher, after all, had set standards of political dominance which *any* successor (even Heseltine) would have found difficult to match. Lamont's choice of villains – 'pollsters and party managers' – was equally double-edged; after all, Thatcher had been reliant on such people to an unprecedented extent. Lamont did not refer specifically to special advisers; perhaps he had no reason to add them to his list because as Chancellor he had been served by very good ones (including David Cameron). Even so, he could easily have mentioned them among the people who were influencing policy despite being 'not very good at politics'; Cameron might have achieved an Oxford 'first' in PPE, but at the time of Black Wednesday he was just twenty-five years old, and was still a political apprentice. More importantly, when he criticized excessive short-termism and over-reaction to events Lamont was taking direct aim at Major, who was hyper-sensitive to negative coverage in the right-wing press. But although it was easy to retort that Major should have grown a thicker skin, newspapers like the *Sun* had enjoyed a licence to spout malevolent propaganda since 1979, with the deliberate connivance of 'Maggie', who had performed valuable services for the proprietor, Rupert Murdoch, in return. Lamont himself had been a victim of gutter journalism, since unfounded stories about this private life had helped to undermine his credibility as Chancellor.

Unfortunately for Major's reputation, his preferred style of government left him with no means of countering Lamont's charges. Thus once 'events' had made Major seem weak – so soon after a Conservative election victory in 1992 which owed much to his personal popularity – the underlying forces which were sapping the authority of British government in general were allowed free play, with gloating commentary from the media outlets which continued to work for their patron, Thatcher.

Apart from controlling inflation, Major's chief policy initiative was the 'Citizen's Charter'. In the right circumstances, this could have been a helpful attempt to 'humanize' Britain's bureaucratic procedures. The unaccommodating, sometimes callous nature of bureaucratic interaction with the public had been a common theme in criticisms levelled from both the political left and the right, so this idea had considerable promise in the abstract. However, the Charter was no less a failure than the Rayner 'reforms'. Its most lasting mark on public memory was created by the 'cones hotline', allowing fuming motorists to complain about motorway lanes which were cordoned off for no apparent reason. The protests were rarely effective since such work was now being done by private contractors rather than public employees (under the arm's-length supervision of yet another new quango, the Highways Agency (1994)). Nevertheless, Major's enthusiasm for the 'Charter' registered with the public, who now expected private-sector-style attention from increasingly demoralized civil servants. In the wake of Thatcher's onslaught on the public service ethos, the initiative could only be seen by government employees as an attempt to make them don a name-badge and a sympathetic smile as they dealt with their 'clients'.

With that, Major had just about shot his policy-making bolt. He managed to achieve the ratification of the Maastricht Treaty, complete with the opt-outs he had negotiated, but only after a bitter struggle which widened the fissures in his parliamentary party. Not even privatization, the policy which had epitomized Thatcherite triumphalism, could provide his government with a sense of purpose. The sell-offs of the Major years (notably the railways and the coal mines) were neither popular nor successful. Even before his bruising experience over pit closures (see chapter 1), Michael Heseltine had been derided by Labour's Shadow Chancellor Gordon Brown for exercising 'absolute power over a department [the Board of Trade] which has become absolutely powerless': the minister had been transformed from 'the king of the jungle' to a 'fireside rug' (Crick, 1997, 384). During an inquiry into the pit-closure fiasco, the Prime Minister was advised in future 'not to fall into the trap of assuming that ministers and officials know what they are doing, or have thought it through' – a remarkable indictment of a very experienced and apparently competent politician and the hollowed-out condition of his department (essentially the former DTI).[12] A later proposal from Heseltine to part-privatize the Post Office was abandoned due to the government's small and dwindling Commons majority.

By the end of his premiership Major was facing a 'perfect storm' – a hostile press, a divided party and an Opposition which seemed highly competent in contrast to 'the man with the non-Midas touch', as the Labour leader John Smith had dubbed him (Stuart, 2005, 260–1). After Smith's death in 1994 Major was faced with an equally effective debater, Tony Blair, who had cultivated the press to make sure that he enjoyed all of the advantages which Major lacked. Major's final handicap was that his party had been in government for eighteen years, making it difficult to offer fresh policy ideas to an electorate which had decided long before that change was overdue. The Conservative manifesto proposals attracted limited attention compared to Major's continuing (and unsuccessful) battle to create an illusion of party unity. He did, though, attract a backhanded compliment from the Labour peer and former special adviser Lord (Bernard) Donoughue, who noted in January 1996 that he preferred Major to Bill Clinton, and that the former 'with all his failings, may prove to be the last old-fashioned Prime Minister, who occasionally looks at the policy and not just the presentation' (Donoughue, 2016, 12–13). This was very different from the view expressed in Lamont's resignation speech. Perhaps it was based on a shrewd anticipation of what life would be like once New Labour took charge.

Tony Blair

Thus when a very new-fashioned Prime Minister took office in 1997 he had been equipped (by Thatcher) with the necessary tools for exercising political control from Downing Street, and a convenient pretext for using them, thanks to the general attribution of Major's failure to his reversion to a more 'collegial' style. Far from apologizing for his 'Bonapartist' approach, Blair claimed in July 2002 that a 'strong centre' was essential for good governance (Allen, 2003, 6). By the 'centre' he obviously meant No. 10 rather than the executive branch as a whole.

For his purposes, Blair was in the fortunate position of being able to exert influence directly, indirectly and by 'remote control'. The first approach is illustrated by the experience of the Home Office (see above). Blair also developed the habit of going above the heads of ministers and announcing policy initiatives in public without consultation. Thus in June 2000, after discussions with Alastair Campbell, he proposed a system of on-the-spot fines for petty offenders. Campbell admitted that this idea was 'pretty last-moment because the Home Office had been so useless'. What he meant was that the Home Office – a regular target for his outbursts – would not have touched the idea with a bargepole. Yet Campbell (and Blair) thought they knew better, assuming that the announcement would win widespread and favourable media coverage. When (inevitably) it aroused a storm of criticism and even ridicule, Campbell decided this was 'in part' the Home Office's fault (Campbell, 2011, 357–9).

The most stunning example of government by remote control was the decision of ministers to approve the Millennium Dome – an expensive project originally (and ominously) championed by Michael Heseltine to mark the year 2000, and widely expected to be scrapped by the incoming government: even the *Sun* was opposed. However, Blair and his key ally Peter Mandelson decided to endorse the project. Before the Cabinet meeting of 19 June 1997 reached the relevant item on its agenda, Blair left for another engagement. In his absence, his deputy John Prescott tried to steer his colleagues towards a favourable decision on the Dome, arguing tacitly that 'whatever Tony wants, Tony gets'. Ministers were unpersuaded, and Prescott was forced to report their negativity to his boss. Later that day journalists were summoned to the proposed site of the Dome, where Blair gave every indication that it would go ahead.

There was no further discussion of the issue in Cabinet: it was policy-making by photo opportunity (Rawnsley, 2000, 54–6).

There was, however, a flaw in the command-and-control strategy. It was easier to bully ministers and officials precisely because the various changes since the Thatcher years had sapped their ability to effect constructive reforms in their policy areas. Thus, the most that the centralizing urge could achieve was an ever-tightening grip on people and institutions which had been rendered 'unfit for purpose' both individually and collectively, making a mockery of 'joined-up' government. Blair's ignorance could be excused on the grounds that he had no previous experience of Whitehall, contravening Harold Wilson's view that the Cabinet was an indispensable 'training ground' for any Prime Minister (Wilson, 1976, 189). But that just made it more important for Blair to heed the advice of veterans like Straw, rather than bombarding them with instructions and planning to remove them at the first opportunity. In February 2002 Straw had a quiet word with Campbell, warning him that 'we had made Number 10 more power-ful but not necessarily more effective across government', not least because 'departments had any number of people calling up and saying what T[ony] B[lair] wanted' (Campbell, 2012, 173). It is extraordinary that anyone felt it necessary to convey this message almost five years after the government took office – but far less surprising that it seems not to have been transmitted to 'TB' himself.

The other serious flaw was that even this kind of control could never be complete thanks to the brooding presence of Gordon Brown at the Treasury. If 'don't fall out with your Chancellor' was a key lesson of the Thatcher years, Blair was never in a position to profit from it because he had fallen out with his Chancellor before either of them moved into Downing Street. They did at least ensure that they could not quarrel over interest rate policy, handing responsibility in that area to the Monetary Policy Committee of the Bank of England (without asking Cabinet for its views on this important reform). After that, their occasional spasms of amity only ever arose when they both remembered the importance of New Labour retaining office. At other times the Blair–Brown relationship had elements of sub-Shakespearean tragedy, with two protagonists so consumed by enmity that they cared not for any collateral political damage. Thus, for example, after Blair had (not for the first time) failed to execute a promise to step aside in his favour,

Brown reportedly said 'There is nothing that you could ever say to me now that I could ever believe' (Peston, 2005, 349). The mere utterance of such words, at the start of what looked sure to be an election year, should have spelled the end of the 'partnership', one way or another.

The duel sometimes looked like a contest to show the greater contempt for collective decision-making. Thus in January 2000 Blair seized the congenial opportunity of an appearance on the BBC's *Breakfast with Frost* programme to announce a commitment to raise NHS spending to the EU average – a promise which would cost at least £12 billion by 2006. This must have produced a violent ejection of cornflakes in the Chancellor's kitchen. But Blair was only repaying Brown in his own coin. Back in October 1997 the Chancellor had announced in a press interview that he had learned lessons from the ERM disaster, and had devised five economic tests which must be met (with the Treasury's adjudication, naturally) before Britain could commit to joining the European single currency. His spin doctor, Charlie Whelan, let it slip (deliberately or not) that this precluded the possibility of Britain joining the Euro within the current Parliament. As a result, Brown was hailed in the right-wing press as the saviour of the pound. However, the Chancellor's role was regarded as less than heroic by No. 10. Amid the ensuing row, senior civil servants were reported to feel relieved at the prospect of Labour finally learning how to act as a government rather than an Opposition. One was quoted as saying that 'When Labour came in, I reckoned it would be three to six months before they appreciated that the virtues we have – civil service virtues – are in a sense protective ones: protecting Ministers from dropping themselves in it.'[13] The civil servant's reckoning was wrong: as we have seen, Labour ministers grew less, rather than more, appreciative of such 'virtues'.

The 'five tests' announcement did evoke some reaction from ministers who found this failure to consult too blatant to pass without comment. But there was no change in the new Whitehall culture; even Charlie Whelan, identified by Blairites as the main mischief-maker, survived until his involvement in another rumpus two years later. The fact that senior Labour politicians were willing – sometimes seemingly anxious – to identify themselves as 'Blairites' or 'Brownites' was further testimony to the erosion of ministerial status since 1979. The team which accompanied Blair into office hardly bore comparison with the Cabinets of Wilson and Callaghan, in terms of personality, ability and public recognition. Yet it did contain some notable politicians – not least David Blunkett (see above) – who might have demonstrated that ministers still enjoyed 'resources' which would prevent Blair and/or Brown from treating them as cyphers. However, the team members seemed eager to divest themselves of any independent status. The tendency of ministers like Blunkett to denigrate their civil servants suggests a realization that their departments gave them no additional political weight under the new dispensation. Rather, their political fortunes depended either on Blair (whom they wrongly regarded as a kind of electoral wonder-worker: see chapter 6) or Brown (whose assiduous management of government money meant that it paid – literally, in terms of departmental funding – either to swear personal allegiance to him or at least to remain on speaking terms).

In respect of the Chancellor's political power, one important difference between the Thatcher and Blair years was the fact that, after New Labour's first years in which Brown tried to win media kudos by keeping a firm hold on public spending, from 2000 he exchanged prudence for profligacy. Although his initial response to Blair's initiative on health spending had been a volley of expletives, the loosening of the purse strings could be put to positive presentational use, and thus increase his hold over ministers. For hollowed-out departments, the traditional measure of policy success – that is, positive outcomes for British citizens – was increasingly difficult to achieve, or even to assess except through the meeting of arbitrary 'targets'. As a result, there was an inevitable tendency for ministers to define 'success' as the ability to secure funding for a particular project, whether or not the allocated money was ever likely to trickle down to the intended beneficiaries. Sometimes it even seemed that ministers were counting the *announcement* of a policy initiative as a 'success', so long as it attracted favourable media comment. In this context, civil servants were worse than useless since their traditional role had been to congratulate ministers for ideas which sounded good, and then talk through the practical implications in the hope of tempering their enthusiasm. Under New Labour, all that ministers needed was an assurance that proposals would win positive short-term publicity, and special advisers were always ready to provide that service.

Brown himself quickly realized that a reputation for generosity would serve his ambitions, so long as he received the lion's share of credit for the disbursements. In his budget speeches he often invited praise for pledges which had already been announced, in the hope that nobody would notice this 'double-counting'. In this respect, at least, a change of tenant at No. 10 was never likely to make much difference.

New Labour's policy-making process in respect of foreign policy has been explored very extensively, not least by the reviews of Iraq headed by Lord Butler (2004) and Sir John Chilcot (2009–16). The findings of those inquiries complement the argument of this section, showing not only the extent to which Blair infringed traditional decision-making practices but also the tendency for supposedly non-political officials (including members of the intelligence community) to serve the Prime Minister's purposes without the need for direct instructions. The preparation of the case for war in Iraq was an excellent example of government by remote control, leading to a predictable disaster for the Prime Minister and the country.

Gordon Brown

Between June 2007, when Brown finally realized his ambition and succeeded Blair, and May 2010, when Labour lost office, there were numerous ministerial resignations, some of which (like that of the Home Secretary, Jacqui Smith) were prompted by the expenses scandal of 2009. Others, though, were intended, calculated departures, to destabilize the Prime Minister. Thus, when the Work and Pensions Secretary James Purnell – a former special adviser to Blair – resigned in June 2009, declaring that the Prime Minister was 'unelectable', the *Guardian* newspaper described his decision as 'a monumental blow' to Brown. With unconscious irony, given Brown's history of dealings with the media, No. 10 expressed displeasure that 'Purnell had chosen to tell newspapers before telling the leader of the Labour Party.'[14] But the fuss was unnecessary, since few Britons could have known Purnell's name, let alone the fact that he had been serving as Work and Pensions Secretary. In 1982, the broadcaster Robin Day described the Secretary of State for Defence, Sir John Nott, as a 'here today, gone tomorrow politician'. Nott, in fact, served in that position for two years, which made him a gnarled veteran by the standards of the Brown Government. Under Brown, few ministers attracted public notice unless they resigned; and even that gesture only made them famous for fifteen minutes.

If Major had hoped to superimpose a 'human face' on Thatcherism but ended up presiding over the exposure of its private parts, when

Brown became Prime Minister in 2007 he was left with the rancid fag end of 'Blairism'. He came to office with ambitious plans to rein in the role of the Prime Minister, which looked well-intentioned at first glance. But the relevant passage in his memoirs merely reveals how bad things had become; although he had wanted to 'empower' ministers, his main concern was to allow them to announce policies themselves rather than letting the Prime Minister take the plaudits (Brown, 2017, 208–9). Only in retirement could Brown appreciate the true extent and nature of the dysfunctionality which Thatcher and New Labour had introduced since 1979. For example, he now realized that special advisers were comparable to 'a kind of unelected cabinet'. He noted, with considerable understatement, that this 'was not, I found, a good system for governing' (Brown, 2017, 226). The role of special advisers was something Brown could have begun to address without legislation, and his failure to do so is explained (though certainly not excused) by the perverse perspective arising from more than a decade of exposure to the New Labour mindset. According to Blick and Jones, the problems caused by Brown's unelected entourage meant that he had to fall back on the civil service, which 'was able to enhance its position in an important historic shift' (Blick and Jones, 2013, 309). The only evidence for the 'historic shift' was the prominence of Jeremy Heywood, who became Brown's Chief of Staff in October 2008. But Heywood had begun his Whitehall career in 1983, at the height of Thatcher's iconoclasm. By all accounts, although Heywood was highly regarded by all the Prime Ministers he served, he acted more like a special adviser with good manners than a traditional civil servant.

As it was, Brown's plans were quickly overtaken by events, particularly the irruption of a financial crisis due to inexpedient banking practices on both sides of the Atlantic. This could be seen as an appropriate form of retribution for Brown, who as Chancellor had tried to cultivate personal support in the City of London by relaxing the supervision of banking activities. The obvious threat to the 'New Labour' project allowed Brown to extend olive branches to senior Blairites, including Peter Mandelson, who rejoined the Cabinet initially as Business Secretary and from June 2009 as de facto Deputy Prime Minister, chairing several key Cabinet committees. But by that time the old feud had been complicated by fears of an impending electoral defeat under Brown, whose personal ratings had slumped. Mandelson helped to stave off attempted challenges to Brown's leadership, but he could not dissuade all of the ministers who wanted to abandon the sinking ship. While this did nothing for the government's stability, ultimately it was less important than a new schism Brown had created – between the Prime Minister and his Chancellor.

When Brown had given this key position to Alistair Darling, it seemed that his intention was to continue as Chancellor in all but name. Darling was a long-standing ally with a low public profile and limited personal ambitions – the ideal candidate, it seemed, if Brown was to avoid a repetition of recent disharmony between Prime Ministers and Chancellors. Yet Brown was to learn that his lengthy spell at the Treasury had not established continuing personal dominance; indeed, it had depended heavily upon special advisers who (like Ed Balls and the future Labour leader Ed Miliband) had already been parachuted into safe Labour parliamentary seats by 2007, or had followed their leader into No. 10. Thus Balls, Miliband and Brown were unable to prevent Darling from falling into the clutches of Treasury officials, who were aided and abetted by like-minded colleagues in the Bank of England. While Brown favoured a quasi-Keynesian spending splurge to stave off the worst effects of the inevitable recession, Darling was alarmed by the existing level of government debt and preferred a much more cautious approach. In fact, Brown had always wanted to appoint Balls rather than Darling, initially earmarking the latter for either the Foreign Office or the Home Office (which Darling had turned down on two previous occasions).

The creation in October 2008 of a National Economic Council (NEC) – another institution whose nature and name were clearly inspired by the US system – was intended to dilute the Treasury's influence and understandably aroused its suspicions. Darling accepted the idea because he 'wanted to keep the peace'; as he noted laconically in his memoirs, 'At the end of the day, the Treasury can always say no' (Darling, 2011, 194). In June 2009 Brown made another attempt to dislodge Darling, at which point James Purnell's resignation became a 'monumental blow' for Brown after all, because the Prime Minister could not afford to lose another colleague and Darling had told him that either he stayed as Chancellor or he would leave the government entirely. He stayed as Chancellor, to the (very) bitter end. By the time of the 2010 general election, the untried Conservatives had opened up a twenty-five-point lead in the area of Brown's greatest policy expertise (Darling, 2011, 247–53).[15]

David Cameron

The final months of Brown's premiership conveyed the odour of decay and policy stasis which had marked the end of the Major years. His successor, David Cameron, had declared himself 'the heir to Blair' before becoming Tory leader, but this was misleading. Even if his party had won an overall majority at the 2010 general election he would not have copied Blair's hyper-interventionist approach to policy. As it was, coalition with the Liberal Democrats suited him admirably.

Cameron was also fortunate in having a trusted friend, George Osborne, as the obvious choice for Chancellor. Osborne knew that Cameron would back his controversial programme of economic 'austerity'. In other areas of policy, the coalition partners published a document which showed a remarkable level of agreement, as well as specifying the issues on which they would agree to differ. Cameron and Osborne used regular meetings with Nick Clegg and his Liberal Democrat colleague David Laws (later replaced by Danny Alexander) to oversee government activity; the so-called 'Quad' was a much better approximation to an orderly 'inner Cabinet' than anything that Blair and Brown had created. This was not a conclave of cronies, but rather a meeting where problems could be addressed by colleagues who represented different interests within the government. As such, one might borrow the language of the 'core executive' school to say that the members of the 'Quad' enjoyed 'independent resources'.

With this system in place, the 'Heir to Blair' believed that he could put into practice what Gordon Brown had fleetingly preached – 'a rejuvenation of a more collective form of decision-making' (Brown, 2017, 209). Of course, Cameron was conscious that John Major's similar attempt had not been an unalloyed success, and his party was even more divided on 'Europe' than Major's had been. However, the need to find Cabinet positions for Liberal Democrats gave Cameron a pretext to disappoint at least some of the Eurosceptics who might otherwise have emulated Major's 'Bastards'. In addition, while Major was bound to be compared to his iconic predecessor, Cameron had succeeded a Prime Minister whose domineering style had not endeared him to the public, attracting media coverage which portrayed him as a bully.

In short, if a 'hands-off' approach to government was ever going to succeed under modern conditions, Cameron was the right person, in the right context, to make the experiment. Overall, one could readily concede that he fared better than Major. However, before the end of the coalition Cameron reflected ruefully that, 'Thinking I was the chairman and letting ministers get on with their jobs might not have been the best strategy' (Seldon and Snowdon, 2015, 193).

Cameron was thinking chiefly of health policy, and the ill-starred reforms of the Secretary of State, Andrew Lansley. The historians of governmental blunders imply that Cameron was 'uninvolved' in this fiasco, but it seems more likely that, along with Osborne, he was attracted by the prospect of 'efficiency savings'. King and Crewe are certainly right to identify a lack of collegiate discussion which could have helped the government avoid embarrassment (King and Crewe, 2013, 400–2). Lansley's proposals contradicted a promise made in the 2010 Coalition Agreement to spare the Health Service from further 'top-down reorganizations': previous speeches by Conservatives (including Cameron himself) had pledged an end to *pointless* reorganizations, but this was a verbal quibble since the clear impression was given that *all* such reorganizations were 'pointless' (Seldon and Snowdon, 2015, 181). Lansley's plan for re-organization was, according to one official, so big that 'you could probably see it from space' (Timmins, 2012). The resulting improvements in the service, however, were difficult to detect from any vantage point without the aid of blue-tinted spectacles. Furious opposition from politicians (including Cameron's Liberal Democrat coalition partners) and various interest groups forced the Prime Minister to intervene, calling a temporary halt to the passage of Lansley's bill, but the ensuing 'listening exercise' consisted largely of listening to Lansley's supporters. Once the damage had been done, Lansley became the victim of another top-down reorganization: Cameron sacked him in September 2012.

Another reason for Cameron to regret his approach to government was the licence this provided to his first Secretary of State for Education (2010–14), Michael Gove. A journalist who had acquired an intellectual reputation, Gove quickly ran into trouble, publishing a list of schools which would be affected by cuts in a rebuilding programme, only to be forced to apologize for numerous inaccuracies. Gove had entered government with a special adviser, Dominic Cummings, whose appointment had been vetoed by Cameron's Director of Communications Andy Coulson. Ironically, it was Gove's blunder over the rebuilding programme that persuaded Cameron, against his better judgement, to let the minister employ Cummings, on whom Gove seemed almost wholly dependent.

After Gove left Education in July 2014, his former ministerial colleague David Laws reflected that, with considerable assistance from the abrasive Cummings, Gove had managed to alienate almost everyone connected with education, as well as provoking numerous rows with other ministers. Yet if Cummings (in Cameron's reported words) exercised 'a Rasputin-like influence' over Gove, the latter had a similar effect on otherwise perfectly rational people, including Cameron himself and the Liberal Democrat Laws (Laws, 2016, 432–5). Eventually even Cameron's tolerance for Cummings was exhausted, but inexplicably he offered Gove the post of Chief Whip rather than sacking him. This is even more mysterious since Gove continued to be on close terms with Cummings, who in the month before the reshuffle had been quoted as insulting several of the Prime Minister's closest colleagues (particularly Nick Clegg), while describing Cameron himself (not inaccurately) as 'a sphinx without a riddle' (Laws, 2016, 434; Laws, 2017, 301–8).

The saga of Gove and Cummings shows that, despite its remarkable success in many respects, the coalition was no exception to the trends identified in this chapter. Rather, the tolerance for so long in an important government department of a two-man wrecking squad suggests that the developments which had begun under Thatcher were now making rational policy-making almost impossible. Gove and Cummings were fizzing with impractical ideas, and impatient of any obstruction. Cummings made no attempt to conceal his contempt for civil servants, and meaningful consultation with representatives of the educational establishment ('the Blob', as Cummings dubbed it) was clearly unthinkable.

Cameron was a 'mood music' man rather than a policy entrepreneur. He took justifiable pride in ensuring that the international development budget reached and stayed at the desired 0.7 per cent of national income. But his favourite theme – the creation of a 'big society' – was never backed up by concrete ideas. He suffered his own spectacular policy-making lapse, over Libya (see chapter 5). The other disaster – the decision to call a referendum on membership of the EU – bears some New Labour hallmarks, since this momentous decision was presented as the Prime Minister's personal initiative at a staged media event. But

Cameron had discussed the issue with his closest colleagues for some time, and only one of these individuals (the Chief of Staff Ed Llewellyn) was unelected. In addition, there is some justice behind Cameron's claim that he was forced to hold the vote – not so much because of the rise of UKIP, but because his party's divisions on Europe were spilling over into other policy areas. Cameron could argue that it was worth a try in the hope of restoring a modicum of sanity to backbench MPs until the next election; if the ploy failed and anarchy persisted, the Conservatives would probably lose office anyway. The flaw in the plan was that Cameron and Osborne had been so effective in their attempts to blame Labour for the need to impose 'austerity' that the voters decided in 2015 to stick to the Tories, divisions and all – but not, understandably, to entrust them with the comfortable majority Cameron needed to govern effectively.

Cameron's second spell in office was dominated – and ended – by the referendum question. Overall, his record was not entirely barren of policy achievements; but the most notable reform, allowing same-sex marriage, was a matter of conscience pushed through in defiance of his party. By the time of the referendum one had to look back more than a decade and a half to find a government which had carried out a significant programme of reforms; and even this (Blair's first term, which had seen the implementation of devolution, human rights legislation, partial reform of the House of Lords, limited freedom of information and the implementation of a minimum wage) represented a stockpile of Labour Party commitments which Blair had inherited in 1994, rather than reflecting a coherent New Labour agenda. The end of constructive governmental reform had virtually coincided with the lavish celebrations of a new millennium, in the majestic surroundings of a Dome which a clear Cabinet majority had never wanted to build. To say the least, the British political system was not in a perfect condition to cope with additional shocks when the public voted in May 2016.

Theresa May

In the 2017 general election Theresa May was associated with the words 'strong' and 'stable', but when she came to office in July 2016 she seemed the epitome of 'compromise' and 'competence'. Her six-year stint at the hazardous Home Office made her the first Prime Minister since 1979 to have undergone the 'standard' apprenticeship for the top job – long service in at least one of the four 'great offices of state'.

Although her obvious over-riding objective was a satisfactory withdrawal from the EU followed by beneficial post-Brexit arrangements, May also signalled a departure from the recent past in that while she stated her policy objectives in general terms – help for those who, since the advent of austerity, had been 'just about managing', etc. – she could also be very specific. One of her pledges – the introduction of worker representatives on company boards – was a throwback to the pre-Thatcher days of 'One Nation' Conservatism. However, in one crucial respect May was more like Thatcher and Blair than Edward Heath or Harold Wilson: she was heavily reliant on special advisers, especially Nicholas Timothy and Fiona Hill. May's plans for domestic reform were heavily influenced by Timothy, to an extent which made it difficult to discern where his thinking ended and her personal contribution began (if it ever did).

We have already discussed the miscalculations which prevented May from making progress with any of the items on her agenda (see chapter 2). Her decision in April 2017 to break the parliamentary logjam by calling a snap election resulted in the destruction of the positive public image which was her last remaining asset. Once this gamble had failed (see chapter 6) May was able to cling to office thanks to a pact with the Democratic Unionist Party (DUP), but was forced to part with 'The Chiefs' – Timothy and Hill. She found a new unelected ally in Olly Robbins, a civil servant who had become Permanent Secretary at the Brexit department despite his evident ambivalence at the prospect of leaving the EU. Now that May had rediscovered pragmatism, Robbins seemed a marked improvement on the jilted Timothy and was equally invulnerable to charges of plotting to replace the Prime Minister, unlike an unsettling number of her Cabinet colleagues. But although the advent of Robbins raised the chances of a deal which would satisfy the EU, it made it even more unlikely that the House of Commons – still divided on party lines, but with the Conservative ranks far more fissiparous than Labour's – would accept it. May had just one more shot in her locker. She knew that many of her Cabinet colleagues had reasons of various kinds to oppose her deal, and were using the post-Brexit status of Northern Ireland as the most convenient way to obscure their real motives. But if she could isolate the Cabinet from the toxic atmosphere of Westminster and persuade them to put aside their personal interests, even the most Europhobic backbenchers might fall into line.

To this end, in July 2018 May invited her Cabinet colleagues to a meeting at Chequers, her country retreat. Britain's second female Prime Minister was improving on a tactic which Margaret Thatcher had used during her own crisis of leadership in 1990. Instead of holding face-to-face meetings with ministers in the hope of intimidating them, as Thatcher had done, May saw an opportunity to induce 'group-think' by staging a collective meeting in an agreeable country house. Harold Wilson had described a Chequers meeting as 'informality at its best', giving ministers 'an ideal place for contemplative discussion, particularly on long-term strategic questions' (Wilson, 1976, 60). However, the passage of time and technological advances meant that certain precautions were necessary in July 2018, particularly the confiscation of mobile phones. Attendees at the Chequers meeting were duly deprived of their social media lifelines, and it was reported that any minister who decided to resign on the spot would not be given a free ride back to London in a government car. Harold Wilson, and even Thatcher, would have been alarmed to know that within a few decades the Prime Minister would effectively use Chequers to place ministers under house arrest.

Given the frailties of human nature, it is not surprising that May, like Thatcher before her, received verbal support which turned out to be meaningless. Since on this occasion (unlike in 1990) Cabinet colleagues could relax over a drink after their deliberations, there was even a fleeting possibility that previous enmities might be forgotten: the Remainer Greg Clark joined Michael Gove in putting his name to a *Daily Mail* article pronouncing that 'We're friends reunited in the Battle for Britain!'[16] But once May's Brexiteer colleagues had been chauffeured safely home in their ministerial cars, they began to weigh the advantages of keeping up a pretence of loyalty to May against the laurels they would receive for resigning over a purported issue of principle. The departure of David Davis – who in truth had little to gain whether he left or stayed, since his reputation had not been enhanced by the Brexit negotiations – acted as a trigger for more calculated exits, notably that of the Foreign Secretary, Boris Johnson (Seldon and Newell, 2019, 433–47). Unsurprisingly, Gove decided that his interests would be best served by maintaining his show of solidarity with his leader, like Brutus suddenly signing up to the Julius Caesar Fan Club.

Although the details of May's subsequent travails need not detain us here, it is worth noting that there were times when her desperation to push through her withdrawal agreement looked sure to inflict lasting damage on the authority of her office. Thus in December 2018 MPs passed a motion which held ministers to have acted in contempt of Parliament by withholding the full legal advice they had received over Brexit. Among those supporting the motion, which passed by eighteen votes, were the DUP whose backing May had bought in such humiliating circumstances the previous year. Then, after May's deal had suffered two crushing Commons defeats, on 29 March 2019 she insisted on another attempt, this time promising to resign if MPs would endorse her plan. In some parallel universe this might have looked like a noble gesture – offering the ultimate political sacrifice in the national interest. In reality, it was difficult to follow the logic of a Prime Minister who was promising to step down in the national interest if MPs would only admit that she had been right all along.

May completed the bingo card of prime ministerial shortcomings by developing a dysfunctional relationship with her Chancellor, Philip Hammond. This was quite an achievement, since at the time of the referendum they had been united in the view that Britain's best interests, on balance, would be served by continued EU membership. However, once May became Prime Minister their Cabinet positions sent them onto divergent trajectories. While May felt it necessary to claim that 'Leave' commanded overwhelming support among well-informed Britons, at the Treasury Hammond was increasingly impressed by the likely downside of the vote. The real poison in the relationship, though, seems to have been injected by Nicholas Timothy, who saw Brexit as a unique opportunity to enact his radical domestic programme. From Hammond's perspective, 'radicalism' of any kind would have to be put on hold until a sensible Brexit deal was concluded; and as an elected politician he was entitled to feel that his judgement should carry more weight than the personal agenda of a special adviser.

Thus when May finally announced her intention to resign on 24 May 2019 she had failed on every front. Feted at the outset as the epitome of competence and the most likely politician to effect a compromise, three years later she had become an object of public pity. On the face of it, the job which had wrought that transformation should have had limited appeal. However, there was no shortage of candidates – ten MPs were formally nominated, and other hopefuls only declined the contest because they were bound to be eliminated at the first hurdle (see chapter 1). The incentive to stand on this occasion was that however badly the winner performed, he or she would almost certainly be regarded as an improvement on the last incumbent.

Conclusion

In terms of policy-making, the relevant picture is not one of increased prime ministerial 'power', but rather the very sharp relative decline of other government institutions (with the exception of the Treasury). This trend arose from a series of developments which began under Thatcher: a reduction in the scope of departmental duties; a deliberate and continuous attack on the integrity and ability of civil servants; an increasingly intrusive and abusive media, making ministers more dependent on the generation of positive short-term publicity; and the growing propensity for ministers to turn for psychological and other forms of support to special advisers with limited policy expertise or political judgement. Although there is no *necessary* connection between these developments, even in the abstract one can appreciate how they could be mutually reinforcing, increasing their detrimental effect.

Prime Ministers have not been immune from these changes. Just as a battered outcrop stands out in a flattened landscape, the incumbent has become more *prominent* by comparison. Prime Ministers have 'hived off' some powers of appointment, but they are still the ultimate source of *political* patronage and promotion. Even the most discredited Prime Minister is not tied to a specific policy area, and can use his or her media prominence to try to shift the news agenda in a more favourable direction. Finally, even though some Prime Ministers might feel constrained by a relative paucity of special advisers based in Downing Street, this is only a consideration for people who look longingly at the superfluous resources available to an American President. As the Blair Government showed, a fairly small number of people can easily cause considerable havoc. So long as they claimed to speak in the Prime Minister's name, special advisers could be sure of arresting the attention of their counterparts in individual departments and shaping (even dictating) their policy agendas. A formal Prime Minister's Department, lavishly endowed with 'the brightest and the best' from Whitehall and elsewhere, might have been a source of *more effective* policies; but this is no longer the obvious priority it should be, for governments who now seem unable to look beyond tomorrow's headlines.

4

Communicator in Chief

The British Prime Minister has been a significant figure in electronic broadcasting since the advent of radio in the early 1920s; indeed, Prime Ministers took advantage of this new means of addressing the nation several years before the first monarchical Christmas broadcast (by George V in 1932). The first Prime Minister to exploit the new medium was Stanley Baldwin (in 1923), who recognized that radio could be not only a vital electoral asset but also a channel of communication with the nation at times of crisis (like the General Strike of 1926).

The nature of broadcasting has been transformed since the 1920s, when radio transmitted by the monopolistic BBC represented an obvious opportunity for a Prime Minister like Baldwin, who had a gift for communication and understood how to turn the authority of his position to partisan advantage. If anything, the technological changes since 1923 are less important in this context that the *cultural* ones; the automatic deference which Baldwin could command as Prime Minister has virtually disappeared, along with the element of choice which he enjoyed. During the General Strike, for example, it was difficult for the BBC to deny the Prime Minister the *right* to speak, even though this national crisis was highly political and Baldwin's ability to address the nation raised serious questions about the BBC's 'impartiality'. By the twenty-first century, the Prime Minister's right to speak had turned into something akin to an *obligation*, not just during election campaigns (see chapter 6) but whenever the media judge that the nation needs reassurance or explanations from its political leader. While Baldwin could address his audiences without fear of unhelpful interruptions, by the late 1960s Prime Ministers could not avoid regular televised interviews; and their interlocutors were becoming more abrasive, insistent and better paid.

While no subsequent Prime Minister could hope to emulate Baldwin's unchallenged mastery of electronic communication, they could stage a fightback by paying closer attention to the timing of their broadcasts, and picking and choosing among an ever-growing number of media 'opportunities'. In other words, while Baldwin had been able to enjoy a walkover in media terms, from the mid-1960s his successors had to recognize that they were engaged in a battle of sorts, and that the media preoccupation with negative stories even when things seemed to be going well meant that they could never feel entirely safe. 'Presentation' therefore became increasingly important; the Prime Minister would have to be good at it, but would also need professional support.

This chapter reviews the records of successive Prime Ministers since 1979 in their use of the media, and the resources they have drawn upon in this increasingly fraught encounter. In particular, it examines their televised speeches at party conferences, which provide them with an opportunity to address multiple audiences.

Margaret Thatcher

Unlike Edward Heath, her predecessor as Conservative leader, Margaret Thatcher was always open to suggestions from media advisers. By the time she became Prime Minister in 1979 her physical appearance had been transformed and even the tone of her voice had been modified.

One thing that had not changed was Thatcher's determination to challenge the prevailing policies of the post-war period. This was always likely to generate an unusual level of controversy – including within her own party – and to place corresponding demands on her media advisers. In this respect she had an early dose of good fortune. When her first Press Secretary left at the end of a temporary contract, he was replaced by Bernard Ingham, a former *Guardian* reporter who had joined the civil service in 1967. Ingham had been suggested on the basis of merit rather than presumed political sympathy with his new boss. In fact, in one respect at least, he was rather like the traditional Conservative Party which was passing into oblivion: his secret weapon was loyalty. In the past he had given unstinting service to the left-wing Labour ministers Barbara Castle and Tony Benn. Significantly, Ingham had worked for them in very different circumstances (at the times in question Castle had enjoyed the support of the Prime Minister, while Benn most decidedly did not); yet he had been equally devoted and valuable to both.

True to form, Ingham quickly established an excellent rapport with Thatcher. Journalists soon appreciated that when Ingham addressed them, either collectively as the 'Lobby' or one to one, he was speaking with the Prime Minister's authority. Indeed, on occasions when Ingham's briefings conflicted with Thatcher's own utterances, it was the Press Secretary rather than the Prime Minister who was believed. Thus in 1982, after the Leader of the House of Commons, Francis Pym, had made pessimistic noises about the state of the economy, Thatcher defended him at PMQs at the same time that Ingham was making derogatory comments at the Lobby briefing (Cockerell et al., 1984, 69–70, 137–8).

Ingham always maintained that he had been careful not to infringe the duty of civil servants to remain politically neutral. However, this rule had always been difficult to observe: hypothetically, press secretaries could announce government activities without enthusiasm, but this approach might not be appreciated by their political masters. The distinction between party and state became even more obscure in the Thatcher years, given the polarization of politics at the time and the ongoing attack on 'impartial' public servants (see chapter 3). Those who were not openly against Thatcher were deemed to be with her in spirit; and Ingham was very palpably *not* against her. In addition, although Ingham had always been very robust in defending his ministers, those infighting skills seemed less appropriate when his official role was to speak for the government as a whole.

As it was, Ingham was so important to the Prime Minister that it became impossible for him to observe a rigid separation between 'governmental' and 'party political' business; he could (and did) ensure his exclusion from Conservative Party meetings, but his presence at any discussion which dealt with presentation was so natural that there were almost certain to be technical lapses. The most serious allegation was that, in January 1986, Ingham had ordered an information officer at the DTI – a junior official – to leak a letter written by the Solicitor-General, which was damaging to the position adopted by the Defence Secretary Michael Heseltine during the Westland Affair (see chapter 3). Ingham argued that he had never authorized the leak. However, the junior official (Colette Bowe) was well aware that he wanted the letter to reach the public domain, but that the leak itself must come from the DTI rather than No. 10 in the interests of 'deniability'. This was a pretty plausible deduction, since Thatcher had asked the Solicitor-General to write the letter and she had no reason to want something which helped her own interests to remain a tightly guarded secret. Thus this seems like an instance of a Prime Minister being able to produce a desired political result by 'remote control': whether or not there was a direct instruction, Bowe knew what Ingham wanted and had every reason to regard his desires as a faithful reflection of the Prime Minister's mind (Campbell, 2003, 489–91; Moore, 2016, 490–3).

While Ingham spoke on Thatcher's behalf to the political media as a whole, the Prime Minister herself was eclectic in the outlets she used to communicate with the nation. Unlike her predecessors, she made no use of special prime ministerial broadcasts – a format which gave Opposition parties the chance to demand a reply, and which had sometimes proved counterproductive (not least for Wilson and Heath). She excelled in televised interviews, particularly with the former Labour MP Brian Walden whose politics had moved sharply in her direction since he had left Parliament. Her favourite sparring partner, however, was the BBC radio presenter Jimmy Young, who was popular with the 'middle England' audience which Thatcher was particularly keen to reach. She was interviewed by Young just a few days after becoming party leader in 1975, and made regular appearances as Prime Minister. She could also access an important segment of the electorate through magazines like *Woman's Own* (which published an interview in September 1987 featuring her notorious 'no such thing as society' remark).

Although, as we have seen, Thatcher was not an assiduous attender at the House of Commons, she could make her appearances count for more now that the proceedings were broadcast on radio. Thus, for example, her announcement that Britain would send a task force in an attempt to retake the Falkland Islands in 1982 was delivered in the proper parliamentary setting. During the war itself, Thatcher's best-remembered media contribution was an unscripted follow-up ('Just rejoice at that news . . . Rejoice') to the announcement that the island of South Georgia had been recaptured. This welcome message, quite properly, had been delivered by the Defence Secretary, John Nott, rather than by Thatcher herself.

However, Thatcher's most reliable opportunity to speak to the nation was the annual Conservative Party conference. Before becoming Prime Minister she had a sound tactical reason for addressing her remarks to voters beyond the conference hall – thus, for example, in 1978 she made a specific appeal to trade unionists who might be thinking of voting Conservative.[17] Between the speeches of 1979 and 1981 she knew that a significant section of her audience would have preferred a more consensual leader. But she could still feel that the grassroots would respond warmly to their party leader and Prime Minister, and her message was sure to be given a positive 'spin' by a highly partisan press, notably Rupert Murdoch's *Sun*. Thus in her 1980 speech she taunted faint-hearted colleagues – some of whom were sharing the conference platform – who were desperate for a significant shift in economic policy: 'You turn if you want to: the lady's not for turning.'

After the Falklands, Thatcher was guaranteed a rapturous reception from party members, who could be manipulated to maximize the impact of the spectacle on television viewers of all parties. Thus in 1982 she began by saying that her speech would not be about the Falklands, and although she immediately broke this promise she lavished praise on British service personnel without mentioning her own role in the conflict. However, viewers were meant to draw the inference that this 'remarkable chapter in our island history' had been inspired by her personal determination to restore British pride. Having established her credentials as the architect of national resurgence, she could devote much of her speech to attacks on Labour which would please her immediate audience, before using the Falklands as a means of restating her 1980 message about the inadvisability of 'U-turns' ('Nothing could be more damaging to our prospects as a nation if this Government [threw] away the reputation it has earned for constancy and resolve'[18]). This was the first of Thatcher's conference speeches to be delivered with the advantage of a specially designed backdrop – blue, to match her jacket as well as the party's colours, with the words 'The Resolute Approach' behind her just in case anyone mistook the verbal message.

After Thatcher's 'constancy and resolve' had been rewarded with a crushing victory in the 1983 general election, the days when coded criticisms of the government attracted media attention at party conferences were over. It was natural for journalists – and, presumably, most of Thatcher's grassroots supporters – to regard the leader's speech as the sole noteworthy aspect of these occasions. This tendency was reinforced by the 1984 conference (held in Brighton, the scene of the 1982 gathering), when Thatcher added physical courage and emotional resilience to her proven qualities by delivering a speech hours after the IRA's attempt on her life. The challenge now was to restrain any 'triumphalist' impulses. In 1987, after her party's third consecutive election victory, she succumbed to that temptation during the main part of her conference speech. Having congratulated herself and her party for creating 'a new Britain, confident, optimistic, sure of its economic strength', she assured her audience in the hall and at home that the blessings she had bestowed were not coming to an end any time soon: 'Our third election victory was only a staging post on a much longer journey.' Despite all that she had achieved, she still had plenty of radical ideas: 'Would "consolidate" be the word that we stitch on our banners? Whose blood would run faster at the prospect of five years of consolidation?'[19]

For some of Thatcher's colleagues, the prospect of five more revolutionary years was likely to make the blood run much colder. By the time of her 1990 speech Thatcher's prospectus of unending radicalism certainly seemed less attractive to the electorate as a whole. Rioting against the poll tax was only the most spectacular symptom of widespread dissatisfaction with the practical results of 'Thatcherism'. Although she managed to deliver her speech without a single mention of the poll tax, the Prime Minister could hardly avoid another painful subject – Britain's membership of the European Exchange Rate Mechanism (ERM: see chapter 3) – because the belated and bitterly contested decision to join the ERM had been announced just a few days earlier, in the hope of diverting media attention from what had been a successful Labour Party conference.

At the time Labour's leadership was annoyed about this ploy, but there was no reason to think that the damage would be more than temporary since Thatcher's defence of the policy was understandably lame: and if the decision had helped to keep the Prime Minister in office until the next election Neil Kinnock and his acolytes should have been punching the air, since by 1990 the Prime Minister had become their chief asset. As it was, despite the standing ovation that she received from the conference of October 1990, Thatcher had been deposed before the end of November. The real lesson for Labour should have been that crude gamesmanship can never save a government in terminal trouble; rather, it can make a bad situation worse. Yet one suspects that this shoddy incident made a lasting impression on some ambitious members of the Opposition, leading to the view that government announcements could be timed in a way which kept less helpful headlines off the front pages of the tabloids. To adapt a favourite New Labour phrase, a big policy announcement could be used to 'bury' good news for the Opposition.

In hindsight, the most arresting feature of Thatcher's valedictory conference speech as Prime Minister was her verbal recognition that her government included other individuals apart from herself. While in previous speeches she had only mentioned individual colleagues by name if they had done something particularly commendable, a short section of the 1990 speech included a favourable namecheck for fourteen ministers – though not, of course, her bête noir Geoffrey Howe, who was on the verge of resignation. If this inveterate individualist now felt it necessary – thanks to the promptings of her Party Chairman, Kenneth Baker – to showcase her team-playing propensities, her government was surely in terminal trouble. Having talked up her ministers, Thatcher invited her audience to shower them with applause, describing them as 'a fabulous team'.

Within a few weeks, the 'fabulous team' stood accused of having forced their beloved skipper out of office. When the result of the first leadership ballot in November 1990 was announced, Thatcher had been attending a European Security conference in Paris, and her decision to let her name go forward to the next round was announced outside the Paris embassy amid a media melee in which the ever-faithful Ingham was a central figure. Back in Downing Street, she simply told reporters 'I shall fight on. I fight to win.' Nothing in her front-line political career – and particularly in her public declarations – became her like the leaving of it.

John Major

Having been chosen as Conservative leader and Prime Minister at least in part because he was so different from Margaret Thatcher, in terms of public communication John Major lived up – or down, according to taste – to expectations. The first clear evidence of the contrast came on the day after his election, when Major stood on the doorstep of No. 10 and spoke of his ambition 'to build a country at ease with itself, a country that is confident, and a country that is prepared and willing to make the changes necessary to provide a better quality of life for all our citizens'. By implication, although he lauded her legacy Major thought that Thatcher had been deficient in these respects. But perhaps the sharpest contrast came in January 1991, when Major delivered a prime ministerial broadcast in order to explain why Britain had joined in the US-led mission to remove Iraqi forces from Kuwait. Having offered his thanks and best wishes to service personnel in the Gulf, he seemed to have the whole nation in mind when (apparently against the advice of his aides) he ended with the words 'Goodnight – and God bless' (Price, 2010, 288).

In keeping with the new tone, while the press secretaries who served Major for most of his time in office (Gus O'Donnell and Christopher Meyer) were very able individuals who went on to hold even higher offices, unlike Bernard Ingham they had never been journalists, so they brought far less professional baggage to the role. This is not to say, however, that Major and his advisers reacted against the media management of the Thatcher years, swearing to tell the plain unvarnished truth without availing themselves of presentational advantages. In June 1994, after the Conservatives had incurred serious losses in European parliamentary elections, the MP and diarist Gyles Brandreth reported that 'Christopher Meyer has had a bright idea. Get the PM to give a presidential press conference *in the* [Downing Street] *garden*. We can't change the play, but we can change the set!' (Brandreth, 1999, 266: italics in original). Evidently Major agreed with Mayer and Brandreth, because he chose the same stage in the following year when he announced his resignation as party leader, challenging his opponents to 'put up or shut up'. He was not the last significant political figure to exploit it.

By 1994, Major was having to exploit previously untapped prime ministerial resources because he could no longer rely on Thatcher's key asset – supportive media outlets which would speak to the country on his behalf. Instead, after Black Wednesday Major was faced with a right-wing press which had returned to its first love (Thatcher), and treated her successor with unconcealed contempt. There was never any chance that the Prime Minister would gain compensation by winning a sympathetic hearing from centre-left papers like the *Guardian*, while the *Mirror* had an umbilical link with Labour. Thus Major had to fall back on his personal powers of communication if he wanted to kindle a positive public response to his 'One Nation' message. Yet although his political approach had much in common with that of Stanley Baldwin, the only time that he came close to the latter's ability to communicate directly with the nation was the Gulf War broadcast of January 1991, when Major was enjoying his 'honeymoon' with the voters. For all his well-meaning rhetoric about building 'a country at ease with itself', after the polarization of the Thatcher years this task could hardly be accomplished by unassisted good intentions. A relevant vision of Britain would have helped, but when Major evoked the essence of his country in a speech of April 1993 it turned out that his ideas were both anachronistic and Anglo-centric: 'Fifty years from now Britain will still be the country of long shadows on county grounds, warm beer, invincible green suburbs, dog lovers and pools fillers.'[20] The final reference will be unintelligible now to anyone born after 1994, when Major's government effectively destroyed 'the pools' as a form of weekly gambling by introducing a national lottery, and Major seemed unaware that the idea of county cricket would not be very evocative for voters outside England. Even at the time, the speech suggested a view of Britain that would have made more sense to Stanley Baldwin himself than to the vast majority of voters in 1993. While Thatcher spoke to a nation which had lost its global status and wanted to blame someone for that 'defeat', Major had been a war baby, part of a generation which had been lulled by successive governments into a feeling that relative decline was in the natural order of things, and could be managed without undue resistance, sacrifice or discussion.

Though easy to mock, Major's eulogy of Britain/England was actually an effective counterblast to Margaret Thatcher, who in her Bruges speech of September 1988 had implied that closer European integration would replace the identity of individual Britons with a kind of 'identikit' European personality. Major, after all, had been addressing a group of beleaguered pro-EU Tories when he prophesied that Britain would remain resolutely dog-loving and pools-filling. Yet by the time of his speech the proprietors of Tory-supporting newspapers had realized that Margaret Thatcher had been a gift which could keep on giving – indeed, that her political martyrdom made her even more alluring, since freedom from the ties of office allowed her to give full vent to a Europhobia based on her hatred for Germany. No right-wing newspaper ever saw a dip in its circulation figures after a bout of 'Euro-bashing'; and the addition of Thatcher's name to the story was sure to boost sales still further. It is unlikely that any of the major proprietors worried unduly about 'national sovereignty', except insofar as it affected their business interests; and the EU was likely to be more of an obstacle to these than an enfeebled, 'hollowed-out' state like Britain.

Thus, for any Thatcherite proprietor or editor, the 'line to take' on 'Europe' was a no-brainer in the 1990s and after. At best, a cascade of anti-European headlines might force Major to abandon his position, in which case the newspapers could claim that they had persuaded him to 'save Britain' from federalism, he would become a passive vehicle for their various whims and they could recommend their readers to vote Conservative next time round. Alternatively, if Major resisted they could hold a watching brief before announcing their partisan preference for the next election. If they sensed that Labour was going to win, they could effect a timely switch of allegiance which (hopefully) would make the new government feel that it was under some kind of obligation. Then, if the Opposition leader Tony Blair followed Major's pragmatic approach to Europe, newspapers like the *Sun* could sell extra copies by subjecting him to the same nationalistic attacks.

While political scientists and scholars in associated disciplines try to measure media influence on voting behaviour through survey evidence, this is a dubious exercise since elections are contests between parties whose policies are shaped, to varying but always significant degrees, by media coverage. This means that, even for the best-informed voter, there can be no escape from media influence. Thatcher had very little interest in daily headlines – she could afford to adopt this lofty attitude since she was sure of support from proprietors like Murdoch – but to keep her informed of public adulation Bernard Ingham fed her with daily digests carefully culled from the newspapers which supported her. John Major could never have been fooled in this fashion; he wanted to read the papers himself, as soon as they reached the news stands, and their headlines certainly had a profound effect on *him*. For normal human beings, Major's response to media criticism was understandable; equally, normal human beings in liberal democracies do not want their political leaders to exhibit 'normal' sensitivities, expecting them to be tough and tender-hearted by turns (and often at the same time).

In Major's case, the damning indictment was delivered by Norman Lamont in his resignation speech of June 1993, when he accused the government he had just left of 'too much short-termism, too much reacting to events . . . Far too many important decisions are made for 36 hours' publicity' (see chapter 3). By the time of Lamont's resignation it was obvious that 'events', which had been so helpful to Major in his elevation to the premiership, had turned decisively against him, The change of approach dictated by Black Wednesday is apparent in Major's subsequent speeches to party conferences. In October 1991, addressing his first Conservative gathering as Prime Minister, Major had envisaged that the party was his primary audience (at one point pausing to say, 'I hope the whole country is listening' as if there was some doubt about this).[21] The 1992 conference should have allowed Major to speak to a party 'at ease with itself', since the Conservatives had won a record vote at that year's general election. Instead, thanks to Black Wednesday Major found himself disadvantaged even compared to Thatcher's pre-Falklands position, trying to appeal over the heads of his immediate audience. Major, indeed, went further than Thatcher had ever done in confessing the true purpose of his speech, saying in 1992 that 'I intend to address myself to the country, the Conference and the Conservative Party.' This stated order of priorities might have been accidental, but it was not misleading.[22]

Major's message to the country was quickly forgotten, as an announced programme of pit closures aroused angry protests from backbenchers and a media which, for once, was united in its condemnation of the government. Then, in early November 1992, Major's ally George (H. W.) Bush was defeated by the Democrat Bill Clinton in the US presidential election. This was a personal setback for Major, who had infuriated Clinton by allowing Conservative functionaries to assist

Bush's re-election campaign. More seriously, the Home Office had taken an interest in Clinton's spell at Oxford University, apparently with a view to discovering whether he had applied for British citizenship in order to avoid the Vietnam draft. Thus, instead of being able to issue a public message of congratulation to Bush, Major was lumbered with the task of sending Clinton a grovelling apology, which the new President snubbed.[23] Any hope of cashing in, like Thatcher, on the media advantages arising from a 'special relationship' with the occupant of the White House had evaporated; rather, these opportunities would fall to Major's political opponents. In addition, Bush's defeat suggested that in the post-Cold War climate candidates who lacked 'the vision thing' would be at a significant disadvantage.

Major was left with no choice but to relaunch his premiership with a vision of sorts – hopefully one which would enthuse his party as well as providing the public at large with the sense that the government shared its concerns. The chosen theme was equipped with a catchy slogan – 'Back to Basics' – and featured heavily in Major's 1993 conference speech. The immediate media reaction was disappointing, but even hostile newspapers showed that they had understood what Major was trying to say; the *Guardian* reported without irony his closing words of thanks to grassroots members for their loyalty to him and to the party.[24] However, under questioning Major's spin doctors exceeded their brief, agreeing that the Prime Minister had been talking about personal morality as well as the 'basic' values which should underpin public policy. As a result, Major's media tormentors were given a licence to print stories about the private lives of ministers and even obscure backbenchers as if this salacious coverage had an obvious connection with government policy and was thus in the 'national interest' (Major, 1999, 555–6).

In June 1995, Major flew to Nova Scotia for the annual G7 summit between the leaders of the world's richest countries. Far from giving the Prime Minister a platform for good publicity as such occasions usually do, the British media seized the chance to hound him with questions about splits within his party. On the return flight, instead of sharing confidences with journalists he ignored them. He was brooding over a last-ditch attempt to restore his authority – wrong-footing his opponents by precipitating an early leadership election. The ensuing contest only exposed the hopelessness of his position; although he received enough support from backbenchers to justify his continuation in office, he was written off as a loser by virtually all the right-wing newspapers. When the result was announced, a posse of supportive ministers was unleashed to 'spin' the result into a magnificent endorsement of the embattled premier. Norman Lamont, who had supported Major's challenger John Redwood, might have reflected that this was a perfect example of a government which had always hungered for '36 hours' of positive publicity. After the 1995 leadership contest it was left with precious few scraps to feed on.

Tony Blair

Early in his premiership, Tony Blair delivered a tribute to a much-loved woman who had suffered grievously at the hands of the establishment, not least because of her involvement in a mixed-race relationship. The woman's tragic fate had provoked an outburst of public anger, and an intervention from the Prime Minister was deemed appropriate.

It was April 1998, and as a former barrister Blair was giving his opinion that Deidre Rachid (formerly Deidre Barlow), a fictional character in the ITV soap opera *Coronation Street*, had been wrongfully convicted of fraud. Blair was on a winning streak with regard to pronouncements of this kind, and he was equally adept when talking about real people. After the death of Princess Diana along with her lover Dodi Fayed on 31 August 1997 he had lauded her as 'the people's princess', a phrase which had been agreed with his Press Secretary, Alastair Campbell, and delivered to the media as Blair arrived at his local church. He had told Campbell, 'What I have to do today is try to express what the country is feeling' (Campbell, 2011, 126). Even a sceptical journalist had to admit that on this occasion Blair had hit exactly the right note: 'He defined public sentiment and by doing so surfed and channelled the emotion that was washing across much of Britain' (Rawnsley, 2000, 62).

Rather than seeing Thatcher as their role model, as is sometimes assumed, Blair and his aides were more influenced by Major's fate and based their strategy on the need to avoid it. Major had been dogged by open dissent, so New Labour's high command took control of ministerial media appearances. Thatcher had enjoyed excellent relations with media proprietors and their editors; Blair tried to emulate her as far as possible (ending up as godfather to one of Murdoch's daughters). But

New Labour had another trick up its sleeve. By constructing its policies on the findings of focus groups, it ensured that even hostile newspaper editors would hesitate before attacking specific initiatives. Where media opposition was guaranteed (e.g. on the issue of the European single currency) Blair decided to pull back rather than undergo the kind of drubbing visited on Major. Then Campbell, who knew how the media worked and was in no danger of over-rating journalistic integrity, could play one outlet off against another, offering special access to ministers and exclusive 'scoops' of various kinds. Almost invariably such favours were bestowed upon right-wing papers rather than Labour's traditional media friends, whose continuing support could be taken for granted.

While implying that Major's media operation had been woefully inadequate, Labour's approach also superseded the Bernard Ingham model, effective as that had been. As we have seen, Ingham was a civil servant who had to exclude himself from formal discussions of Conservative Party business. He was not allowed to instruct other members of the Government Information Service (GIS), although in practice junior officials understood that it was advisable to act on his unspoken wishes. Ingham's ability to exert 'remote control' was impressive, but Blair left nothing to chance, giving Campbell the right to instruct civil servants and in some cases to engineer the removal of any members of the GIS (now renamed the Government Information and Communication Service) who showed insufficient enthusiasm for the new regime (Price, 2010, 340–1). Previous doubts concerning the propriety of the government's mouthpiece attending 'political' meetings – including Cabinet – had been buried under the Labour landslide.

While some commentators described Campbell as the real 'Deputy Prime Minister', this attempt to gauge his influence missed essential points, since previous 'deputies' had been parliamentarians rather than former journalists, and the title had been awarded either because of existing influence (Whitelaw) or to fob off senior politicians who were outliving their usefulness (Geoffrey Howe and, under Blair, John Prescott). A closer parallel, perhaps – and one which would have appealed to Campbell as an ardent football fan – would have been Assistant Manager. Campbell was always ready to argue with Blair, and undoubtedly affected some key decisions, but understood the limitations of his role and was willing to 'spin' on behalf of policies he had opposed in private. In some circumstances this arrangement could have worked very well, but the Manager and his gifted Assistant had to cope with someone who could be compared to a Director of Football – Gordon Brown, who had his own retinue of media manipulators. As a result, too much of Campbell's time was occupied with unscheduled matches between rival spin doctors. More generally, the battle between 'Blairites' and 'Brownites' contributed to a feeling in the Campbell camp that the party was still in Opposition, and had to squeeze every presentational advantage out of any encounter with the media. Wherever possible, this advantage should accrue to the Prime Minister rather than to Brown or any subordinate colleague. Bending the truth – or even disseminating outright falsehoods – was acceptable if it scored points for New Labour over the media. It seemed not to worry Labour's spin doctors that by misinforming elements of the media they were effectively deceiving members of the public.

In 2002, after New Labour had won its second landslide, Stuart Weir, the Director of 'Democratic Audit', told the Commons Committee on Public Administration that thirty-seven out of the government's eighty-one special advisers 'were either primarily employed to manage and protect the government's (or a minister's) image, or ready to do so'. Campbell himself headed a phalanx of Whitehall 'spinners', deployed within a number of 'units' and 'offices'.[25] While New Labour's policy advisers tended to be recent university graduates, brimming with enthusiasm but devoid of experience, Campbell knew that presentation was too important to be left to novices. He recruited seasoned journalists, often BBC employees who either sympathized with New Labour or realized that this government would make life dull (but professionally dangerous) for anyone who worked within a Corporation which was meant to be impartial (Jones, 2001, 82–7). When critics complained about the spreading tentacles of Campbell's empire, he tended to retort that such commentators were fixated with 'process' – that is, with the message, not the substance of policy. But, for New Labour, the message *was* the substance; not least because previous governments had 'hollowed out' Whitehall departments and made it impossible for them to oversee the implementation of policies in the customary fashion (Foster, 2005, 185: see chapter 3). Thus the right to make 'announcements of intent' became jealously guarded; and since Blair wanted to take full advantage of the Prime Minister's licence to roam in policy terms, any minister whose department happened to 'deliver' on New

Labour promises was liable to have the glory stolen at the last minute – either by the occupant of No. 10, or by his surly neighbour.

In this context, 'joined-up government' could only mean co-ordinated *presentation*; and unfortunately for New Labour, practical results still mattered, even to a media which retained a strong (if short-term) interest in policy failures, provided that they could be given a 'human interest' angle. Long before the catastrophic failure of the Iraq War (see below) the self-defeating nature of the New Labour project had been exposed in a fashion which could easily have brought it to an end if Blair had not (like Thatcher) been blessed with an ineffective Opposition. In September 2000 well-organized protests against the price of fuel brought Britain to a standstill within less than a week. According to Campbell's diary, Blair spent much of the time fulminating about his inability to fight back against the protestors, even blaming a reaction against onerous fuel taxes on a deeply laid right-wing conspiracy rather than identifying the real problem – namely, a drastic and deliberate reduction in the authority of the state under Thatcher and Major, which New Labour had only compounded. Thus when Blair demanded factual evidence about the extent of the crisis rather than 'all the blather that departments pumped out', neither he nor Campbell seemed to realize that they had made ministries into factories of 'good news' stories rather than reliable sources of information (Campbell, 2011, 396). The 'facts', thanks to the combined efforts of every government since 1979, were grim. Despite Britain's dependence on petrol there had been no contingency planning for protests involving the disruption of supplies, the Treasury had sold off emergency reserves and the government didn't even have a map of the country's refineries (Straw, 2012, 311–12). Those who remember the 2000 fuel crisis will not have been surprised by the inadequate response to the coronavirus pandemic twenty years later (see chapter 8).

Blair had been warned about the strength of feeling against fuel taxes by his pollster Philip Gould, but had paid insufficient attention to the issue. The man who had 'surfed' so skilfully when Diana died seemed in danger of being engulfed on his first encounter with choppy waters. Some kind of address to the nation was imperative. However, like Thatcher, Blair eschewed old-style straight-to-camera broadcasts. Instead, he held press conferences on three consecutive days. On such occasions, he admitted much later, all that a Prime Minister could do was to 'give a general appearance of being in charge, whatever the panic underneath' (Rentoul, 2001, 570–2; Blair, 2010, 269). His appearances were ineffective; the protestors only began to melt away when they became alarmed by the possible consequences of their success, with vital public services coming close to collapse due to lack of fuel.

At the time, Campbell and other advisers were working hard on Blair's speech to the 2000 Labour Party conference. Since Blair became leader in 1994, the annual conference had been 'hollowed out'; although the original Labour constitution had made it the party's key decision-making body, this authority had been eroded over time and now it was extinguished altogether, turning the conference into an opportunity for party members to exhibit adulation for the leader. Nevertheless, for Blair and his team the task of composing a text which would appeal to multiple audiences 'produced agony, consternation, madness and creativity in roughly equal proportions', and what Campbell described in 1997 as an 'exhausting and tortured process' never got easier (Blair, 2010, 23; Campbell, 2011, 162). In 2000 the need to get things right was more acute than ever, not just because of the fuel crisis but also thanks to a public relations disaster in June, when Blair had been slow-handclapped by the Women's Institute after ignoring advice that his speech should eschew party politics. It was a far cry from Blair's conference speech of 1996, which had been aimed squarely at first-time voters. Blair, who had associated himself with the short-lived 'Britpop' phenomenon, spoke of Britain as a 'young country', and adapted a popular football anthem by declaiming that 'Labour's coming home' (much to the annoyance of Gordon Brown, who had wanted to pull a similar stunt in his own speech (Campbell, 2010, 536–7; Harris, 2004, 303)). Discarding any pretence that the speech had been prepared for the enlightenment of his party, at one point Blair ranted, 'I say to the British people: have the courage to change now.' His command of the audience in the hall was demonstrated by the applause which greeted his disclosure that 'businessmen say to me, "Tony, I never thought I'd be doing this but here's a big cheque to help you beat the most negative, dishonest campaign in history".' When the Ecclestone affair came to light six months after New Labour was elected, it seemed more likely that such conversations had proceeded along the lines of, 'Tony, here's a big cheque which you should bear in mind whenever one of your ministers is thinking of taking a decision which will hurt my business interests.'

Within a few seconds of bragging about his first-name relationships with businesspeople who were desperate to reward him for his honesty, in his 1996 speech Blair promised the country that under New Labour there would be 'No more sleaze . . . No more lies.' In 2000, his conference oration was rewritten at the last moment to include a mea culpa, attributing the fuel protests to an uncharacteristic inattention to the public mood. For good measure, Blair decided to use the season of apologies to rid himself of any responsibility for the Millennium Dome fiasco: 'Hindsight is a wonderful thing, and if I had my time again, I would have listened to those who said governments shouldn't try to run big visitor attractions.' As Blair knew very well, this was not the reason why a majority of his Cabinet colleagues had opposed the Dome: they had argued that it would be a colossal waste of public money. By a miracle of mendacity, Blair had turned his own failure of judgement – which could be, and was, identified as such without the benefit of hindsight – into an attack on the public sector. Yet Lance Price, who had left the BBC to join New Labour's spin machine, recorded in his diary that 'Blair's speech was superb', marred only by his choice of shirt, whose colour made it all too obvious to television viewers that he was sweating profusely (Price, 2005, 255).

By the time of the 2001 general election, the essence of New Labour had been exposed in more than one book – particularly Andrew Rawnsley's *Servants of the People*, which was being serialized during the 2000 Labour conference – and voters had few illusions when New Labour was re-elected on the lowest voter turnout of the democratic era. Yet before the full implications of this tacit vote of no confidence in the Blair project could be digested, the terrorist attack on America (September 11, 2001) had taken place. The attacks claimed sixty-seven British victims, yet Blair framed 9/11 as an assault on an abstraction – Western civilization – and he declared his readiness to 'stand shoulder to shoulder with America' in its defence.

It was Blair's 'Brighton Bomb' moment, except that the attacks had not been directed at himself and had happened an ocean away. In 1984, Thatcher had stayed at Brighton after the attempt on her life to deliver her planned conference speech (with a few topical adjustments). On 11 September 2001 Tony Blair was in the same Brighton hotel, preparing for a speech to the annual Trades Union conference, when the news from the US came through. If Blair had been among kindred spirits at a conference of business leaders, he might have collected his thoughts and delivered a passionate, impromptu speech. But the TUC was 'Old Labour', and its 2001 gathering had already shown hostility towards Blair's government. It was not the right setting for an address to the nation, so after a few remarks Blair excused himself and hurried back to the sanctuary of Downing Street to give a speech – delivered rather like the political broadcasts of old, except with the Prime Minister standing and not looking straight to camera, to enhance the sense of drama – which conveyed the same message that he had given at the TUC.

The road from 9/11 led to Blair's departure from office in June 2007, although there was a pause in the journey when New Labour won a third consecutive general election in 2005. Blair was also able to convince a parliamentary majority to support British participation in America's war on Iraq, after a speech which was an address to a divided nation as well as to the House of Commons (see chapter 1). While Blair's admirers (and even some critics) thought that his speech in the key debate of 18 March 2003 was one of his best, he failed to win backing from a majority of backbench Labour MPs and the outcome could have been even worse if Robin Cook, the former Foreign Secretary, had made his impressive resignation statement on the day of the debate rather than the previous evening (Straw, 2012, 390; Kampfner, 2004, 304–9). The subsequent 'spin' operation was reminiscent of the concerted attempt to shore up Major's position after the 1995 leadership election; as Campbell put it, the official 'line' was 'we won the vote, because we won the argument, and now the country should unite' (an anticipation of the 'Leaver' refrain after the 2016 referendum, in which both Blair and Campbell were prominent on the losing side). Since the overwhelming majority of Conservative MPs had supported Blair it was not surprising that most of the press was happy to follow this narrative (Campbell, 2012, 512). As British troops went into action, Blair tried to spin away the issues at stake in a televised address which evoked pride in Britain's armed forces and presented the alternative to action as a shameful retreat. This ignored the inconvenient fact that a retreat would only be necessary because troops had been already been dispatched to the area in accordance with the prearranged timetable for war.[26]

Two inquiries into the government's handling of the case for war were conducted in its immediate aftermath (a judicial inquiry under Lord Hutton, and a review of intelligence by privy counsellors, chaired by the former Cabinet Secretary Lord Butler). The evidence collected for these inquiries revealed a government which was 'unfit for purpose', and whose dysfunctional nature arose chiefly from its obsession with positive presentation. However, Butler and his team pulled their punches because they felt it was not their place to express their findings in a way which might undermine an elected government, while Lord Hutton chose to rain punches on the BBC rather than Blair. Although Hutton's attempted 'whitewash' backfired in terms of public opinion – without Alastair Campbell to guide him, Hutton was unable to give his findings a veneer of impartiality which might have made them more credible – the government could claim to be vindicated, while a Corporation which had been guilty of errors in judgement concerning a single broadcast was forced to make significant changes in procedure and personnel. The repercussions of the Iraq intervention included the London attacks of 7 July 2005 – hours after Blair had hailed the 'momentous' decision to award Britain the 2012 Olympic games. It was the Royal Family, rather than the Prime Minister, which spoke for Britain after '7/7'.

A few days before he stood down as Prime Minister, Blair delivered an extraordinary speech in which he compared the media to 'a feral beast, just tearing people and reputations to bits'. This was followed by a typical Blair apology – an apparently candid admission of error coupled with a contorted gloss which, while not shirking his personal responsibility, insinuated that the Prime Minister himself had been more sinned against than sinning. Blair's admission that 'We paid inordinate attention in the early days of New Labour to courting, assuaging, and persuading the media' was arresting enough, although the vague chronology conveyed the misleading impression that Blair had quickly changed his ways. In any case, there had been no alternative to the creation of a spin machine: although other people in public life were afraid to admit it, 'a vast aspect of our jobs today . . . is coping with the media, its sheer scale, weight and constant hyperactivity. At points, it literally overwhelms.' Therefore, Prime Ministers have no choice but to mount a 'proper press operation'.[27]

Blair's speech raised serious points about the media of 2007, which was increasingly driven to seek 'sensational' stories because of emerging competition from the internet. However, that had not been true of the media between 1994 and 1997, when New Labour looked on with quiet satisfaction as newspapers ripped 'people and reputations to bits' and Blair and his party were the beneficiaries of 'feral' behaviour from the Murdoch press. Since then the media had indeed changed, but to a considerable extent its new willingness to expose New Labour scandals arose from the personal and policy failures of ministers. These would have been newsworthy at any time since 1979, and had increased public cynicism precisely because Blair had been believed when he claimed to offer a sleaze-free style of politics. Even as he prepared to leave office Blair could not relinquish his old habits, singling out the *Independent* newspaper for attack rather than more egregious outlets, and inviting his listeners to believe that the Hutton Inquiry had only been discredited because 'its verdict was not the one its critics wanted'. These belated and ineffectual attempts to settle old scores betrayed the real problem with Blair and New Labour: they had campaigned and governed for a tabloid audience, and could not forgive people who (notwithstanding the emergence of twenty-four-hour news) still preferred to base their political opinions on solid evidence rather than short-term sensations and crude propaganda.

Gordon Brown

In part, Blair's salvo could be read as an invitation to his successor to introduce more rigorous regulation of the media. Almost certainly he knew that Gordon Brown would not take the hint, because his own record of dealings with the media since 1994 was no better than Blair's.

In his battle to ensure that at least some positive headlines came his way, as Chancellor between 1997 and 2007 Brown had focused on the budget, traditionally delivered near the end of the financial year (5 April), but moved by his predecessor Kenneth Clarke to the late autumn. Brown restored it to April, and made sure that he had at least two annual dates at the centre of the political stage by renaming the old Autumn Statement a 'Pre-Budget Report'. His performances on these occasions were designed to signal that while Blair might be New Labour's show-man, Brown was the indispensable producer/director. Sooner rather than later, Brown hoped, the warm-up act would grow tired of the limelight, allowing the real star to step into his rightful place.

Unfortunately for Brown this proved to be a painful and protracted process, during which the Chancellor found himself compelled to imitate Blair's populist approach to communications. He recruited media operatives who were only too keen to beat Blair's team at their own game, and although his policy advisers (notably the 'two Eds', Balls and Miliband) were at least the intellectual equals of anyone working directly for Blair, they learned very quickly that servants in Brown's retinue were expected to fight at a much less elevated level.

Shortly before leaving office, Blair had come closest to endorsing Brown as his successor by warning the Opposition leader, David Cameron, that he would soon be facing a 'great clunking fist' at PMQs. This was unlikely to intimidate Cameron, since it implied (rightly) that Brown was a pretty 'clunky' communicator, at least when compared to Blair. Thus it came as an unpleasant surprise to the Conservatives (and presumably to Blair) that in his first weeks as Prime Minister Brown created a very favourable impression through his decisions, and public pronouncements, in response to floods and a terrorist attack on Glasgow Airport. An important reason for this positive presentation was that Brown made a conscious attempt to speak to the nation as the leader of a team, rather than a 'presidential' figure; thus one of his televised interviews on the terrorist incident was conducted outside the Cabinet room, and he ensured that all of his senior colleagues were fully briefed on the situation (Brown, 2017, 205).

However, Brown's early success as Prime Minister rested on fragile foundations; when he spoke to the country, many of his colleagues denied that he had earned the authority even to speak for his party, since he had become leader without a contest. A possible way around this problem was Brown's understandable and genuine interest in the concept of 'Britishness' in the post-devolution context. It is more difficult for opponents to deny you the right to act as a national spokesperson if you have been the first politician successfully to *define* the nation itself. It is also helpful to establish your credentials if your definition makes the public feel good about itself. Brown's list of British values included fairness, tolerance, belief in liberty and a sense of decency; it was, in fact, an update on Major's 'Back to Basics' vision, now featuring a (partial) recognition that Britain was not just England and that its society contained many people with roots outside the UK (for a critique, see Lee, 2009, 134–64). Perhaps fortunately for Brown, it did not capture the public imagination even in the negative sense achieved by 'Back to Basics', allowing him to escape media comment on the apparent conflict between the boasted British values and the nature of his media operation, where 'fairness, tolerance and decency' were in very short supply.[28] For example, Damian McBride, who had worked for Brown at the Treasury as a civil servant, moved with him to No. 10 and earned the nickname of 'Mad Dog', with an apparent licence to savage the premier's opponents in all parties.

If Britishness failed, the obvious alternative was the ballot box. Calling a 'snap' election on the wave of initial popularity was an obvious temptation for Brown, but the potential hazards were equally apparent. Brown's situation was far more complicated than the one facing Major in 1990; in order to claim a personal mandate, Labour would not just have to win, but to win big (see chapter 6). Since the polling data were ambiguous, Brown prevaricated despite a well-received speech at the 2007 party conference, in which he had heaped praise on the British people and associated himself with the country's values, speaking directly to the voters and insisting that 'I will not let you down.'[29]

After the conference Brown flew to Iraq, to visit British troops still stationed there and announce a significant pull-out before Christmas. This turned out to be a disaster for Brown, and again the comparison with Major is instructive. In 1991, the newly elevated Major visited British forces in the Gulf, and certainly did his image no harm. But Major, unlike Brown, had become Prime Minister after a leadership contest; in 1991 the troops were preparing to fight, rather than hoping to leave the scene of an earlier and highly controversial action; and there had been no speculation that the Prime Minister was hoping to use the occasion as the prelude to a general election campaign. Brown's camp denied that his visit had been staged to impress voters, but the media, acting on their own interpretation of British 'fairness', refused to give the Prime Minister the benefit of the doubt.

Almost immediately after Brown had 'bottled' the election, he was handed another chance to cement his authority. All things being equal, early symptoms of serious malaise in the world's banking system should have made Britons grateful that their Prime Minister had spent so long at the Treasury. However, this particular ex-Chancellor could be deemed at least partly responsible for Britain's vulnerability to a financial crisis. To make matters worse, Brown's relations with his appointed Chancellor, Alistair Darling, came under increasing strain as they differed over the severity of Britain's position. In September

2008 – days before Labour's party conference – Darling gave an interview to the *Guardian* in which he predicted that the economic crisis would be the worst since the Great Depression. Although he had tried to emphasize that this was a global, rather than a uniquely British, problem, the published interview gave a different impression. It had been conducted at Darling's Outer Hebridean home, and featured pictures of the Chancellor amidst a desolate landscape. In flagrant violation of New Labour's handbook of media management, the interview was a verbal and visual contradiction of Brown's ongoing attempt to reassure voters that he could ameliorate the worst of the crisis. After the story broke, it seems that Brown and Darling held a constructive conversation about a damage-limitation exercise. But Darling was already very wary of Brown's spin doctor Damian 'Mad Dog' McBride, who had never treated him with respect since he knew that his master would have preferred to appoint Ed Balls as Chancellor (see chapter 3). When someone in Brown's camp began to brief the media against him, Darling suspected that McBride was behind it and later claimed that 'the forces of hell' had been unleashed against him. Actually it seems that the chief culprit was Brown's former spin doctor Charlie Whelan, but this hardly exonerated Brown since Whelan, who had been forced to resign in 1999, was still an outspoken loyalist with continuing ties to the Prime Minister (Rawnsley, 2010, 563).

It was a partial re-enactment of the Thatcher–Lawson–Walters confrontation of 1989, but with two significant differences. Whether or not an ideologue like Walters was fit to be a special adviser to a British Prime Minister, he did at least enjoy a reputation for economic expertise. McBride, by contrast, had been a relatively junior civil servant before being promoted as a Treasury spin doctor. If such an unelected individual had been licensed by No. 10 to traduce the Chancellor, the pecking order in Whitehall had clearly undergone an unhelpful change over the years since 1989. The other difference was that in 1989 both Lawson and Walters had resigned; in 2008 Darling and McBride stayed (although the latter's role was reduced). Unlike Lawson in 1989, Darling really was 'unassailable' for the time being, since the sacking of the Chancellor at a time of economic peril would have had disastrous consequences.

Continued friction between the residents of Downing Street hampered Brown's attempts to inspire public confidence. Although he is rightly credited by economists as the most important political actor in the co-ordinated international response to the global financial crisis, for voters at home it was all too easy to remember his oft-repeated claim to be the 'prudent' Chancellor who had 'abolished Tory boom and bust'. In December 2008 he was mocked after a slip of the tongue at PMQs, in which the intended phrase 'saved the world's banks' was mangled into a claim to have 'saved the world'.[30]

Brown might have salvaged some dignity on that occasion if he had given a self-deprecating smile to acknowledge his mistake, but his public demeanour had always belied his warm private personality. Realizing that he needed to soften his image, in April 2009 he released a video in which he smiled frequently, albeit in the least appropriate places. Brown was giving his government's response to growing public criticism of the misuse of MPs' expenses. His toe-curling performance went public just days after Damian McBride had been forced to resign after revelations that he had been planning to run 'smear' stories about senior Conservative politicians. At least, for once, the Mad Dog had been soiling the Tory lamp post rather than relieving himself in Labour's kennel, but this was limited compensation for Brown, who had just returned from a successful G20 summit when the bad news broke. Despite the clearest evidence that McBride was a liability to the Prime Minister and the government as a whole, Brown was reluctant to dispense with his services and took several days to apologize, in a fashion which implied that he was unaware of McBride's methods. In his memoir he barely mentions McBride except to thank him for writing 'a very penitent and honest book blaming only himself' (Brown, 2017, 18). It might have helped Brown's reputation if he had followed suit.

David Cameron

At the time of McBride's departure, David Cameron called for a change of culture in Downing Street. Although Cameron's No. 10 did not forswear the assistance of spin doctors, between 2010 and 2016 the worst excesses of the Blair–Brown years were avoided; the toxicity created by special advisers arose from other departments (particularly Education: see chapter 3).

This relative harmony, however, was at least in part the result of a dubious development. Cameron and his Chancellor, George Osborne, had nothing to learn from unelected spin doctors because they were very talented representatives of the breed, who had themselves worked as special advisers. When they were confronted at the despatch box by Ed Miliband and Ed Balls, their respective 'shadows' between 2010 and 2015, it was essentially a clash of the ex-special advisers, and no more 'edifying' as a result. Margaret Thatcher's sound bite, 'Advisers advise; ministers decide!' had become 'Advisers advise; ex-advisers decide!'

In fact the advent of special advisers in an elected rather than a hired capacity had a practical downside beyond its worrying implications for those who bemoaned a new class of 'career politicians' (Oborne, 2007). Blair had been criticized for his intimacy with media figures, but Cameron's dealings were even more dangerous. For example, in 2009 his long-standing friend, the former racehorse trainer Charlie Brooks, married Rebekah Wade, who had edited both the *Sun* and the *News of the World* and was now a senior executive in Rupert Murdoch's media empire. In 2011 Cameron's Director of Communications Andy Coulson – himself a former *News of the World* editor who had once been Rebekah Brooks' lover – was forced to resign amid allegations of serious malpractice involving phone hacking, which led in 2014 to a prison sentence. Yet Cameron continued his friendship with the Brookses, leaving him hopelessly compromised when he was forced to order an inquiry into the conduct of the press, under Lord Justice Leveson. The Leveson Inquiry exposed embarrassing exchanges of messages – embarrassing for Cameron, at least – between the Prime Minister and Rebekah Brooks. Having promised that he would implement the inquiry's recommendations 'provided they were not bonkers', Cameron broke his word and rowed back from statutory regulation. The 'Heir to Blair' had failed to tame the 'feral beasts', and could not provide an adequate answer to the charge that his judgement had been swayed by a demeaning mixture of fear and misplaced friendship.

Through training as well as natural aptitude, Cameron was certainly a skilful communicator. At least in part, he owed his position as Conservative leader to the engaging speech which he had delivered, without notes, at the 2005 party conference. However, his best performances as Prime Minister were early ones; indeed, his personal best was the offer of a 'big, open and comprehensive' arrangement with the Liberal Democrats, which effectively secured the keys to No. 10. His subsequent double act with Nick Clegg in the Downing Street garden was a memorable piece of political theatre; the original intention was to hold the press conference in the Cabinet room, but Cameron and Clegg both realized that the garden would give an appearance of informality to match the knockabout banter between the pair (Seldon and Snowdon, 2015, 27). Cameron could also address the nation – or at least a significant part of it – effectively in the House of Commons. On 15 June 2010 he delivered a heartfelt and eloquent apology for the 'Bloody Sunday' atrocity of 1972. This was warmly received by the nationalist community in Northern Ireland. Cameron was certainly much more eloquent than Brown when apologizing for other people's mistakes.

Over time, however, Cameron's effectiveness was impaired by his inability to conceal his satisfaction with his own performances. This was also true of George Osborne, who contrived to sound triumphalist even when delivering budgets which condemned the country to years of 'austerity'. Osborne, in fact, had begun by delivering a tacit rebuke both to Brown and to the Treasury, establishing an independent Office for Budget Responsibility (OBR) to provide economic forecasts. This implied that the informed guesswork of Osborne's own department could no longer be trusted. This new commitment to impartiality and substance over spin was somewhat undermined by the fact that Osborne and Cameron peddled partial truths (or worse) in blaming New Labour for Britain's economic plight. Thus while Brown's budgets had invariably contained some seriously misleading claims, Osborne's entire economic approach had arisen from a successful exercise in 'spin'.

Unlike Thatcher, Cameron was a temperamental conservative out of the Major stable. This was reflected in his powers of persuasion, which were most potent when he was trying to prevent change, notably in the first two of the referendums for which his premiership will always be remembered. In the first, on limited electoral reform (May 2011), he only intervened under pressure from backbenchers who feared that the change would have adverse consequences for the party. His speeches, which wildly exaggerated the likely costs of reform and claimed that, in comparison to first-past-the-post, the Alternative Vote was 'inherently unfair', probably helped to tip the balance in favour of the status quo; they certainly enraged his Liberal Democrat partners. While Cameron was careful not to insult Clegg in public, Conservative strategists were encouraged to take full advantage of the Deputy Prime Minister's drastic drop in popularity thanks to his broken promise on tuition fees (Seldon and Snowdon, 2015, 118–20). In his final speech before the referendum on Scottish independence (September 2014) Cameron showed genuine emotion as he emphasized the likely costs to Scotland of a 'Yes' vote.[31] His feelings were understandable; while he and Osborne put their faith in 'Project Fear', a vote for independence was certainly a fearful prospect for Cameron, whose premiership, as well as the future of the UK, was on the line. His efforts might have been unavailing were it not for a late oratorical intervention from Gordon Brown, whose genuine belief in the Union allowed his 'great, clunking fist' to be put to effective use.

The relief felt by the British establishment – shared, Cameron inadvertently revealed, by the Queen herself – was understandable, since the outcome had looked too close to call in the days before the poll. Yet instead of showing magnanimity, on the following day Cameron stood outside No. 10 and announced that 'We have heard the voice of Scotland and now the millions of voices of England must be heard' – an astonishingly cack-handed way of telling the nations of the UK that it was a good time to address constitutional anomalies arising from the devolution settlement.[32] This uncharacteristic lapse of judgement was clearly influenced by Cameron's need to throw some red meat in the direction of restive English nationalists within his party. The impression that the Prime Minister was losing his presentational touch had already been illustrated by his failure, in August 2013, to persuade the House of Commons to authorize military action against the Assad regime in Syria. Cameron had failed where the master, Blair, had succeeded; indeed, he failed at least in part *because* Blair had succeeded, with Labour MPs understandably reluctant to give their support to another military adventure. Nevertheless, the vote was a serious reflection on Cameron's authority as well as Blair's legacy.

Cameron had already sealed his fate with a speech of 23 January 2013, promising to hold an in/out referendum on EU membership if his party won the next election. In the referendum campaign itself Cameron delivered numerous speeches which outlined a pragmatic case for 'Remain'. However, the relative failure of his negotiations with the EU made it difficult for him to address the nation as a guarantor of 'sovereignty' for a Britain which stayed in the EU. Cameron also refused to be drawn into personal attacks on Conservative colleagues, even those (like Michael Gove and Boris Johnson) whom he now despised (Oliver, 2016, 186). He seemed always to be conducting the campaign with a view to the aftermath, when having secured the expected victory he would still have to deal with 'Leavers' and a vehemently Eurosceptic party rank-and-file. More aggressive tactics were left to George Osborne, who took to the task with relish and paid the inevitably penalty once the referendum was lost. In this context, Labour could not have had a less helpful leader than Jeremy Corbyn, whose own ambiguous position was combined with a general distaste for personal attacks.

After the vote, Cameron decided that his position was untenable, and crafted his resignation speech, delivered outside No. 10, as a graceful exit from the political stage. Unfortunately, as he delivered his parting lines he began to smash up the scenery. In the course of a very brief statement, he included three curious comments: that he had 'held nothing back' in the campaign, which as we have seen was definitely untrue; that 'the British people have made a very clear decision', which might be defensible in terms of raw numbers but was a strange way to describe an outcome which was very close in percentage terms; and, finally, that Britain was 'a parliamentary democracy where we resolve great issues about our future through peaceful debate'. If this was meant sincerely rather than as a rhetorical flourish, one was entitled to ask why this particular 'great issue' had been decided by direct, rather than representative, democracy – an exercise which was generally 'peaceful' but in which a 'Remainer' MP had been assassinated.[33]

Theresa May

David Cameron and Theresa May were Prime Ministers with sharply contrasting personalities and leadership styles, and there was little love lost between them. However, there was one striking similarity; in terms of public communication, their best performances came at an early stage. The difference was that while Cameron continued to impress for a few months after becoming leader, May was never able to match the standards she had set in running for the leadership and accepting her new responsibilities. In short, her best days as a communicator were behind her as soon as she started work as Prime Minister.

In launching her candidacy to succeed Cameron on 30 June 2016,

May tried to dispel any suspicions that she might seek to defy the declared will of the people, ruling out a second referendum and unveiling a slogan which would become over-familiar – 'Brexit means Brexit.' To murmurs of approval from her audience, she also declared that the next general election would not be held until 2020, in line with the provisions of the 2011 Fixed-Term Parliaments Act. In other respects, though, it was a competent performance which justified her position as front runner (thanks to Michael Gove's decision, announced minutes earlier, to ditch Boris Johnson and run for the leadership himself). As well as highlighting her record as a long-serving Home Secretary, May revealed a previously unsuspected passion for 'One Nation' Conservatism, claiming that there was a 'great hunger' in her party for an agenda which would serve the interests of Britons who 'just about manage'. This would have been an unwelcome surprise to the hyperglobalist hedge-fund beneficiaries who now sponsored the Conservative Party and had infiltrated its higher ranks. But even to them May must have seemed like a safe pair of hands to guide the country through the Brexit process; she admitted that she was not 'a showy politician', and simply got on with the job in front of her.[34] It was reminiscent of the advertising pitch launched in 2007 by Thatcher's favourite agency, Saatchi and Saatchi, this time on behalf of a Labour premier: 'Not flash, just Gordon'.

On arrival in Downing Street, May virtually ignored Brexit, speaking instead about her commitment to the United Kingdom and her resolve to address the 'burning injustices' suffered by ordinary people. This sounded more like Clement Attlee than any of his successors, Labour or Conservative. However, it was probably written by her special adviser Nicholas Timothy.[35]

Preparing for May's first conference as leader, her advisers decided that she should make two speeches – one on Brexit, the other on her domestic agenda. The first speech was one of the most extraordinary performances in British political history. May used it to answer the question raised by the departing Cameron. Britain was not a parliamentary democracy, nor indeed a direct democracy (since the public would be given no opportunity to revisit the Brexit decision), but something more akin to an authoritarian state. Having softened up her audiences in the hall and watching on television by repeating Cameron's claim that the referendum result had been decisive – when launching her leadership bid she had been more careful, merely alluding to the high turnout – the Prime Minister insisted that neither House of Parliament could interfere with her right to trigger the withdrawal process by activating Article 50 of the EU's Lisbon Treaty. Constitutional purists, and people who prefer their politicians to deal in facts, would have been well advised to hit the 'mute' button as she declaimed, 'the people gave their answer with emphatic clarity. So now it is up to the Government not to question, quibble or backslide on what we have been instructed to do, but get on with the job.' To make sure that her coup succeeded, she claimed that those who upheld Parliament's constitutional role were merely trying to delay or prevent Brexit, and were 'insulting the intelligence of the British people'. By resorting to this cheapest of shots, May was deliberately inflaming one of the more grievous sores inflicted by the referendum – the indisputable fact that 'Remainers' tended to be better educated (and informed about the EU) than 'Leavers' (Evans and Menon, 2017, 84). She was also effectively insulting her own intelligence, since her main contribution to the referendum debate was a speech in which she had stressed that her own belief that continued EU membership was in Britain's national interest arose from rigorous and rational reflection.[36]

May, like anyone else, was entitled to change her mind; but it was all too evident that her mind had been changed on this subject by the fact that, between her referendum speech and her address to the party conference, she had become Prime Minister of a sharply divided country. In the remainder of her speech she sketched out an inspiring vision of the kind of 'cherry-picking' Brexit which had been promised by the 'Leave' campaign but which the EU was never likely to accept.[37] The Prime Minister whose elevation had been greeted with widespread enthusiasm and relief had decided to reinvent herself as the political beneficiary of a schism which had divided families and friends.

The idea of two speeches fitted Timothy's mindset perfectly – the first would give him the chance to exult in the defeat of 'Remain', while the second would sketch out a way to reunite a fractured country under the 'One Nation' banner. The flaws, however, were apparent to anyone outside No. 10. Even the most optimistic Brexiteer acknowledged that there might be some short-term damage to the British economy before the country embraced its future as a prosperous, happy escapee from the European yoke. What would happen to the people who had voted for Brexit in the expectation of immediate dividends, in the months or years before the benefits started to roll in? Second, under Timothy's tutelage May had learned to recite the characteristic Brexiteer script about national sovereignty, and 'taking back control'. The Prime Minister was willing to churn out this anachronistic claptrap because, as Home Secretary, she had yearned for the old days when Britain could control its borders. But in reality there had never been a 'golden age' in this respect; among a multitude of examples, the grandfather of another Brexiteer, the previous Conservative leader and Home Secretary, Michael Howard, had settled in England in defiance of strict immigration laws (Crick, 2005, 1–22). On the wider issue of 'sovereignty', Timothy/May seemed to understand this in the nineteenth-century sense of an independent nation able to make its own laws free from constraint. But in case anyone had overlooked the long succession of post-war developments which disproved this simplistic doctrine, the true story of the banking crisis which began in 2007 should finally have disabused them. Many of the people who voted 'Leave', and rejoiced in its victory, were themselves victims of a global crisis which began in America, not in London; and it had been the Conservatives, not Gordon Brown, who had argued that there was no viable policy alternative to economic 'austerity', whose effects fell heavily on the 'just about managing'.

At London's Lancaster House in January 2017 May clarified, though she did not soften, her position. Once Britain left the EU, she promised, it would not be part of the single market (whether or not this had been the considered preference of 'Leave' voters). Nicholas Timothy took the opportunity to unveil another fateful slogan, making May announce that 'no deal is better than a bad deal' for Britain. Thus the Prime Minister and her advisers had embarked on a course which forced all of them to leave office before a withdrawal agreement had passed through Parliament. In the process May herself incurred public ridicule for her 'robotic' manner of communication; while this certainly did not help her, it should not deflect attention from the mistaken decisions which would have made things very difficult even for a charismatic leader with a golden tongue.

Conclusion

This chapter has looked at the attempts of Prime Ministers since 1979 to communicate with the nation. In their different ways, and for very understandable reasons, all of them have been anxious to influence the media's 'agenda'. The New Labour example shows that, given the right circumstances, a relatively small number of people working for the Prime Minister can exert a profound influence over the presentation of a government's activities; the fact that the Chancellor of the Exchequer had his own team, trying to do the same thing, does not affect this argument. Latterly, Prime Ministers have used social media and other resources in a bid to contact voters directly, but the old battle between traditional media and politicians has continued unabated. Television and radio are still vital means of communication, and the verdict of the 'dead tree press' on these performances still matters. In particular, speeches to party conferences are vital tests of a Prime Minister's ability to convey direct messages to the country; the audience in the hall is not irrelevant, but is normally a secondary consideration. A Prime Minister, whether 'weak' or 'strong', is always newsworthy, and in demand for comment on important national developments. The next chapter continues the 'communication' theme before discussing the Prime Minister's role in foreign policy.

5

Speaker for Britain

As we have seen, when Prime Ministers address their party conferences they are acutely aware that they are speaking to more than one audience. Ideally they hope that their words and style of delivery will enthuse party members while impressing the country as a whole. They are not so unrealistic as to expect a very substantial worldwide audience, but there will be at least some interested observers in other countries.

It goes almost without saying that, regardless of their different personalities, outlooks and speaking styles, every Prime Minister feels obliged to convey a positive view of Britain – usually in the peroration, which they hope will bring the audience in the hall to its feet. The task is usually quite easy for a Prime Minister in the first two or three years after leading an Opposition party to an election victory. The relevant section of the speech almost writes itself, or can be plagiarized from conference performances when the party was out of power: 'Britain is a great country but our opponents have dragged its reputation into the gutter; now that we're back in power things are improving/have already improved.' Speech-writing tends to get trickier after mid-term, unless something has happened which can be cited as proof that the country is already on the way back to its former status. Just as a rock band has trouble following up a successful first album, British Prime Ministers who have been elected with a workable majority live in fear of that difficult third or fourth conference speech. In this respect, Margaret

Thatcher was in an ideal position in 1982, when she was able to disclaim any intention of talking about the Falklands War (but nevertheless did so for several minutes). Prime Ministers who take over when their parties have already been in office for a decade – like John Major and Gordon Brown in the period under review – are in an even more ticklish situation. They have to pay fulsome tributes to the achievements of their predecessors, while implying that they themselves have something distinctive and essential to add to an ongoing success story.

If they were laid end to end, with the names and dates of the orators removed, the speeches of Britain's Prime Ministers at their party conferences would present an unsettling, even surreal picture with the greatness of their country and its people as the single constant theme. Using excerpts from the speeches as the basis for a game of 'guess the speaker, guess the date' might be fun, but not even the best-informed participant would have much chance of getting both answers right without some unsubtle clues. For example, 'We are building the greatest success for this nation that we have known in our lifetime . . . We know no other Party can win the battles for Britain that lie ahead' and 'Wherever I went abroad, I found the same story. Britain is respected again' both sound like Thatcher, probably one soon after the Falklands, the other at the beginning of her third term. In fact, the orator on both occasions was John Major, and the second speech (from 1991) was earlier than the first (1995). In between those speeches Major had told his conference (in 1993, when the party had been in office for nearly a decade and a half) that 'it's time for this country to set our sights high again'.

The game, unfortunately, gets even trickier after 2000. Here are the quotations: (a) 'That's our dream – to help you realise your dreams. A Greater Britain – made of greater hope, greater chances, greater security'; (b) 'this is our generation's moment . . . To build a stronger, fairer, brighter future . . . here in Britain'; (c) 'Let us fulfil our duty to Britain. Let us renew the British dream'; (d) 'Ours is a great country . . . Together, let's build a better Britain.' They all sound like Tony Blair, but the answers are: (a) David Cameron, 2015; (b) Theresa May, 2016; (c) Theresa May, 2017; and (d) Theresa May, 2018. Anyone following these speeches closely would have been struck by the slow progress of May's building project; indeed, judging from the phrase she used in 2018 it seems not to have made it past the drawing board. By 2018, of course, her party had been in office, either in coalition or alone, for the best part of a decade. Having said that, in 2008 Gordon Brown had told his first conference as Prime Minister that 'This is our country, Britain. We are building it together, together we are making it greater.' Perhaps the work of construction over eleven years of New Labour was being conducted as one of Brown's ruinous public–private partnerships (PPPs), to be completed (if at all) long past the deadline and way over budget.

Prime Ministers do occasionally refer back to their own previous conference speeches – particularly if they featured specific pledges which (through luck or judgement) ended up being fulfilled. But it is doubtful that any of them ever look back at the morale-boosting clichés, which are only ever intended as 'mood music'. However, their words do have consequences, not least in terms of public expectations. As Richard Crossman once put it, 'One of the difficulties of being British is that we believe our own propaganda' (Crossman, 1972, 35–6). If a country is inherently great, but great things are not happening to it, voters will want to know why – and will look to the Prime Minister for answers.

The consequences of prime ministerial rhetoric extend beyond its impact on voters. It also has an effect on a Prime Minister's dealings with other world leaders. If Britain really is 'great', it must be shown to matter on the world stage. This has been a problem for all post-war Prime Ministers, and if anything the requirement for holders of the office to say something intelligible on the subject increased after the mid-1970s, thanks to the intensified media focus on events like party conferences. Margaret Thatcher's view after the Falklands was that Britain had given the lie to any notion of national decline, breathing new life into its 'special relationship' with the United States, which was already stronger thanks to her personal and ideological affinity with President Reagan. Yet this argument was not necessarily an effective answer to critics who argued that Britain had yet to settle into a sustainable post-imperial role in world affairs. For example, in a famous speech of December 1962 – just weeks before General de Gaulle's rejection of Britain's belated bid to join the EEC – the American Secretary of State Dean Acheson remarked that Britain had lost an empire but was still seeking a role, stressing that the 'special relationship' was not a sustainable basis for global relevance (Brinkley, 1990).

In his speech to the 1994 Conservative Party conference, John Major addressed Acheson's charge directly:

a generation ago it was said that Britain had lost an empire but not yet found a role. It may or may not have been true then, but it surely isn't true today, because economically and militarily Britain remains in the top league – a member of the permanent five of the United Nations, a leading member of NATO [the North Atlantic Treaty Organization], of the European Union, and of a Commonwealth that covers one-third of all the people on earth, a member of the Group of Seven of the world's most powerful economies and one of only five significant nuclear powers in the world, and we have too as a priceless asset, perhaps the finest professional armed forces anywhere.[38]

Major's patriotic puff might have satisfied his immediate audience, but it left Acheson's argument unanswered. Britain had enjoyed all of these accolades and advantages *before* Thatcher came to office in 1979; the only difference was that, since then, the European Communities (EC) had become more integrated within the European Union (EU) – but that was a development which many of Major's party colleagues *opposed*. In any case, Major's list might have shown that Britain was not a global irrelevance – very few people took the contrary argument that far – but that only showed that the country *could* find a meaningful role from a position of relative strength, if it finally applied itself to the problem after an open-minded debate about its true place in the world.

Far from encouraging a national conversation of that kind, Major had already shown that his attitude to international politics was unduly influenced by the need to demonstrate 'strength' to his domestic audience. In December 1991, after negotiating British 'opt-outs' from the terms of the Maastricht Treaty, he allowed his spin doctors to claim that this constituted 'game, set and match for Britain' (Gowland, 2016, 133). This showed Major's fellow leaders that, although he might have been sincere in his vow to place Britain 'at the very heart of Europe', his personal intentions were far less important than his desire to manage his party, which was becoming increasingly hostile to Europe in fealty to Margaret Thatcher. Dean Acheson, like most US diplomats of his era, had hinted that Britain could find a secure global role by accepting its status as a leading European player, while retaining those extra-European ties which suited its national interests. Whether or not Acheson was right, Thatcher had made it much harder for any of her successors to explore the possibility.

In the post-war years up to 1979, all but two of Britain's Prime Ministers had either served as Foreign Secretary or worked closely with the Foreign Office. Churchill (1951–5) had unrivalled experience in international politics. Anthony Eden (1955–7) had twice served as Foreign Secretary. Harold Macmillan (1957–63) only held the position for a few months in 1955, but had played an important diplomatic role during World War II. Lord Home (1963–4) was a controversial Foreign Secretary before becoming an improbable Prime Minister. Edward Heath (1970–4) had overseen Britain's first attempt to join the Common Market, and was responsible for Foreign Office business in the House of Commons at that time (the Foreign Secretary (Home) was in the Lords). James Callaghan (1976–9) was Foreign Secretary for almost exactly two years; like Home and Eden, he was serving in that role when he became Prime Minister. The two exceptions among the eight post-war Prime Ministers up to 1979 were Clement Attlee (1945–51) and Harold Wilson (1964–70 and 1974–6). The first was served for most of his first term by Ernest Bevin, a Foreign Secretary whose judgement he trusted; although during the wartime coalition Attlee had concentrated on domestic politics, he had served briefly as Under-Secretary of State for War in 1924 and had a long-standing interest in colonial matters. Wilson was shadow Foreign Secretary for two years (1961–3); his spell as President of the Board of Trade at a time of soul-searching about Britain's role in the world (1947–51) meant that he was hardly a stranger to the kind of dilemmas which would face him in Downing Street.

By contrast, since 1979 only two of seven British Prime Ministers have previously served as Foreign Secretary. The first, John Major himself, held the post for just three months – an experience which made him all the more grateful that he inherited the seasoned diplomat Douglas Hurd as Foreign Secretary when he succeeded Thatcher. The other, Boris Johnson, lasted for two years, but his promotion was emphatically not a recognition of diplomatic skills, whether instinctive or acquired, and his tenure of the office tended to confirm rather than allay the fears of those who had questioned his appointment. Indeed, although with hindsight Johnson's time as Foreign Secretary could be seen as a reversion to the pre-1979 position, when the job was recognized as a stepping stone to No. 10, at the time Theresa May's decision to appoint Johnson seemed to be part of a cunning plan to keep him quiet.

That supposition might be regarded as an unjust reflection on the calibre of other post-1979 politicians who have served as Foreign Secretary – notably Douglas Hurd (1989–95) and William Hague (2010–14). However, even under the first Wilson Government (1964–70) it was possible to detect a tendency for Prime Ministers to regard the Foreign Office as a consolation prize for politicians who deserved a senior position, but had not quite measured up to expectations in other important roles. In the Wilson/Callaghan Governments of the 1970s, two people who seemed ideally equipped for the job of Foreign Secretary (Roy Jenkins and Denis Healey) were successively denied the position; Callaghan, in particular, felt able to appoint two unlikely candidates (first Anthony Crosland, whose expertise lay in economics, then David Owen, who was highly promising but far less qualified than Healey). In another Prime Minister, this approach to Cabinet-making might have been attributed to desperation or frivolity; but Callaghan, a machine politician to his fingertips, was not given to such emotional decisions. Having held the post so recently, he knew very well that the Foreign Secretary no longer deserved to be classed among the 'great offices of state'; and he acted accordingly.

Hollowing out the Foreign Office

If anything in political life can be described as 'inevitable', that word is rightly applied to the post-war decline of Britain's Foreign Office (formally, since 1968, the Foreign & Commonwealth Office (FCO)). The history of this Whitehall department was itself testimony to Britain's relative decline; over the twentieth century it had gradually mopped up other government bodies which had been deemed necessary when the country ruled about a quarter of the world's population. Thus after 1945, Britain's imperial retreat spelled the end for the India Office (1947), the Colonial Office (1966) and, finally, the Commonwealth Office (1968). The magnificent Foreign Office building, a product and symbol of Britain's imperial power in the mid-1860s, was scheduled for demolition a hundred years later; it was saved partly by a public outcry, but also (significantly) because a replacement would have been too expensive (Garnett et al., 2017).

The creation of the FCO was thus a *result*, rather than a *cause*, of a decline in Britain's global influence and responsibilities, from a position which had been shown to be unsustainable by the ruinous expense of the wars of 1914–18 and 1939–45, turning Britain from the world's greatest creditor into a heavily indebted nation. Nevertheless, there were some people whose ideological perspective led them into a confusion between causes and effects. Certainly by 1979 the FCO tended to take a sombre view of Britain's prospects, based on a dispassionate view of global realities, whereas the incoming Prime Minister's analysis of the post-war experience convinced her that the national malaise was mainly psychological – a temporary aberration associated with the vogue for 'socialism' and reflected rather than contested by the FCO.

Thus when Thatcher took office in 1979 the prospects for a comfortable relationship between Downing Street and the FCO were bleak. The situation was complicated by longer-term developments affecting every industrialized country. The collapse of the post-war 'Bretton Woods' economic framework in the early 1970s was just one of several factors which stimulated more regular meetings between heads of government (e.g. the G7, which has been convened annually since 1975). Such events were attended by other senior ministers, but nothing of real significance could be signed off without the agreement of the heads of government; and, thanks to the ease of international travel, national leaders could be present in person without undue inconvenience. A similar situation arose through Britain's admission into the EEC (1973); although routine business was conducted in the Council of Ministers (and the FCO took a very active organizational role), the big decisions were reserved for biannual meetings of heads of government (the European Council) which were formalized in 1975. Thus, whether the British Prime Minister liked it or not, she or he was going to have to take a closer and continuous interest in diplomacy from the mid-1970s.

For the first three years of Thatcher's government the Prime Minister's suspicion of the FCO was held in check. She had appointed Lord Carrington as Foreign Secretary, rather than her shadow spokesman Francis Pym, and this was a shrewd decision not least because Carrington, unlike Pym, had limited interest in domestic matters, rarely expressing his doubts concerning Thatcher's economic approach outside private conversations. Under Carrington, the FCO was able to steer Rhodesia towards majority rule (1980), despite the Prime Minister's deep reservations, and even used her pugilistic attitude on the subject of Britain's disproportionate contribution to the EC budgets as a bargaining tool (Hurd, 2003, 256–60; Carrington, 1988, 280, 285).

This period of relative amity came to an abrupt end in April 1982, when Argentine forces invaded the Falkland Islands. The FCO's critics held it responsible for the absence of adequate warnings of Argentine intentions, and for its previous support for a compromise over the future of the islands despite the clearly expressed preference of residents for continued British sovereignty and administration. On the day (5 April) that the British task force sailed to reclaim the Falklands, Carrington braved a hostile meeting of the 1922 Committee of Conservative backbenchers, whose 'cat-calling, derision and jeers' clearly reflected contempt for the FCO as an institution (Nott, 2002, 268–9). He had already contemplated resignation because of vehement press criticism, and decided to go in the hope that he would serve as an adequate scapegoat for a policy failure whose causes went far wider (and higher) than the FCO.

Thatcher felt she had no alternative but to replace Carrington with Francis Pym. Although he had never actually served in the FCO, Pym epitomized the qualities which the department's critics loathed – a preference for compromise based on a fatalistic outlook. On 25 April he recommended that the War Cabinet should accept a Falklands settlement which had been negotiated by the US State Department. Had other colleagues sided with Pym, Thatcher recorded in her memoirs that she would have resigned (Thatcher, 1993, 202). With diplomatic resources now effectively exhausted, Thatcher could show her preference for military advisers and the Ministry of Defence, whose Secretary of State John Nott announced the recapture of South Georgia on the day of Pym's defeat.

Thatcher could not easily celebrate the Falklands victory by sacking Pym, whose dismissal had to wait until after the 1983 general election. While effectively serving out his notice, Pym had managed to prevent Thatcher from creating a foreign affairs unit in Downing Street, although she did appoint a part-time adviser (Sir Anthony Parsons, who had excelled as Ambassador to the United Nations during the Falklands crisis), in addition to her existing Private Secretary for Foreign Affairs, Sir John Coles. Her first choice for Pym's replacement was Cecil Parkinson, who had been a staunch and effective supporter in the War Cabinet. Parkinson had no ministerial experience in foreign affairs, which no doubt enhanced his credentials in Thatcher's eyes; as Party Chairman at the time of the 1983 general election he had overseen a campaign which showcased the Prime Minister's virtues.

To her considerable chagrin, difficulties in Parkinson's personal life thwarted Thatcher's intentions. However, for the purposes of the post-election reshuffle there was a silver lining to this setback. Thatcher had found it difficult to think of a new position for Geoffrey Howe, whom she had decided to move from the Treasury. She could now resort to the Wilsonian device of offering the position of Foreign Secretary as a consolation prize to someone who was superfluous to more important requirements. It was a decision which she came to regret, not because Howe acted as an effective check on her own foreign policy priorities, but because she found him so irritating that she could not treat him with the respect due to a senior Cabinet colleague. As she explained in her memoirs, this was really Howe's fault, since he allowed himself to fall 'under the spell of the Foreign Office' and to adopt 'the habits which the Foreign Office seems to cultivate – a reluctance to subordinate diplomatic tactics to the national interest and an insatiable appetite for nuances' (Thatcher, 1993, 309).

It would be an exaggeration to say that the FCO's influence over Britain's foreign policy ended with Howe's appointment. Nevertheless, notwithstanding the occasional appointment of considerable figures like Hurd and Hague, there was a marked change in the tenure (and stature) of Foreign Secretaries after Howe himself was demoted in July 1989 (and this includes Major, whose lack of experience made him very uneasy about his appointment as Howe's replacement). If spending power is a gauge of Whitehall clout, even under Hague the FCO was overshadowed by the Department for International Development (DFID), whose functions had been the subject of a Whitehall tug of war since its inception in 1964. Between 1967 and 1997 the FCO enjoyed the upper hand in this battle, subsuming international aid within its responsibilities; in 1997, however, DFID regained its independent existence, and its budget was protected by David Cameron in spite of his government's commitment to 'austerity'. On coming to office in 2010, Cameron established a National Security Council (NSC) which further diluted the FCO's influence; his Foreign Secretary, Hague, seemed happy to acquiesce in the creation of a body in which his would just be one amongst a multitude of voices, presumably because in reality this situation had been reached long before his appointment. When Theresa May became Prime Minister in 2016 she established two new departments to handle 'Brexit', both of whose functions overlapped with the duties which, at one time, would have been entrusted to the FCO.

In 2019, when Boris Johnson became Prime Minister, he followed May's example by giving the post of Foreign Secretary as a 'consolation prize' to an unsuccessful rival in a leadership contest. This time it was Dominic Raab, who in November 2018 had confessed to ignorance about the volume of UK trade which passed through the port of Dover – a deficiency in relevant knowledge which had not deterred him from campaigning vigorously for Brexit in the 2016 referendum. In the strange post-referendum climate this was not seen as a reason to deny Raab a job which brought a very nice office, but no influence in normal times. And Raab could console himself with the thought that Johnson himself had been the recipient of the FCO consolation prize, in 2016. In 2020, when Johnson fell victim to Covid-19, Raab stood in for him, as Deputy Prime Minister; subsequently it was announced that his department would resume control of the overseas aid budget, which Johnson described with typical flippancy as 'a giant cashpoint in the sky'.

The Prime Minister and foreign policy since the Falklands

In 1969 Ian Gilmour – a very astute political observer, who went on to serve as Lord Carrington's deputy at the FCO until Thatcher lost patience with his coded 'wet' criticisms of government policy – explained why Prime Ministers feel tempted to set themselves up as authorities on foreign policy, while they are usually content to leave economic decisions to the Chancellor of the time: 'Most people have strong views on foreign affairs ... whatever their knowledge of the subject. On economics people are not as a rule similarly opinionated' (Gilmour, 1969, 199). For understandable reasons, Gilmour was unable in 1969 to anticipate the emergence of a Prime Minister like Thatcher, who was equally 'opinionated' in both areas, despite a very partial acquaintance with either economic or foreign policy. As we have seen (chapter 3), after her third general election victory Thatcher thought she had a licence to second-guess her Chancellor; she had begun to treat her Foreign Secretary in the same fashion as soon as Lord Carrington resigned in 1982.

Anthony Parsons and his successor as special adviser, Percy Cradock (who helped to persuade Thatcher, against her instincts, of the need to pave the way for a smooth transfer of sovereignty in Hong Kong), forged constructive partnerships with the Prime Minister. But they were quintessential products of the FCO, and Thatcher needed an adviser who would reinforce her own instincts. On the retirement of Sir John Coles in 1984 she appointed Charles Powell, who had served the FCO in Washington, Bonn and Brussels, as her Private Secretary for Foreign Affairs. Despite his orthodox FCO background Powell was no ordinary civil servant. Instead of following the departmental script and reining in the Prime Minister, Powell gave every impression of agreeing with her views, bolstering her intuition that the FCO was an obstacle rather than a diplomatic asset. While Powell is often regarded as a malign background influence over Thatcher – the foreign policy equivalent of her Press Secretary, Bernard Ingham – his appointment coincided with the Prime Minister's growing exasperation with Geoffrey Howe, and it is possible that any Private Secretary appointed in 1984 would have been asked to play a similar role. Like Ingham, Powell certainly proved that a Prime Minister did not need a vast entourage of advisers to help her operate in the way she wanted; the only requirement was for an individual she trusted implicitly and who could match her own remarkable appetite for work.

Thatcher's official biographer notes that 'The suggestion that Powell and Ingham were the two most powerful people below the Prime Minister, and in effect ran her government, was explosive, especially as it was not completely untrue' (Moore, 2016, 487–9). Thatcher's appreciation of Powell's services was so great that, unlike previous holders of his position who had returned to the FCO after two or three years in Downing Street, he stayed with her until the end (and was even retained by Major for a final year). Thatcher resisted repeated attempts to move him. After the Westland Affair, when his prominent role (along with that of Ingham) aroused considerable media interest, he offered to step down; but far from accepting his resignation Thatcher became increasingly reliant on his advice. After Thatcher's third consecutive election victory, Chris Patten (at the time responsible for Overseas Development within the FCO) told the journalist Hugo Young that Powell was 'very, very influential . . . Across the board. He and Ingham are the heart of the Court, and the Court may in the end be her downfall' (Young, 2008, 268). Ingham and Powell certainly resembled courtiers in finding each other increasingly irksome; Ingham, in particular, resented Powell's interference in presentational matters (e.g. Ingham, 2019, 170).

Powell's support was vital in fostering Thatcher's confidence in her personal diplomacy. In this respect there was a crucial development in February 1984, when Geoffrey Howe suggested that the new Soviet leader, Chernenko, should be invited to London. Powell seconded Thatcher's own view that this would be premature, and suggested instead that the Prime Minister should cultivate 'rising stars' in the Kremlin, particularly Mikhail Gorbachev. By October 1984 Gorbachev had agreed to visit Britain and was invited to Chequers, where he and Thatcher indulged themselves in their shared passion for verbal combat, to considerable mutual satisfaction. Although Howe was present, it was Charles Powell (or Ingham – typically the querulous duo disputed the parentage of the phrase) who came up with the line Thatcher used to sum up the encounter: 'I like Mr Gorbachev. We can do business together' (Moore, 2016, 229, 235–41).

In May 1985 there was a much less successful rendezvous at Chequers, between Thatcher and the West German Chancellor, Helmut Kohl. Kohl's personality (and even his dietary preferences) confirmed Thatcher's deep-seated prejudice against Germans. There is no evidence that Powell discouraged this, and the tone of their conversations can be gauged from a memo he sent to Thatcher before the Chequers meeting, advising her to make ritual noises about the virtues of co-operation while insisting that she would not 'succumb to the drivel about European Union' (Moore, 2016, 397). Although the FCO was involved in the preparation of Thatcher's fateful Bruges speech of September 1988, the main draftsman was Powell.

By the mid-1980s it was evident that, egged on by Powell, Thatcher had come to see herself as the only true custodian of Britain's national interests (abroad as well as at home), and to resent those who disputed her vision. Understandably she took a dim view of her domestic critics, but increasingly this disdain extended to foreign leaders and diplomats when such individuals pursued their own perceived national interests in ways which conflicted with her priorities. In particular, Thatcher was unable to understand the motivations of leaders like Kohl, who regarded the idea of a European Union as something more than 'drivel'.

She was far more sympathetic to the worldview of leaders she liked, such as Reagan and Gorbachev; but even they could let her down, as they proved at the Reykjavik summit in October 1986 (held, ironically, at the former British consulate) when in ill-mannered contradiction of Thatcher's Cold War outlook they came perilously close to agreeing to scrap all of their nuclear weapons.

Although in this instance Reagan and Gorbachev stepped back from the brink of sanity, their combined efforts in Europe were unstoppable. In June 1987 Reagan pleaded with Gorbachev to 'tear down' the Berlin Wall, and in November 1989 Gorbachev's relaxed attitude to the collapse of the Soviet Empire forced the East German government to allow demolition to take place. Before the advent of Gorbachev, the idea that this potent symbol of East–West divisions might disappear almost overnight would have seemed like 'drivel'. Now that it had happened, Thatcher was faced with the unwelcome prospect of German reunification. Notoriously, she embarked on a lonely and unsuccessful crusade to prevent it, confiding to the Irish Taoiseach Charles Haughey her fear that German attitudes were becoming increasingly 'Germanic' and reportedly telling fellow leaders before an EC Summit 'Twice we've beaten the Germans! And now they're here again!' Thatcher's admirers would have been dismayed by her omission of the 1966 World Cup final from the list (Moore, 2019, 500–1).[39] Her attitude provoked a similar outburst from Kohl:

> Thatcher says the European parliament can have no power because Whitehall cannot yield a bit of sovereignty. Her ideas are simply pre-Churchill. She thinks the post-war era has not come to an end. She thinks history is not just. Germany is so rich and Great Britain is struggling. They won a war but lost an empire and their economy. (Moore, 2019, 496).

While it included some perceptive points, this analysis of Thatcher's position was little better than the Prime Minister's own wilful misreading of Kohl and his fellow Germans. However, while Thatcher's diatribes cost her vital goodwill and exposed the real weakness of her diplomatic position, Kohl's remarks were made in a private conversation with a very sympathetic George H. W. Bush, who had succeeded Reagan in 1989. Conscious that international politics were turning in an unhelpful direction, at the 1989 Conservative conference Thatcher had tried to claim credit for the trends: 'We Conservatives were the pathfinders. We did not know it at the time but the torch we lit in Britain, which transformed our country – the torch of freedom that is now the symbol of our Party – became the beacon that has shed its light across the Iron Curtain into the East.'[40] It would have been a fitting prelude to a declaration that the time had now come to pass the torch to someone else, but retirement was far from Thatcher's mind.

It was left to the FCO – now headed by Douglas Hurd, since Thatcher had run out of excuses to debar him – to mend fences with Kohl. In February 1990 the West German Chancellor asked him 'to act as his political contact' (Hurd, 2003, 384). If Thatcher had known about this conversation it would not have improved her opinion either of Kohl or of the FCO; in a prudent precaution, no officials were present. The Prime Minister's wrath would have been even greater had she learned that, in a subsequent conversation with the journalist Hugo Young, Hurd had conceded that 'She remains very useful' as a conduit between Bush and Gorbachev (Young, 2008, 297). If even the Foreign Secretary felt able to patronize Thatcher in such terms, it was obviously time for her to go.

John Major

Commentators (including Ian Gilmour, quoted above) have stressed that prime ministerial interference in foreign policy began long before Thatcher. But the most recent precedent for a Prime Minister who tried to run his own foreign policy without relevant ministerial experience was Neville Chamberlain, whose forays into the field yielded patchy results. Even Anthony Eden, with all his knowledge of world politics and of the Middle East in particular, came a cropper when he tried to bypass the established machinery of government during the Suez crisis (1956). The examples of Chamberlain and Eden paled by comparison with Thatcher's strategy in her third term, which was to second-guess the Treasury and the FCO at the same time, having already satisfied herself that, by placing dutiful people in the relevant departments, she could exert decisive influence over the rest of Whitehall by 'remote control'.

Thus when John Major undertook the salvage operation in the

aftermath of Thatcher's German miscalculations, he had no inclination to emulate her approach to foreign policy, which in any event he deemed to be very safe in Hurd's hands. Initially it looked as if his low-key approach, as exemplified by his conduct during the Gulf War, would satisfy the public. The same seemed to be true, at first, of his handling of Thatcher's other pressing foreign policy legacy – Europe.

Yet Major had to deal with a more general bequest from Thatcher – the impression that a Prime Minister *ought* to be in charge of all policy matters, and of foreign affairs in particular. Thatcher had also managed to create the expectation that a Prime Minister worthy of the name should not just be ready and able to 'speak for Britain', but to demonstrate the country's global influence. In this respect sterling's ejection from the ERM in September 1992 (see chapter 3) was a double disaster for Major; it discredited him domestically, since he had been outspoken in his support for membership, while also exposing Britain's inherent economic weakness to an international audience.

During his whistle-stop tour of the FCO and the Treasury, Major had recognized the emptiness of Thatcher's rhetoric; the Falklands had certainly arrested Britain's declining international reputation, but it had *not* restored its former position as a great global power, and there had been *no* 'economic miracle', despite the advantages which the country had briefly possessed thanks to North Sea oil. From Major's perspective, it could only be hoped that Thatcher had provoked one last post-colonial spasm amongst voters, who might now resume their possession of solid good sense and realize that Britain could still exercise significant influence in world politics if it would only adopt the role which Dean Acheson had envisaged – that is, as a leader, along with Germany and France, in a Europe which co-operated in essential respects but which left other arrangements to national governments. In the abstract, the task of persuading Britons to accept a European destiny should have been far less demanding than Thatcher's self-appointed role of launching a national revival on the basis of willpower alone. Yet Thatcher had been preaching to a very receptive audience, composed largely of voters with a limited interest in foreign policy and whose post-war leaders had never provided an adequate explanation for Britain's relative decline. Major, for all his virtues, lacked the eloquence for such a task; and the humiliation of 'Black Wednesday' made it impossible for him to try. Even before the ERM fiasco, and in the aftermath of the government's early foreign policy successes, Douglas Hurd had illustrated the unique difficulties facing Britain's foreign policy-makers when he argued that 'In recent years Britain has punched above her weight in the world' (quoted in Wallace, 1994, 292–3). Unwittingly, his metaphor recognized that Britain was no longer in the top fighting division; but it was also a tacit promise that the country could keep over-performing on the world stage.

The government's task was made no easier by the activities of Thatcher herself, whose 'back-seat driving' consisted chiefly of directives regarding 'Europe', and foreign policy more generally. Thatcher had been dogged by criticisms from her own predecessor, Edward Heath; but he had focused on economic policy, and (in line with Gilmour's rule) the true nature of the disagreement would have been lost on most voters, so that the over-riding impression (strengthened by Heath's unappealing public persona) was that Thatcher's predecessor was just 'sulking'. As Gilmour had written, on foreign policy everyone tends to take a position, however ill-informed; and since 1969 the so-called 'CNN effect', giving television viewers vivid second-hand evidence of the sufferings of non-combatants in wartime, had greatly increased the attractions of armchair commentary. Thatcher was particularly outspoken in her remarks on British policy towards the former Yugoslavia, accusing the government of complicity in the slaughter of innocent Bosnian Muslims. Throughout the Balkan crisis Hurd was the recipient of regular advice (or, rather, instruction) from the ex-premier (Hurd, 2003, 445). Her most vehement public criticisms were provoked by ill-advised words from the Foreign Secretary, who had insisted that providing arms for the Bosnian Muslims would merely create 'a level killing field'. Privately she went even further, accusing Hurd of making 'Neville Chamberlain look like a warmonger'. In return, the Defence Secretary, Malcolm Rifkind, claimed that Thatcher was peddling 'emotional nonsense' (Simms, 2001, 50). In reality, Major and his colleagues had been caught off guard when a US President (Bush) who agreed with their policy of non-intervention was replaced by Bill Clinton, who was much more sympathetic to Thatcher's position.

In his memoirs, Major defended his Balkan policy and explained that a more forceful approach had only paid off (in 1995) when the diplomatic context changed. Whatever the rights and wrongs of the government's position – and most observers accept that it was both wrong and shameful – it is a mistake to confuse British inaction with a reduction of prime ministerial influence over foreign policy. Although Hurd was a very active participant in policy-making, Major was equally involved (as he was in another decision to do nothing despite advance warnings in 1994 of possible genocide in Rwanda). Indeed, Major chaired two international conferences on Bosnia (1992 and 1995), and describes them in detail in his memoirs (Major, 1999, 536–8, 545). While Hurd's approach to the Balkans was based on a 'realist' understanding of international relations – that is, basing decisions on narrow calculations of national interest – Major brought to bear 'realism' of a different kind: that is, the likely reaction of public opinion if Britain became embroiled in a bitter and protracted conflict. These differing motivations fed into a shared hope that the inevitable Serbian victory should be allowed to happen without undue outside obstruction and with minimal casualties. Siding with the strong against the weak is not normally the way to 'punch above one's weight'.

Tony Blair

Tony Blair's determination to make his government as different as possible from Major's was based on genuine conviction rather than tactical considerations. The contrast was particularly marked in respect of foreign policy. In place of hard-headed (or cold-hearted) 'realism', policy would now have a pronounced 'ethical dimension'; rather than looking for reasons to keep out of conflicts in obscure places, the new government would start from the premise that inaction in the face of proven evil was itself an evil.

Blair's dominant role in decision-making with regard to Iraq and the 'War on Terror' more generally has been heavily documented. It is worth noting, however, that his initial approach to this policy area was different. It was Blair's Foreign Secretary, Robin Cook, who led negotiations with Iran which facilitated a restoration of diplomatic relations (1998). Over Kosovo (1999) Cook played an important role – co-chairing a last-ditch attempt to avoid conflict, helping to persuade Russia not to intervene on Serbia's behalf, and liaising with the US Secretary of State Madeleine Albright (Kampfner, 2004, 39, 41, 43). Cook had also been allowed to take the initiative on Sierra Leone, a former British colony whose democratic government had been overthrown. However, this had gone badly for Cook, who was forced to deny all knowledge of an arms shipment by a British company (Sandline) to the displaced government, in apparent contravention of a British-sponsored UN resolution. Cook's faltering defence exasperated Blair, who complained that he was surrounded by 'weak vessels' (Campbell, 2011, 388). In television interviews, Blair argued that whatever the legal niceties, supporting the democratic government was the right thing to do. When in May 2000 British forces took the lead in restoring the government's authority, it was Blair and his Defence Secretary Geoff Hoon who received the political plaudits.

When Labour came to office Cook had attracted media attention with an FCO 'mission statement' promising an 'ethical dimension' to British foreign policy – a pledge which, by the time of the Sandline controversy, Alastair Campbell was describing as 'RC's bloody ethical foreign policy statement' (Campbell, 2011, 391). This had backfired on the government whenever its actions seemed morally dubious (e.g. when it permitted the sale of arms to distasteful regimes). In April 1999, with the NATO intervention in Kosovo still ongoing with Britain's prominent support, Blair used a scheduled speech in Chicago to set out his own thinking. In fact the speech had been drafted by the London-based scholar of international relations Lawrence Freedman, although Blair came up with the grandiloquent title 'The Doctrine of International Community'. FCO input was zero – a significant shift from the scenario in 1988, when the department was allowed to exercise considerable (though far from decisive) influence over Thatcher's Bruges speech. In his memoirs, Blair claimed that the Chicago speech was intended to set out the terms under which intervention would be justified 'to bring down a despotic dictatorial regime' – a very significant reinterpretation of the text, which is concerned with intervention on humanitarian grounds rather than 'regime change'.[41] As so often, one of Blair's aims was to distance himself from Major; thus the speech entailed 'a specific rejection of the narrow view of national interests' (Blair, 2010, 248).

As the US presidential election of 2000 approached, Blair was anxious to avoid yet another of Major's mistakes – backing the wrong American horse. The Prime Minister was right to hedge his bets, since the controversial winner – after a prolonged steward's inquiry – was the Republican George W. Bush. Before the result was confirmed, Campbell in particular was working out the best strategy for establishing a close working relationship. Blair secured an invitation to meet Bush at Camp David soon after his inauguration, and they got on well. Possibly Clinton – a lawyer who could easily have been a professional actor, and whose domestic outlook was vaguely 'progressive' – had resembled Blair too closely. By contrast, Bush had a business background, limited charisma and some views which would have been difficult to accommodate even within the increasingly right-wing British Conservative Party.

Any doubts about the relationship were dispelled when Bush showed genuine gratitude for Blair's wholehearted expression of support for America in the wake of 9/11. Although US reprisals against the Taliban regime in Afghanistan already enjoyed widespread backing, Blair willingly undertook diplomatic missions (e.g. to Assad's Syria) at the risk of incurring humiliating snubs. Presumably Blair was already looking beyond Afghanistan, hoping to maximize his influence over US policy towards other potential targets, notably Iraq. But his efforts were deemed worthwhile for their own sake, resulting in vivid testimony to the strength of the special relationship.

In September 2002 Robin Cook – who had been demoted from Foreign Secretary to Leader of the House of Commons after the 2001 election – advised Blair to 'remember what happened to Anthony Eden' (Cook, 2003, 203). Blair could brush this warning aside, since Eden's downfall arose from his failure to win unequivocal approval from the US administration before Suez, whereas Britain would be supporting America in Iraq. There were, though, some common features, in that British action (as at Suez) ultimately arose from a secret agreement in which the Prime Minister had been the chief British actor. When Blair promised Bush that Britain would support his war on Iraq, at the President's Texas ranch in April 2002, only his foreign policy adviser David Manning and his Chief of Staff (Charles Powell's brother Jonathan) were present on the British side.

Although Blair was still in danger of sharing Eden's fate – toppled because of a Middle Eastern adventure – his situation in September 2002 was in some ways closer to that of Neville Chamberlain prior to the 1938 Munich Agreement. Blair, like Chamberlain, was a foreign policy novice who considered himself an astute judge of character. While Chamberlain imagined that Hitler's promises were credible, Blair believed that his personal friendship with Bush would ensure British influence before and after the war, if not during the conflict itself. He was right to the extent that Bush did try to secure a new UN resolution to justify hostilities, but Blair could not convince the President to persevere in this fruitless effort to the point that it jeopardized the predetermined timetable for military action. As for the aftermath, just days before the crucial House of Commons debate the US Defense Secretary Donald Rumsfeld had unhelpfully disclosed that the military action would proceed even if Blair's domestic difficulties prevented British participation. In short, contrary to his hopes Blair had not been able to charm away America's unilateralist preferences, and since the US did not need British military support, he lacked the necessary leverage to persuade his ally to fulfil the 'Chicago principles' by developing a workable plan for post-war Iraq.

While Blair might not have suffered from the self-serving delusions which marred Chamberlain's encounters with Hitler, evidently he failed to detect any evidence that Bush was under the control of his neo-conservative colleagues, and could thus only be trusted in so far as his promises were consistent with their agenda. In part, this was because Britain's best contacts were with people like the Secretary of State, Colin Powell, who had been appointed as apolitical 'window dressing' for an administration which was gripped by ideological fantasies. Blair should have acquainted himself with the true nature of the Bush administration before committing British forces beyond the point of no return (Dyson, 2009, 123–6).

Indeed, one plausible line of argument is that far from being the dupe of Bush's neo-con controllers, Blair shared their millenarian visions. By his own admission, he rejected the 'realist' argument that Saddam was a necessary evil if the over-riding priority was the continued existence of Iraq as a nation-state. Even before Blair's notorious meeting with Bush at the latter's ranch, Colin Powell had sent a memo to his President in which he noted that Blair had made a clear commitment of support, for two reasons: 'the threat is real; and success against Saddam will yield more regional success'.[42] If Powell had read Blair's thoughts correctly, this would mean that the Prime Minister had bought into the neo-con idea that the fall of Saddam would trigger a domino effect, hurling tyrants across the Middle East from their palatial residences and (among other things) enhancing the potential profits for Western oil companies. From this perspective, planning for the aftermath of an invasion (a key 'Chicago' principle) was not of crucial importance;

the only disruption likely to follow the removal of Saddam would arise from unbridled nationwide rejoicing.

Throughout the Iraq crisis, Blair's Foreign Secretary Jack Straw had been supportive, despite his exclusion from effective decision-making and his considerable doubts about the wisdom of the policy. In September 2004, when the government almost lost its Commons majority on the issue of university tuition fees (see chapter 1), Straw had warned the Prime Minister that if he continued to flirt with disaster, "'Your luck will run out'. "Jack," he replied with his blue eyes blazing, "I'm always lucky'" (Straw, 2012, 489). Notwithstanding the blazing eyes, Blair was probably at least half-joking. Certainly, and as usual, he ignored Straw's advice. In May 2006 Straw was sent on the career trajectory previously experienced by Geoffrey Howe and Robin Cook – from the FCO to Leadership of the House of Commons. His replacement, Margaret Beckett, was 'stunned rather than elated with the promotion'. Looking back, Blair reflected that 'you should always promote or demote for a purpose, not for effect' – cautionary words which readers should commit to memory in case they ever become Prime Minister and are tempted to make really stupid appointments. Blair's excuse was that he had been 'determined that we should make a splash, show we still had vigour, show I was still governing for the future'. It was, of course, welcome that a role which had once been very important was entrusted for the first time to a female politician, but any short-term presentational effect was spoiled by the fact that Beckett had shown no appetite or aptitude for the job (Blair, 2010, 594).

Blair, in fact, had been hoping to replace Straw with one of his trusties – Charles Clarke or David Miliband – but decided against this. Straw was marked for a move because he had never been part of the charmed circle, and had been showing 'untrusty' symptoms by seeing more of Gordon Brown, and acting more like a real Foreign Secretary by strengthening his ties with Condoleezza Rice (Colin Powell's replacement as US Secretary of State). Blair wanted to reassert his control of foreign policy, so the person with formal responsibility for that task had to make way for someone who seemed more malleable.

Blair had started a process which bears an eerie similarity to the downfall of another lucky Prime Minister who pushed things too far – Margaret Thatcher. In July 1989 Thatcher had removed Geoffrey Howe – like Straw, another long-serving senior minister – and replaced him with John Major, on the assumption that he would be more obedient. In Thatcher's case, Howe's removal from the FCO allowed her to give full vent to her obsessional dislike of Germans. Blair's replacement of Straw with Beckett was an attempt to write himself a blank cheque with regard to the Middle East and the 'War on Terror'. He duly wrote the cheque, but it bounced.

In July 2006 the Syrian-backed terrorist group Hizbullah captured two Israeli soldiers, and Israel threatened a degree of retaliation which, on any understanding of the word, would be 'disproportionate', starting with air strikes on Hizbullah's bases in Southern Lebanon. On 19 July, at PMQs, the Liberal Democrat leader Menzies Campbell challenged Blair to adopt an even-handed approach to the Lebanese crisis. This Blair refused to do, and when Campbell repeated his question the contorted reply only made it more apparent that, following Bush's lead, Blair was prepared to allow Israel a few days to wreak its disproportionate vengeance. This evidence that Blair was now fully enlisted in the neo-con camp came just a few days after a G8 summit meeting, when Bush had been overheard accosting Britain's head of government with the over-familiar words, 'Yo, Blair!' For Straw, the exchange between Blair and Menzies Campbell was a head-in-hands moment, and he began to resolve the 'conflict of loyalty' which had caused so much agony for Howe when he heard Thatcher give equally unhelpful parliamentary answers in October 1990. He did not emulate Howe by resigning, instead releasing a statement making his objections clear. Other ministers were pressing Blair to change his position, and there were strong rumours of a rift between the FCO and No. 10 (though diplomatic efforts were conducted by a junior minister, Kim Howells, rather than Beckett: Straw, 2012, 485–8).[43]

Even in his memoirs, Blair refused to budge from the position he had adopted in July 2006. The apostle of international morality was apparently unmoved by the idea of massive civilian casualties in Lebanon; he could even write, with the opportunity to measure his words, that 'The occupation of Palestinian land may be an injustice, depending on your viewpoint' (Blair, 2010, 596–7). As Straw put it, by July 2006 'The gap between Tony's "world view" and that of most other people was now beyond conciliation' (Straw, 2012, 488). Even then, Labour's senior figures were unable to put an immediate end to Blair's tenancy of No. 10, allowing him to announce in September 2006 that he would step down in the following year. Blair had transformed himself from Bush's 'poodle' to Labour's lame duck.

Gordon Brown

When Brown finally took the position which Blair had denied to him for so long, his foreign policy priority was to wind down his predecessor's military commitments in Iraq and Afghanistan. His approach to international politics was no less interventionist than Blair's, but his primary focus was on the relief of poverty rather than the removal of despotic governments. As a consequence, his main interest fell within the remit of the Department for International Development (DFID), not the FCO. He was willing to appoint the Blairite leadership aspirant David Miliband as Foreign Secretary, on the well-founded assumption that this would keep him busy without raising his public profile. Indeed, Miliband was quite useful to the Prime Minister, as a Europhile who could deputize on occasions which Brown would rather not handle himself for fear of offending the right-wing press. Thus in December 2007 Miliband, rather than Brown, attended the official signing of the EU's integrationist Lisbon Treaty; the Prime Minister also included Miliband in his first official trip across the Atlantic (July 2007), doubtless to reassure Bush that his government would not be a Blairite-free zone. In his speech to the Labour Party conference the following year, Brown took a swipe at both of his youthful rivals – Miliband and the Conservative leader David Cameron – by saying that it would be a mistake to hand over to a 'novice' at a time of economic crisis. Although the Prime Minister could not supress a smirk as he delivered his killer line, he had just admitted that he had appointed a 'novice' to one of the great offices of state.

Within his preferred sphere of economic diplomacy Brown actually proved a remarkable success, prompting fellow leaders to 'forgive' the debts of developing nations and, in particular, providing the most imaginative and persuasive proposals for dealing with the worldwide financial crisis which began in 2007. However, his drive for global justice was not universally appreciated in Britain, whose right-wing newspapers presented generosity towards developing nations as a waste of taxpayers' money, and his drive to recapitalize the banks fell foul of 'Gilmour's Law'; the proportion of voters who recognized and understood his achievement was smaller than those who had been taught by the Conservatives that he had caused the problem in the first place, and minuscule compared to those who would have hailed him if he had led the country to victory in a post-colonial war.

While Tony Blair resembled Thatcher in feeling that his luck would never run out, Brown (like Major) quickly exhausted his supplies of that invaluable commodity. Having established a reasonable working relationship with Bush – despite disagreements about the British commitment in Iraq – Brown had reason to hope for even better when the Democrat Barack Obama won the 2008 presidential election. However, apart from being anything but an instinctive 'Britophile', Obama was focused on developments beyond Europe. Brown did receive the honour of being the first world leader to visit Obama after his inauguration, and was invited to address both Houses of Congress (although he was beaten to Washington by Miliband, who had been the first foreign minister to hold talks with the new Secretary of State, Hillary Clinton). But Obama did not agree to hold a full press conference after their talks, which was taken as a snub. While Brown had brought with him an ornamental pen holder, fashioned from the timbers of a British ship which had been used to enforce the prohibition of the slave trade, in return Obama presented Brown with a collection of middle-brow DVD recordings which would not even play on British-made machines (Brown, 2017, 326).[44]

David Cameron

Although David Cameron came to office without ministerial experience of any kind, as a special adviser he had been a first-hand observer of Thatcher's last years, as well as being an MP through 9/11 and Iraq. As a result, he was in an admirable position to profit from other people's mistakes. The fact that he headed a coalition government made no difference in foreign policy terms; the Foreign Secretary was always going to be William Hague, who had been an impressive Opposition spokesperson and, as a former party leader, brought considerable political weight to the job. In their 2010 manifesto the Conservatives had espoused a 'liberal Conservative' approach to foreign policy, combining support for liberal values with a steady eye on the national interest. The relevant section of the manifesto was free from bombastic claims about

Britain's role in the world, and eschewed 'grand utopian visions'. The only allusion to a 'special relationship' referred to India, not the US, whose dealings with Britain were aptly characterized as 'strong, close and frank'. The country would be a significant but reforming influence within the EU, and would look beyond both America and Europe for its allies. Cameron's personal commitment to raise assistance to developing countries to the UN target of 0.7 per cent of national income was retained, despite the need for spending cuts in most other departments.

When the coalition issued its 'programme for government' this general prospectus, which implied that politicians would not emulate the excesses of Thatcher and Blair, was unchanged. As we have seen, Cameron also instituted a National Security Council (NSC), with a shifting but wide-ranging membership. The name of the new institution – and that of the National Security Adviser whose position was created at the same time – conveyed an unsettling impression of 'Americanization'. From the FCO's perspective, a potential dilution of influence in the new body was balanced by an assurance that the department would be guaranteed a voice of some kind in key decisions – something that was certainly not true under Blair. However, the FCO could not be certain that its voice would carry much weight if, after Hague's departure from office, he was replaced with a less respected figure.

In 2010, though, it was possible to think that the prestige of the FCO within Whitehall might be restored by Hague, making it impossible for future premiers to give the position of Foreign Secretary to a 'novice' or a has-been. In July 2010 Hague delivered an impressive speech about Britain's position in a 'networked world', showcasing the opportunities for quiet diplomacy which would cement the country's existing ties, revive some neglected old ones (notably with Commonwealth countries) and establish new links. Even at a time of 'austerity', the FCO would be opening offices around the globe rather than closing them down.[45] The primary purpose of this activity would be the advancement of British economic interests, in which task the FCO was seconded by the Chancellor, George Osborne, who was particularly enthusiastic about fostering trade with China and other emerging powers.

Why, then, did it all go wrong? The chief and predictable answer is the Prime Minister's decision in January 2013 to promise an in/out referendum on membership of the EU. Even at the time, this enforced decision suggested strongly that Cameron and Hague were at best level-headed leaders of an ungovernable party. Although Cameron (like Thatcher and Blair before him) evidently expected that his persuasive powers would produce the desired result – even if he did not achieve all or most of his goals in preliminary talks with fellow EU leaders, he would convince the public that it was more risky to vote 'Leave' – the decision looks even more reckless when viewed from the perspective of the coalition's programme. That document presupposed that Britain could deepen and even widen its global interests on the basis of its EU membership, as well as its relationship with the US. Far from presenting alternative choices between which Britain could choose from a position of strength, as Eurosceptics persistently argued, these two foundations of British interests stood or collapsed together; if Britain left the EU, non-European countries (including those in the Commonwealth) would regard it as a less desirable trading partner, while the US (insofar as it paid much attention to Europe) would turn more decisively towards Germany (and even France).

As we have seen (chapter 3), Cameron did at least embark on his gamble after consulting elected politicians, including Hague. His other significant failure – Britain's intervention in Libya – was preceded by discussions within the NSC. This was particularly worrying for anyone who hoped that the replacement of Blair's 'sofa government' with a formal institution would spare Britain from ill-conceived decisions: that if in future British initiatives proved to be mistaken, this would be the result of unforeseen circumstances rather than ineptitude. The 'Arab Spring' of 2010–11 was indeed an unforeseen development; but once it began British policy-makers, led by Cameron, had a duty to keep cool heads and remember the manifesto's injunction against 'grand utopian visions'. Instead, the NSC was unable to restrain Cameron as he found his 'inner Blair', at considerable cost to Britain's international reputation as well as lasting misery for the Libyan victims of his 'liberal Conservatism'.

Beginning in March 2011 as a mission to protect civilians who had been threatened by a brutal dictator (Muammar Gaddafi), air strikes on Libya spearheaded by France and Britain (and later nominated an official NATO operation) escalated into an attempt to promote 'regime change' in a region which had already been destabilized by the early events of the Arab Spring. In August Gaddafi fled from the capital,

Tripoli, and on 5 September Cameron delivered a statement to the House of Commons, claiming (in words which he would later hear in a less pleasing context) that the Libyan people had 'taken their country back'.[46] A few days later, Cameron and the French President, Nicolas Sarkozy, paid a surprise visit to Tripoli, where they received a rapturous reception. It seemed that the country could be left in the safekeeping of a National Transition Council, which had been established in the early stages of the conflict and recognized as the official Libyan government by France. It was aptly named, because it oversaw the transition from Gaddafi's despotism to anarchy; the country was engulfed by a second civil war in 2014.

In September 2016, the Foreign Affairs Committee of the House of Commons published its report on the Libyan intervention. If David Cameron had still been Prime Minister, the report would have made him reconsider his position. As it was, Cameron chose to announce his resignation as an MP two days before the Libya report appeared, contravening his previous pledge to stay on as a backbencher until the next general election. The report noted that Cameron had taken a 'decisive role' during NSC discussions of the intervention, whose ultimate failure arose from inadequate advance intelligence, a failure to explore political solutions to the crisis and inattention to possible problems in the aftermath of Gaddafi's overthrow. In short, Cameron's Libya was a repeat performance of Blair's Iraq, which only attracted less public attention because few British troops had been involved in the ground war, and they were not required to act as an army of occupation.[47]

In August 2013, Cameron suffered the indignity of defeat in a Commons vote on intervention in another war zone caused by the Arab Spring – Syria. In March 2011, British military action to protect Libyan civilians had been approved by 557 votes to 13 (the handful of 'noes', predictably, including the future Labour leader Jeremy Corbyn). The very different outcome of 29 August 2013 was, in effect, a vote of no confidence by the legislature in the executive's handling of 'liberal interventionism' since 2001 (see chapter 1). Cameron had done his best to argue that Syria would not be a replay of Iraq (or Libya), but a majority of MPs felt unable to trust him. In the aftermath of the defeat, fears were expressed by government ministers that the vote would damage the 'special relationship' (the phrase which the party's 2010 manifesto had carefully avoided) and there was considerable angst when the US Secretary of State John Kerry referred to France, which had continued to support the idea of strikes on Syria, as America's 'oldest ally'. The literal truth of this remark should really have been evident to the British public, since the last time a government had been defeated on a matter of war and peace had been in 1782, while Britain was at war with the American colonies and their French allies. In the scramble for scapegoats there were calls for Hague, who had not even spoken in the Syria debate, to resign. This would have been far more quixotic than Carrington's gesture in April 1982, because on this occasion the reputational damage fell squarely on Cameron, who had decided to recall Parliament in the expectation that he could swing the vote, and had encouraged President Obama to think more seriously about military intervention on the assumption that, like Bush before him, he could count on British support. Although Cameron did manage to win backing from the Commons in December 2015 for military action against Islamic State (or Daesh) in Syria as well as Iraq, public opinion was sharply divided even on this question, when the argument for action seemed less contentious. At least the vote meant that the Prime Minister could embark on the final stages of his attempt to renegotiate Britain's EU membership without the fresh memory of another personal setback.

Theresa May

In sharp contrast to the 2010 document, the foreign policy section of the 2015 Conservative manifesto was shameless and shoddy. Headlined 'A Britain Standing Tall in the World', it claimed that Britain's global position had been 'strengthened' since 2010, and that the NSC had ensured 'proper, strategic decision-making at the top of government'. The 'special relationship' was back – indeed, it was now a Special Relationship, adorned with capital letters (and without inverted commas). Although Libya was gripped by the new civil war, British intervention there was claimed as a success. The EU was only mentioned in passing; there was no attempt to argue that membership was helpful to Britain's global status.[48] In other respects, though, the manifesto followed on from the 2010 version, boasting about Britain's burgeoning ties with China and its developing networks with other 'fast-growing economies'. The Home Secretary Theresa May might have noticed one of the 2015 subheadings: 'We want a strong, stable and secure country' (presumably in order to distinguish the Conservatives from any rival party which might be arguing that Britain should be 'weak, unstable and vulnerable').

Under Cameron, the FCO and Hague had been at the forefront of the 'Global Britain' project. It might have been expected that this would continue, with even greater impetus, in the wake of the 2016 referendum. However, as we have seen, May immediately established two new government departments (for Exiting the European Union, and for International Trade) whose remits would naturally have fallen to a resurgent FCO. The fact that May envisaged a very limited role for the department was underlined by her appointment of Boris Johnson as Foreign Secretary.

In fact, the game of ministerial musical chairs was designed to give 'Brexiteers' who doubted May's credentials the impression that a team of true believers had been assembled to steer the withdrawal process (see chapter 3). The truth, though, was that May wanted a dominant role for herself (and her special advisers). Accordingly, in November 2016 she headed a trade mission to India. There she discovered that India had regarded Britain as a key partner not least because of its EU membership. As such, May (who had already set out her vision of a 'hard Brexit' at the 2016 Conservative conference: see chapter 2) had very little to offer; the Indian government wanted significant relaxation in visa requirements, but May's long-standing opposition to mass migration made this impossible.[49] It was thus unsurprising that May's ideas on Brexit began to soften, which in turn made it more imperative for her to keep personal control of the process.

At least there was positive news for Brexiteers from America, where President Obama, who had been persuaded by Cameron to deliver a counterproductive warning against the consequences of withdrawal from the EU, had been replaced by a Leave-loving President. The downside, however, was that the new President was Donald Trump. In January 2017 May was given the usual favour of being the first head of government to visit the newly inaugurated Trump. May's biographers claim that the visit 'showed May at her very best on the international stage' (Seldon and Newell, 2019, 167), but that was a distinctly backhanded compliment. She did, at least, manage to retain some dignity (despite Trump's insistence on holding her hand), and stuck to previous

British policy (particularly on Iran) although this would be unwelcome to a host whose diplomatic talents made Boris Johnson look like Talleyrand. However, within hours of her departure Trump announced restrictions on migration (aimed at Muslims, and affecting some British nationals), forcing the Prime Minister to describe the policy as 'divisive and wrong'. May's attempt to curry favour with Trump by offering him a state visit to Britain obviously pleased a man with a profound veneration for the country's golf courses, but it could only have verified the President's existing hunch that Britain was desperate for a trade deal. When Trump came to London in July 2018 he criticized May's handling of Brexit and lavished praise on Johnson, his British alter ego.[50] Trump was also very free with his comments on senior Conservatives during his subsequent state visit (June 2019), but at least by that time May had already announced her schedule for leaving office. One of her few consoling thoughts must have been the unlikelihood of having to spend any more time with Mr Trump.

At least Trump had played down the significance of a very recent row concerning the involvement of the Chinese company Huawei in the development of Britain's 5G communications network. The US administration had warned that this would have serious consequences, especially in future security co-operation (an area where Britain and America really did have something like a 'special relationship'). In April 2018 Britain's NSC had discussed the implications, and details of the meeting (at which several key ministers, including the Foreign Secretary and the Home Secretary, had raised strong objections) was leaked to the *Daily Telegraph*. Apart from the acute sensitivity of the topic, the incident also suggested that, far from being a forum for 'proper, strategic decision-making', the NSC could not even ensure its own security. It also seemed as prone as the Cabinet to prime ministerial dominance, since May had over-ruled the concerns of her colleagues and used her 'casting vote' in favour of a 'limited' role for Huawei. An inquiry into the leak, conducted with suspicious speed, identified the culprit as the Defence Secretary, May's one-time ally Gavin Williamson, who was promptly sacked.

While Cameron had begun with a sensible approach to British foreign policy and ended in disaster because (like Blair) he departed from his own guidelines, May's position in this respect was always dire and she made it even worse by acting as if she believed her own rhetoric.

Even after confronting reality on her various foreign trips, May continued to mislead voters, in her party's 2017 manifesto (which boasted of Britain's 'global leadership' in almost every conceivable area) as well as her cliché-ridden speeches. This was not pardonable, given the gravity of the decisions she had to take, but it was at least understandable. Having adopted the negotiating posture of a hard-line Brexiteer, May had to keep talking like one in the hope that reality would never catch up with her (and her beloved Conservative Party). If it occurred to her that this performance was suited to a natural populist rather than a pragmatist painfully lacking in charisma, the thought would have been abhorrent because the perfect candidate was all-too available. Having auditioned successfully for the wrong role, May had no alternative but to keep acting out of character until the final curtain.

Conclusion

The main conclusion arising from this discussion is that, while Prime Ministers in the past have chosen to take a leading (even dominant) role in foreign policy-making, it is now difficult to envisage a Prime Minister being allowed the luxury of choice in the matter. This is partly because of the continuous need for the Prime Minister's presence at international summit meetings, the regularity of official trips to individual countries and the requirement to hold talks with visiting leaders. However, it is also connected to the relative decline of the FCO as an institution. This has come about for a variety of reasons, including a general blurring of the boundaries between 'domestic' and 'foreign' policies, and the emergence of issues (notably climate change) which clearly transgress the old departmental denominations.

Yet the most important factor in FCO fortunes is Britain's relative decline on the global stage. As we have seen, the FCO itself was created in response to that decline, coming as it did in the year after Harold Wilson's Labour government had announced the closure of British military bases east of Suez. Arguably the most vivid testimony to this loss of status came very near the beginning of our period. In April 1980, ITV screened a drama-documentary entitled *Death of a Princess*, portraying a nineteen-year-old member of the Saudi ruling family who had been executed for adultery. The television company realized in advance that the programme would be highly controversial in parts of the Middle East, and changed the format from a purely factual piece to a drama involving actors to dilute its likely impact. Nonetheless, the Saudi government was outraged at this exposure of barbaric practices, threatening a breach of diplomatic relations and other sanctions. The British Foreign Secretary at the time – Lord Carrington, an hereditary peer who represented the country's old governing class – could not halt the broadcast without provoking an outcry at home, so he merely stated that he 'wished the programme had never been shown' and that he found it 'deeply offensive'. Both of these remarks were true; Carrington certainly *did* wish that the programme had never been made, let alone broadcast, and the subject *was* 'deeply offensive' to anyone with a vestigial respect for human rights. But his statement was intended as a grovelling apology, and in that spirit it was taken. Although other countries tried to prevent their citizens from viewing this gruesome illustration of the Saudi establishment in action, Britain's attitude was particularly shameful since the programme had been made by a British company. It is difficult to imagine a similar governmental response if *Death of a Princess* had been shown at any time before the oil crisis of 1973–4, which suddenly made Saudi Arabia an important (and vastly rich) global player, and one whose friendship was now vital for Britain.

Margaret Thatcher herself had a lively appreciation of the value of Saudi friendship, in terms of Middle Eastern politics and arms contracts. Nevertheless, she saw the FCO's general appraisal of Britain's place in the world as a symptom of defeatism, promoted by the 'socialist' outlook of post-war British governments. To her mind, the Falklands War proved that Britain was still a 'Great Power'. Her leading role in that conflict convinced her that she alone possessed the moral fibre which was all that Britain required to rediscover its old vitality. As a result, the 'natural' decline of the FCO – no longer the diplomatic arm of a government which gave laws to far-flung nations, but rather a Whitehall department which responded as best it could to the things which foreign powers did to Britain – was accelerated by a Prime Minister who believed that the national interest would best be served if she conducted diplomacy herself. Although she would have liked a separate Unit in Downing Street to assist her, in practice she only needed Charles Powell, assisted (and occasionally hampered) by Bernard Ingham.

Unfortunately for Thatcher, her time in office did not mark a sudden revival in Britain's status. At most, the Falklands reminded world leaders that the country was no pushover, but victory over the conscript army of a corrupt and despotic government was not exactly Agincourt. Just after the Thatcher Government had been re-elected in 1983, US forces toppled the government of the Commonwealth country of Grenada, without prior consultation with Britain. Although President Reagan subsequently apologized, the episode should have demonstrated to Thatcher that, even with a close friend in the White House, American and British interests could diverge. In her second term, the Reykjavik summit made the same point even more clearly. After Reagan's departure, American acquiescence in German reunification, against Thatcher's vehement protests, merely demonstrated that although Britain's relative economic decline had been arrested thanks to its exploitation of North Sea oil, on the diplomatic front it was just a noisier, more obtuse version of the country Thatcher had inherited in 1979.

Although he did have relevant ministerial experience – which had not been enjoyable, largely thanks to Thatcher – John Major was happy to work in harness with a real expert, Douglas Hurd. In a world of counterfactuals, where Thatcher had never existed but Major still became Prime Minister in 1990, the British public would almost certainly have grown accustomed to seeing their country as essentially a regional power which still enjoyed interests and a degree of influence beyond Europe. Instead, when the real John Major succeeded the all-too real Margaret Thatcher he tried to make up for lost time by acting in accordance with a 'realistic' assessment of Britain's global position. However, in respect of the Balkans the resistance of Major and Hurd to the 'something must be done' school took the form of obstructing important things that really *could* be done; and Lady Thatcher was on hand to underline this point. Thus although Major did not buck the trend, and played a significant role in the making of foreign policy, he used his influence in a manner which could be presented as hopelessly *inactive* and defeatist by Thatcher and her allies in the right-wing press.

This lesson, among many others from the Major years, was not lost on Tony Blair. Although his outlook was different – he wanted to root his foreign policy in moral considerations, while Thatcher had been a moralist and a 'realist' by turns – Blair realized that he would have to revert to the Thatcher model at least to the extent of making it look as if Britain 'mattered' on the world stage. Although initially he copied

Major by talking up Britain's role in Europe, he knew that this would bring him into unwanted conflict with the right-wing press, while an attempt (however improbable) to bring British influence to bear on the 'special relationship' was sure to protect him on that vulnerable flank. Blair's plan worked while President Clinton was in office, and he thought he could pull off a similar trick if only he could work his charm on Clinton's successor. The terrorist attack of 9/11 seemingly gave him his chance, but he overlooked the possibility that George W. Bush was totally unlike his 'realist' father, and was instead under the control of neo-conservatives. Even after Blair's strategy of conscripting the US into conflicts which he approved on moral grounds had backfired on him, he continued to reject criticism of his conduct. The rejection of culpability answered to his personal, psychological need, since he had no one else to blame; throughout the pre-war period his Foreign Secretary had been a (semi-)innocent bystander.

The records of Cameron and May are far more instructive than the brief Brown interlude. Cameron had already made a mockery of his party's sensible manifesto, lurching into 'liberal interventionism' in Libya, by the time that he decided to appease his unruly party by promising an EU referendum. In sharp contrast, May came to office with an outlook which was wholly unrealistic, and quickly contrived to make a very difficult situation impossible.

All of the Prime Ministers since 1979, regardless of previous experience or relevant knowledge, took a leading role in the making of British foreign policy, and in every case (with the arguable exception of Brown) their records of failure include avoidable mistakes. Leaving aside the differing factors of individual temperament and international context, the common thread through all these years is a tendency for Prime Ministers to present an unrealistic picture of Britain's role in the world to their domestic audiences. Sometimes the Prime Ministers seem genuinely to have believed their own words, which in a way is even more troubling than the examples of calculated distortion. But even the ones who spoke with sincerity would have felt a compulsion to mislead because not to do so would have been deemed 'unpatriotic' by the right-wing press. If anything, Labour Prime Ministers would be under a greater compulsion than their Conservative counterparts, in order to keep the media moguls onside.

In the immediate aftermath of the Syria vote, the Chancellor, George

Osborne, said that Britain was likely to engage in some 'soul searching' to decide on the role it wanted to play in the world. This sounded promising: a well-informed debate about Britain's post-war experience was exactly what was needed if political leaders of all parties wanted to break the depressing cycle of raising public expectations and then failing to meet them. However, Osborne was a foreign policy 'hawk' who was much admired in US Republican circles; as such, it was obvious that he wanted the 'soul searching' to result in a continuation of the approach which had just provoked a humiliating parliamentary rebuff. Osborne, who hoped to succeed Cameron in due course, evidently believed that Britain should be presented as a Great Power which would never 'turn its back on the world's problems', but would instead approach unfolding tragedies like Libya and Syria with a predisposition to take an active role without a full examination of the likely repercussions. There was some justice, then, in the major setback Osborne suffered over Brexit, when his attempts to focus the debate on practical considerations were easily repelled by Eurosceptics and their media allies, who gratefully co-opted the vacuous nationalistic rhetoric which the public had learned to expect from their Prime Ministers since 1979.[51]

6

Election winner

Explaining British general election results after the event has become no easier than predicting them in advance. Not even the most sophisticated survey data can allow us to draw confident conclusions about the *independent* impact of specific factors; for example, even voters who claim to have based their electoral choices purely on the merits of rival policy programmes will have been affected to some extent by their impressions of the competing parties, while most of the people who think their votes are pure expressions of emotional attachment to a party will take some notice of the key campaign themes. This problem also applies to evaluations of the importance of party leaders, including the serving Prime Minister, as influences on electoral outcomes.

Until the 1960s life was less complicated (though far from trouble-free) for electoral analysts. Although more than two political parties contested general elections, only Labour and the Conservatives stood any chance of winning overall majorities, because they enjoyed the consistent support of significant socio-economic groups. In every election, Labour was backed by around two-thirds of working-class voters, while the Conservatives could depend upon a similar proportion of the middle class (Denver et al., 2012, 57). In order to win a workable parliamentary majority under a first-past-the-post electoral system, the main parties needed to ensure that their 'core' supporters turned out to vote; but they also had to attract 'floating voters' who felt no strong sense of partisan allegiance.

The importance of the connection between social class and voting preferences was underlined in David Butler and Donald Stokes' pioneering study of voting behaviour, *Political Change in Britain* (first published in 1969). The title of the book's first edition was somewhat misleading, since the importance of deep-rooted social factors suggested that elections in Britain should produce political *stability* rather than significant change. Although the two main parties rotated between government and Opposition, they had little incentive to change the rules of the political game (particularly the electoral system, which normally ensured a secure parliamentary majority for the winning side), or to deviate very far in policy terms from 'centrist' or 'consensual' proposals in case this alienated crucial floating voters. One corollary of this assumption was that both main parties must be wary of an attractive 'third force' which sought to occupy the ideological middle ground between Labour and the Conservatives. Since it could not hope to emulate their solid demographic bases of support, such a party was unlikely to win a general election; but it could fare well enough to cause serious damage to a major party which adopted a radical policy programme, or indeed in certain circumstances to defy the logic of first-past-the-post and deny an overall majority to both of its bigger rivals.

Even in the 1950s, when the two main parties broadly agreed on fundamental issues of domestic and foreign policy, the potential potency of uncommitted voters was manifested in by-election successes for the Liberal Party, which was regarded (somewhat to its chagrin) as a moderate alternative to the Conservatives and Labour and thus a congenial receptacle for protest votes. This phenomenon suggested that the partisan allegiance of a significant proportion of voters was weakening, not because the main parties were becoming polarized on ideological grounds but because a growing section of the electorate was disillusioned with their performance. The tendency became even more pronounced in the 1960s, when the increasing vigour of nationalist movements outside England gave voters in Scotland and Wales additional options if they wanted to lodge a protest against the conduct of politics at Westminster (Denver and Garnett, 2014, 19–20).

Despite their understandable focus on *long-term* influences (like social class) on voter preference, Butler and Stokes were aware of developments within the electorate which related to *short-term* factors – for example, political developments at the time of an election and the course of the campaign itself. Butler and Stokes coined the term 'valence voting' to designate the tendency to express party preferences in line with evaluations of party competence (Butler and Stokes, 1974, 292). For these writers, this phenomenon should be distinguished from 'issue voting', where preferences arise from 'rational' assessments of contrasting policies on offer from the competing parties. Valence voting was better described as 'a-rational', since it was based on an *impression* (whether well founded or otherwise) that the preferred party would be better than its rivals at delivering policy outcomes which most people wanted. The classic 'valence' issue was economic prosperity, which, it was safe to assume, most people preferred to the alternative. On the Butler–Stokes approach, valence voters would thus include people who lacked a lasting *identification* with any political party, and would opt for the one which gave the impression of being most likely to make the country better off. This distinguished valence voters from 'issue' voters, who would not be content with mere impressions and would pore over every detail of the election manifestos. To the consternation of democratic theorists, there had never been many of these 'rational' voters, and even in the age of free education for all there were few signs that they would ever constitute a majority of the electorate.

Valence voting, by contrast, was potentially important even at the time that Butler and Stokes conducted their research. The existing tendency to punish governments (or/and the main Opposition party if it was perceived to be equally incompetent) in by-elections could easily spill over into general elections and become a very significant factor – but only if social class ceased to exercise the overwhelming influence on overall electoral outcomes that was still evident in the 1960s. In fact, when Butler and Stokes were writing, that change was already taking place, thanks to various factors including technological developments, the growth of consumerism and a less class-bound education system. Britain was embarking on a painful shift from the traditional extractive and manufacturing industries which had underpinned its brief but spectacular spell as a global superpower. While trade unions were, apparently, more powerful than ever, they could no longer take for granted the solidarity which came from under-rewarded toil in hazardous workplaces. On the other hand, the protest movements of the 1960s had seen members of the middle classes ranged prominently on either side of the various debates. In other words, the circumstances were ripe for a decline of long-term influences on voting behaviour, and the emergence of a more volatile electorate.

Where does the electoral role of the Prime Minister fit into this picture? Before the 1960s, that role was considered to be significant, but far from decisive. Afterwards, it was impossible for Prime Ministers (and other party leaders) to avoid being presented as the centrepiece of election campaigns. It is easy to cite charismatic premiers from the distant past, like Disraeli and Gladstone, and conclude that nothing had really changed. But those electoral titans were exceptions to the rule. Gladstone's Liberal predecessor and successor (Lord John Russell and Lord Rosebery respectively) are not so readily remembered as vote-winning leaders. Disraeli was preceded as Conservative leader by the Earl of Derby, who was very far from being a crowd-pleaser outside his Lancashire heartland; and his successor, the Marquess of Salisbury, thought that democracy was a very bad idea. True, as long ago as 1938 the socialist commentator and academic Harold Laski thought that a general election 'is nothing so much as a plebiscite between alternative Prime Ministers' (Laski, 1938, 241). That is indeed how the battle might have seemed to obsessive consumers of political news at the time. But it is unlikely that the majority of voters saw things that way.

In the 1960s, political scientists like Butler and Stokes considered that admiration for individual leaders tended to arise from pre-existing identification with their parties (Butler and Stokes, 1974, 35–68). Rather like supporters of football teams, voters would tend to approve of 'their' manager at any given time, whatever his personal qualities. If their team happened to recruit a real star (like Gladstone or Disraeli) to the dugout, their enthusiasm might be shown on a continuous basis, and not just on the day of the biggest match. A really attractive leader might, in certain circumstances, even make a difference to the overall result; but for the most part, voters would express their allegiances in elections regardless of the personnel. They would simply cast their predetermined votes with more enthusiasm if they thought that their leader was particularly attractive.

By the early 1970s even Butler and Stokes were having to reassess the electoral importance of party leaders. In the second edition of their classic text, they accepted that such individuals were 'extraordinarily salient in British politics'. Nevertheless, the empirical evidence suggested that the electoral influence of leaders was 'easily outweighed by other issues and events of concern to the public' (Butler and Stokes, 1974, 360, 368). As such, the perceived qualities of leaders were not even high among 'transient' influences on voting behaviour identified by Butler and Stokes, let alone deserving a rank alongside long-term factors like social class.

For party leaders, an important consolation arising from the Butler–Stokes view was the thought that, if their 'team' lost, they could not be blamed and, if they so desired, would be allowed to fight another day. However, even before the appearance of Butler and Stokes' first edition there had been a deviation from this pattern. In chapter 1, we argued that Harold Macmillan's decision to back Lord Home as his successor in 1963 implied that prowess in parliamentary debate was no longer of cardinal importance for potential Prime Ministers. However, Macmillan himself was very conscious of the ability of television to affect political reputations, not least because he was the first Prime Minister to be subjected to mockery by the medium (in the BBC's *That Was The Week That Was* (Thorpe, 2010, 489)). If television was going to be increasingly important as a source of information for voters, Macmillan's preference for Lord Home over more media-friendly candidates – when an election had to be called in the following year – becomes almost inexplicable. True, in face-to-face television interviews party leaders (and the Prime Minister in particular) were still treated with deference in 1963; but even under such tender handling it was obvious that Home was clueless on domestic policy issues except, perhaps, agriculture and field sports. In the House of Commons, Home was unable to match Labour's quick-witted Harold Wilson, and in the television studios it was no contest at all.

In fact the result of the 1964 general election lent support to the orthodox argument that leaders were secondary factors, since the Conservatives almost clung on under their improbable champion. However, this made the subsequent course of events particularly instructive. In 1964 there was no provision for a challenge to an incumbent Conservative leader, and in any case Tory MPs feared that Wilson would exploit any evidence of division, so criticism of Home was muted. However, in the summer of 1965 Wilson confirmed that there would be no election that year, giving the Conservatives an opportunity to deal with the leadership question at leisure. Home was promptly persuaded to relinquish his position, to the dismay of 'traditionalist' Tory MPs who convinced themselves that he had been treated shabbily (Garnett and Aitken, 2002, 68).

Home might be regarded as an unrepresentative case since he should never been made party leader in the first place. After the party's 'men in grey suits' had induced him to stand down, it might seem as if normal Conservative service was resumed; after all, his successor, Edward Heath, managed to fight four elections (1966, 1970 and the two 1974 contests), of which he won only the second. Heath was easily forgiven for the first of those defeats (1966) because Wilson had held all of the electoral cards. However, a second failure (in 1970) would have resulted in a visit from the grey-suited delegation. The party's 'grandees' understood that electoral fortunes now depended heavily (if not crucially) on the image of their leader. If he was deemed to be a 'loser', uncommitted voters were likely to use this as a convenient (if unscientific) indicator of competence – of the party as well as its leader. Even if the majority of voters were still basing their choices on deep-rooted influences, practitioners had clearly reached the view that 'valence voting' had arrived and was here to stay. The growing importance of leaders cut both ways: if the Conservatives had lost in 1970, Heath would have been held responsible and forced to step down, but instead his party's victory prompted over-excited commentators (and supporters) to present the result as a personal triumph for the new Prime Minister.

The idea that Heath had 'won' in 1970 against all odds had fateful consequences for him and his party. It proved impossible to persuade him to step down after two further defeats in 1974, leaving even some of his closest allies in despair. The party's rules were duly changed – fittingly, in a process overseen by Lord Home – to allow for a challenge to an incumbent leader. In February 1975 Margaret Thatcher was the first beneficiary of a system which would eventually bring her down and make life very difficult for her successor.

The Thatcher effect

Although it is a cliché that Conservative MPs constitute 'the most sophisticated electorate in the world', it is pretty clear that in 1975 a majority was acting with the very basic intention of ending up with a leader who was not Ted Heath. If leaders really were becoming increasingly important arbiters of electoral fortunes – the notion which explained why MPs voted to get rid of Heath in the first leadership ballot of 1975, when the majority of their grassroots members continued to support him – it seemed counterintuitive to let the Thatcher 'bandwagon' roll through to victory in the second round of voting. When Thatcher became Conservative leader, the BBC had yet to appoint its first permanent female *newsreader*; the notion that, as leader of one of Britain's two main parties, a woman could be *making* the news on a regular basis seemed outlandish. In addition, Thatcher had not been regarded as a successful minister in the 1970–4 Heath Government.

Enoch Powell once noted ruefully that while he was unable to realize his ambition of leading the Conservative Party, Thatcher 'was opposite the spot on the roulette wheel at the right time, and didn't funk it' (Shepherd, 1996, 462). He could have extended his own metaphor, because having gambled at exactly the right time Thatcher stayed in the casino and just kept on winning. Heath had become Conservative leader when it looked certain that he would have to fight an unwinnable election in the very near future – hence the ready forgiveness of the 1966 Tory defeat. By contrast, by the time that Thatcher succeeded Heath in February 1975 a minority Labour government had already called one 'snap' election in the hope of winning a more comfortable parliamentary position. Its failure to do this in October 1974 made it most unlikely that it would ask the voters for a new mandate until 1978 at the earliest. Thus Thatcher, unlike Heath, could anticipate several years in which she would lead the main Opposition to a government waist-deep in difficulties.

A few weeks before the 1979 general election, James Callaghan's special adviser Bernard Donoughue tried to raise the Prime Minister's spirits by reminding him that the opinion polls had been improving, so Labour might 'sneak through' after all. According to Donoughue, Callaghan replied: 'I should not be so sure. You know there are times, perhaps once every thirty years, when there is a sea-change in politics. It then does not matter what you say or what you do . . . I suspect there is now such a sea-change – and it is for Mrs Thatcher' (Donoughue, 1987, 191). The oddity of this justly famous remark is that a 'sea-change' was indeed happening, but the tide was moving in favour of Callaghan, not Thatcher. According to surveys conducted by the MORI organization, at the beginning of April Callaghan was considered a 'more capable' person to be Prime Minister than his Conservative opponent, by a narrow margin (44 to 42 per cent). In the days before his fatalistic reflections on an unstoppable sea-change, the gap widened to 8 percentage points (47 to 39), and before the election it had increased to 19 points (50 to 31).

The fact that, notwithstanding the public's apparent preference for Callaghan over Thatcher, the Conservatives secured a comfortable overall majority in 1979 is usually interpreted as evidence that the public evaluation of leaders was still relatively unimportant. However, Callaghan was not impressed by the apparent public 'swing' in his favour. A few days after his 'sea-change' remark, for example, Donoughue recorded him as saying 'that Mrs Thatcher was, in his own view, the dominant character of the campaign. For good or ill, she was what the campaign was about and what people were talking about.' As a result, he refrained from personal attacks which might draw extra attention to her. When the Opposition leader turned down a challenge to take part in a televised debate – saying that 'We're not electing a president, we're choosing a government' – Callaghan was delighted (Donoughue, 2008, 490, 477). Thatcher herself was eager to confront Callaghan, but had been dissuaded by her public relations adviser Gordon Reece. Nevertheless, the public would probably assume that Thatcher had backed away because she thought she would fare badly. Callaghan had therefore 'won' the debate without having to take part in it.

Nevertheless, Callaghan's attitude can be questioned. A televised debate in those days – when voters had only three channels to choose from and thus almost literally constituted a 'captive audience' – would have dominated the campaign. With Labour lagging behind the Conservatives in opinion polls, a televised showdown could have been a 'game changer' for his party. Callaghan, who had first been elected as an MP in 1945, was scarcely a novice in his observation of political trends. But he had made a fateful error in not calling a general election in the autumn of 1978, when his Labour Party would have been in a much better position to win sufficient seats to stay in office than it was by the spring of 1979. Was his judgement equally at fault when he welcomed Thatcher's decision not to take part in a TV debate?

The more likely explanation is that Callaghan had detected a 'sea-change' in British politics which went beyond the personalities and issues of the 1979 general election. Indeed, the circumstances leading up to the vote showed the significance of the social and political changes which Britain had undergone since the 1960s. In the 'Winter of Discontent' of 1978–9 many trade unionists had participated in industrial action which affected the interests of other members of the working class. Low-paid workers who assembled on picket lines could argue that they had been left with no alternative, since their living standards were being eroded by inflation. But this argument suggested that the government was to blame; and since Labour was in office, this implied that the workers' party was responsible for undermining working-class solidarity. The impression had already been fostered by the Conservative poster campaign of summer 1978, featuring a lengthy dole queue under the slogan 'Labour Isn't Working.' It was not surprising that even 'tribal' Labour supporters began to reconsider their loyalties. And as they wondered how to cast their votes in May 1979, they were helped into the Conservative camp by the *Sun* newspaper, which had swung to the right under the ownership of Rupert Murdoch and now made no secret of its partisanship.

Months before the general election the *Sun* had targeted Callaghan directly, realizing that he was Labour's only remaining weapon. On 10 January 1979 the Prime Minister returned from a summit meeting (involving the US, France, West Germany and the UK) held on the Caribbean archipelago of Guadeloupe. While the industrial situation deteriorated in freezing Britain, the *Sun* lambasted Callaghan for lazing his time away on a tropical beach. When he returned and denied that Britain's situation had caused concern among his fellow conference attendees, his remarks were translated into a vivid *Sun* headline: 'Crisis? What Crisis?' The whole of the front-page report was designed to undermine Callaghan's considerable personal appeal among disaffected Labour voters. There can, of course, never be any proof that the *Sun* exercised a decisive influence over the 1979 general election or any subsequent contest. It certainly made no dent in Callaghan's opinion poll ratings. However, its presentation of the political battle in the run-up to the 1979 election is particularly significant, since it was clearly based on a calculation that it could launch an unfair attack on the Labour leader without losing readers, even though its primary audience was the traditional working class.

Thus in the first general election of our period, certain trends could be identified whose significance was likely to grow rather than diminish. The fading significance of long-term influences on voting behaviour, notably the link between social class and partisan support, increased the importance of factors which had previously been regarded as both secondary and temporary. Such factors, particularly the media, now had to be regarded as primary influences; and if their impact was transient, this hardly mattered, if the goal for political leaders was to win the next general election. The 'partisan realignment' of the *Sun* during the 1970s presupposed and reinforced a weakening of ties between its working-class readers and the Labour Party. With television now available to almost every British household, newspapers were under increasing pressure to retain their agenda-setting prominence; thus tabloids like the *Sun* increased their focus on individual personalities, which could engage the interest of readers more readily than policy issues. A strongly supportive tabloid was an invaluable asset to any political party, since the style of such newspapers lent itself not just to uncritical praise of the favoured party leader, but also (and perhaps more importantly) the vilification of opponents. Thus the tabloid press reinforced another supposedly 'secondary and short-term' influence on voting behaviour – the party leaders, and the Prime Minister in particular.

Even this general argument is still disputed by some political scientists, who are sceptical of any phenomenon unless it can be subjected to precise measurement. Such academic observers would be left unmoved even by meticulous enumeration of headlines and column centimetres devoted to party leaders; if media coverage cannot be proven to affect voters, who cares about the level of attention which various outlets waste on such ephemeral figures? However, for our purpose the key point is that all media outlets operate on the assumption that leaders *are* important: and leaders repay the compliment. Believing that their fortunes depend crucially on media support, political leaders are prepared to place their reputations in what would be serious jeopardy if their tabloid allies were not on hand to rescue them. This tendency did not begin with Margaret Thatcher, but she made strenuous efforts to propitiate her ally Rupert Murdoch, preventing adequate investigation of his proposed takeover of the *Times* newspaper in 1981 and, five years later, ensuring that the full power of the state was mobilized in defence of his decision to move the printing of his newspapers to a union-free plant.

In itself, the favour bestowed on Murdoch is compelling testimony to Thatcher's recognition of the media's importance. Thatcher was not a 'prude' by any means, and her reading of the 'Victorian values' which she equated with Britain's rise to greatness was strictly selective.[52] But the hedonism celebrated by the *Sun* newspaper was difficult to square with Thatcher's Methodist conscience. Presumably she spared herself the ethical quandary by entrusting the task of scanning the newspaper to her faithful Press Secretary, Bernard Ingham.

James Callaghan might have been mistaken in his view that Thatcher was the dominant factor for voters in the 1979 general election. However, Thatcher was eminently newsworthy, not least because of her forthright views on domestic and international questions. Whether or not the Falklands conflict determined the outcome of the 1983 general election – most likely, it simply increased a majority which the Conservatives would have secured anyway – it ensured that Thatcher would certainly be the central figure second time round. At the start of the 1983 campaign the *Economist* pronounced that 'The issue is Thatcher.' What this meant, to 'rational' readers of a specialist journal, was that the election was likely to be decided by voters for whom all of the political issues of 1983 (the economy, nuclear weapons, etc.) were somehow subsumed or transcended by a single personality. Right-wing tabloid journalists, well aware that their readers would not wish to follow the nuances of the economic debate which had ravaged the Conservative Party since 1979, replaced the old journalistic deference towards Prime Ministers with slavering subservience. One *Daily Express* writer opined that 'The PM is the sun around which all other politicians orbit' (Butler and Kavanagh, 1984, 206–7).

With this level of adulation fresh in her memory, it is not surprising that Thatcher was taken aback by the relatively low profile she was asked to adopt in the next general election campaign (1987). Although she understood that some of her colleagues – notably the Chancellor, Nigel Lawson – had contributed to the supposed 'economic miracle' which had taken place since 1983, she surely deserved a central role as the person whose iron resolution had rescued the country from the turmoil of the late 1970s. When on 'Wobbly Thursday' (4 June 1987, just a week before the election) opinion polls suggested that the overall Conservative majority might fall – or disappear entirely – Thatcher began to suspect malevolent intentions even in previously trusted colleagues like the party's Chairman, Norman Tebbit. Indeed, before the campaign began she had given an important role to the Secretary of State for Employment, the former special adviser Lord Young, who could not be suspected of any ulterior motives in serving her since (unlike Tebbit) he owed his political position entirely to Thatcher's favour (see chapter 2).

Tempers boiled over in Conservative Central Office on Wobbly Thursday; even her admiring official biographer concedes that the Prime Minister behaved irrationally as the bubble of positive publicity which Ingham provided for her was pricked by polling evidence reflecting the real world (Moore, 2016, 702). In the most dramatic incident of that day, Young physically accosted Tebbit and told the Party Chairman in no uncertain terms that unless he changed his strategy the party would lose the election. In any other setting, a physical confrontation between Young and Tebbit would probably have been somewhat one-sided. On this occasion, however, Tebbit knew that his opponent enjoyed prime ministerial favour, so he stayed his murderous hands. Thatcher duly returned to her rightful place at the forefront of Conservative press conferences, and despite her erratic performances on these occasions the party easily won a third consecutive parliamentary majority.

The battle for control of the 1987 Conservative election campaign can be seen as a conflict between those who wanted the party to win by whatever means, and Thatcher loyalists who were hoping for a victory which could be presented as a personal mandate for the Prime Minister. But if the latter camp would always have preferred a 'presidential' campaign in 1987, their case was strengthened by the fact that Labour had already adopted that approach. The party's leader in 1983, Michael Foot, was not an image-maker's dream. But his much younger successor, Neil Kinnock, took a starring role in a 1987 election broadcast which was judged to be so successful that it was shown twice. Directed by the Oscar-winning Hugh Hudson, the broadcast (dubbed 'Kinnock: The Movie') sought to exploit the fact that the Labour leader was more popular than his party. Kinnock was portrayed as a sensitive family man who was also sufficiently tough to stand up against extremists within his own party. The obvious problem here was that footage of Kinnock defying the Militant Tendency would remind voters that his party contained a substantial contingent of extremists. However, during the campaign Kinnock's ratings as 'best person for Prime Minister' edged upwards, and although on polling day he still trailed Thatcher by around twenty points, this was enough to make even some sensible judges think that Labour had 'won' the presentational battle – a considerable boost to the reputations of the strategists Peter Mandelson and Philip Gould, and an incentive for them to repeat the personalized approach in future.[53]

Nightmare on Murdoch Street

The apparent lessons of 1987 were not lost on the Conservatives, either. The 1987 Labour Party manifesto had sported on its front cover a photograph of Kinnock receiving acclaim after one of his speeches. By contrast, the only image on the Conservative offering, as in 1983, was the party's symbol of a torch. In 1992 the Conservative leader was a much less divisive individual. A close-up, blue-tinted photograph of John Major looking his consensual best duly dominated the cover of the party manifesto. The supposedly bashful Prime Minister was willing to be photographed holding aloft a copy of the solipsistic document, and to claim at its launch that the contents were 'all me' (Major, 1999, 300). He also co-operated with the shooting of 'Major: The Movie' – an election broadcast directed by another award-winner (John Schlesinger), featuring a return to Major's humble childhood haunts in Brixton, South London. But this time the Tories and their media allies were ready to take revenge for Wobbly Thursday by giving Kinnock a serious whacking. Voters' judgements on the competence of party leaders were necessarily *relative* – even a leader of proven incompetence would come out well in the polls if her or his main rival was judged to be utterly hopeless. While the official Conservative line, as in 1987, was to take on Labour's policies – which meant distorting their tax policies, rather than lampooning their approach to defence issues as they had done in 1987 – the Tory tabloids unleashed all of their venom on Kinnock, to reinforce pre-existing impressions that he was not 'prime ministerial'. Predictably the *Sun* took the lead. On the morning of the election (9 April 1992) the newspaper's front page featured a picture of Kinnock, not looking at his most 'prime ministerial', superimposed on a light bulb. The contrived, unamusing but nevertheless striking tableau was partially explained by the headline:

'If Kinnock wins today will the last person to leave Britain please turn out the lights.'

After the election, the *Sun* bragged that its character assassination of Kinnock had swung the election in favour of the Conservatives. In reality, right-wing newspapers had been doing their best to undermine Kinnock's claims to 'governing competence' in all of their political coverage since he became leader in 1983; and in 1992 Kinnock had inadvertently lent support to their efforts by indulging in premature celebrations at Labour's eve of conference rally.[54] At the time, Conservative strategists downplayed the impact of their media attack dogs, attributing the 1992 victory to their own skilful tactics (Butler and Kavanagh, 1992, 255). In his retrospective account Major himself made no mention of the press campaign, insisting that Kinnock had alienated voters through his unaided efforts, and that the government's perceived competence on the economy and other issues had been decisive. Shedding crocodile tears for his defeated rival, Major merely conceded that 'Neil was a more forceful leader than the Tory Party or the press ever acknowledged' (Major, 1999, 303, 307). Had Major not been wearing the blinkers of partisanship even when writing his memoirs, he might have reassessed the role of the right-wing press in the 1992 campaign. Within a few months of the election he had replaced the ex-Labour leader as the *Sun*'s punchbag of choice. Now that he was the victim rather than the beneficiary, his estimate of press influence changed dramatically: the daily press attacks 'ripped into my premiership, damaged the Conservative Party and came close to destroying the government', he lamented (Major, 1999, 360).

Whether or not it was the *Sun* 'Wot Won it', as its front page declared the day after the election, in 1992 both major parties had run 'presidential' campaigns, and the most widely read newspapers were doing the same thing, even if their preferred game was 'Trash your rival.' Broadcast media, bound by rules of impartiality, were compelled to follow an agenda set by the press and the parties rather than keeping the focus of debate on issues. Thus, whatever survey respondents might report about their reasons for voting in 1992, the people who were not affected significantly by impressions of the party leaders in that general election can only have been a tiny minority of media-shunning mavericks.

On the face of it, between 1992 and 1997 the main parties chose divergent paths. Kinnock's successor, his Shadow Chancellor John

Smith, was a serious politician, whose honest presentation of Labour's 1992 tax policies had provoked a crude but nevertheless effective Tory counterattack. In one respect, Smith was fortunate in that the obsessive focus on Kinnock in the election campaign meant that he was not pilloried as the chief architect of defeat, and he won almost unanimous support in the subsequent Labour leadership contest. However, the strains of leadership proved too taxing for his fragile health. After his death in May 1994, Labour faced a choice between a candidate of considerable substance, who nevertheless could not be guaranteed to attract 'floating voters' given his deep Labour roots and relative lack of charisma – and Tony Blair, whose commitment to Labour seemed (and was) the product of biographical accident more than conviction, but who was ideally suited to an era of 'presidential' electioneering. The preference of the party's image-makers was predictable, and instantaneous. Their only problem was to persuade Gordon Brown that, if he chose to contest the leadership against Blair, they would somehow cancel each other out and let an unelectable 'Old Labour' dinosaur seize the crown. The idea that, whoever stood in the 1994 leadership contest, the winner would be someone other than Brown or Blair was even more implausible than the myth that Thatcher had been toppled by a Cabinet plot. The fact that Brown allowed himself to swallow the story suggests that, on grounds of gullibility at least, Blair's advocates might have made the right choice after all.

Under Blair, Labour embarked on the process of removing any distinctive (i.e. potentially vote-losing) policy positions; the acceptance of these changes by the success-starved rank and file effectively disproved the idea that a candidate who revealed a bias towards working-class interests could possibly have beaten Blair or Brown. By sharp contrast, between 1992 and 1997 the Tories transformed themselves into a party which was fixated on a single issue – Europe. Thus while Labour was doing too much to make itself 'electable', its chief rival was straining every sinew to turn off the average voter and to undermine its own leader, whose struggles against Eurosceptics made Kinnock's battle to purge Labour 'militants' look like a walk in the park. Nevertheless, the same 'presidential' impulse was at play. Unfortunately for the Conservatives, in their psychological meltdown after 1992 they had become a discordant tribute act to a presidential candidate who could no longer run for the highest office, since in

1992 Margaret Thatcher had accepted a life peerage from John Major's unworthy hands.

By the time of the 1997 general election, it seemed unlikely that the Conservatives would want to copy the presidential blueprint of 1992. Yet the party's manifesto still carried a picture of the long-suffering Major on its front cover, albeit in a format which gave more prominence to the uninspired and self-evidently misleading slogan, 'You can only be sure with the Conservatives.' Skilled photographers had managed to make the Prime Minister forget his manifold problems, including the certainty of electoral defeat, and to smile for the camera. In an advertising campaign the previous year the Conservatives had tried to discredit Blair by superimposing demonic eyes on a picture of him grinning inanely. In an interesting reflection of the public relations industry of the time, this was acclaimed by *Campaign* magazine, and condemned by the Advertising Standards Agency. On its target audience of voters it had nugatory effects. Tony Blair's real face, sporting a serious but optimistic expression, dominated the cover of the Labour manifesto. On the basis of the pictures alone, it was almost embarrassingly easy to pick the likely winner; and during the campaign itself Major's engaging smile was rarely on display.

Things can only get better?

Blair's victory speech, in which he promised to 'govern as New Labour', was widely interpreted as an attempt to dampen the hopes of long-suffering party members who imagined that he would use his bloated parliamentary majority to reverse key Thatcherite policies. The phrase also implied that a party which had been forged into an election-winning machine would retain that ethos – that is, it would evaluate its performance against indicators of popularity, as if its first term in government would be an elongated re-election campaign. If the diaries of New Labour operatives are reliable – which in this respect they most probably are – opinion polls were always awaited with trepidation. The potential for this attitude to spill over into the policy-making process was obvious. Ideas which seemed likely to produce almost instantaneous results were sure to be preferred to suggestions which might take years or even decades to fructify. Since a promising idea might not work out in practice – either because it was 'too clever by half', or because the hollowed-out state machinery was unable to realize its practical potential – there was a clear temptation for New Labour ministers to regard policy *announcements* as the most important part of their remit. This tendency was sure to be reinforced by special advisers, whose role was to boost their employers' public profiles.

Blair himself had been doubtful of the 1997 result until the first constituency declaration. When it was clear that his party had secured a landslide, for understandable reasons he was euphoric. But a moment's reflection would have made him wish that the electorate had been less emphatic in its rejection of the Tories. Even if it won more individual votes in future – and there was scope for improvement here, since Labour fell short of the overall number secured by the Conservatives in 1992, while its proportion of support was just over 43 per cent, almost identical to its share when it lost in 1970 – it was unlikely that the party could emulate, let alone exceed, its overall parliamentary majority (179 seats).

A more reflective Blair might have wondered if his attempts to woo Rupert Murdoch had been counterproductive. The Australian-born American citizen had bided his time, until it became obvious that his newspapers would look ridiculous if they continued to back the Tories. As soon as Major named the date for the 1997 election the *Sun* announced that it would be switching its allegiance. But it endorsed Blair, rather than the Labour Party; and its special relationship with the Prime-Minister-in-waiting was emphasized by a photograph of a beaming Blair, sitting in his kitchen with a mock-up of that day's newspaper. The copy Blair held was open, and one can only hope that his moral sense, composed as it was of a unique blend of Christianity, political correctness and superficial knowledge of youth culture, was not offended by a glimpse of the *Sun*'s infamous Page 3. The newspaper, its editor Stuart Higgins explained, considered that 'Mr Blair has all the qualities of leadership required to take this great country forward. The Tories are tired, divided and need a good rest to regroup.'[55] Taken literally, this meant that the country should vote for a different *individual* because the opposing *party* had run out of steam. If their editor was in such a state of confusion about the nature of the British political system, his readers could be forgiven for thinking that they were voting for a Prime Minister rather than constituency candidates.

Stuart Higgins had been too kind to the Conservatives, presumably in the expectation that the *Sun*'s owner might want to switch back to them in the near future. Instead of 'a good rest', the party required a long lie-down in a darkened room. In July 1995 John Major had been challenged for the party leadership by the unelectable, allegedly Vulcan-like John Redwood, who nevertheless adopted as his campaign slogan 'No change, no chance'. Only one Conservative-supporting newspaper, the *Daily Express*, voiced support for Major. Redwood's campaign manager issued a leaflet headed, 'Save Your Seat, Save Your Party, and Save Your Country.' This was a telling order of priorities, which also took it for granted that MPs understood their personal electoral fortunes to depend on the identity of the leader, rather than their party affiliation or record of service to their constituents. After fending off Redwood's extra-terrestrial challenge, Major was granted an audience with Murdoch. The British Prime Minister was warned in advance that he might not be allowed more than half an hour to plead his case, because the objectionable Antipodean was a very busy man.[56]

As we have seen, Major was hyper-sensitive to media criticism, and his willingness to subject himself (unsuccessfully) to this demeaning political speed-dating could be regarded as a reflection of his personal vulnerability. Yet his rival, Blair, had already endured a similar going-over by Murdoch. Thus whichever of the pair emerged as the 'winner' of the 1997 general election, the result from Murdoch's point of view would be the same: he would still enjoy the privileged access to Downing Street which he had earned by his previous services to the Conservative Party, and in any case could be confident that the next government would continue Major's 'Thatcherism with a human face'. If Thatcher had been opposite the spot on the roulette wheel at the right time, Britain's politicians had ensured that Murdoch would win wherever the ball came to rest.

By the time that Blair himself was persuaded to 'rest and regroup' in 2007 he had learned to regret his initial cultivation of the media. However, in the 2005 general election he was let off relatively lightly by the press; the *Sun* thought that Blair deserved one last chance, and not even the *Independent*, which Blair despised because of its opposition to the war on Iraq, came out for the Liberal Democrats without reservations (Bartle, 2006, 140). While the Conservatives had quickly disposed of Anthony Eden after Suez for his own sake as well as the country's, Labour allowed Blair to stay in office because he was still seen as a vote-winner, thanks to the limited electoral salience of foreign policy issues. In 2001 he had led his Tory rival William Hague by almost forty points as preferred Prime Minister. Despite the sharp decline in his ratings once voters had registered the extent of his miscalculation over Iraq, he could still rely on the Conservatives to choose leaders whose appeal barely extended beyond 'core' supporters. At the time of the 2005 general election, he was preferred to the Tory leader Michael Howard by around twenty points.

When he was finally allowed to take over from Blair, Gordon Brown had been socialized into a style of politics which he would have viewed with considerable distaste when he was first elected in 1983. As we have seen, whatever his private views, Brown was complicit in the worst excesses of New Labour, employing spin doctors who made even Alastair Campbell look like Richard Dimbleby. Once again, there was an instructive parallel between New Labour and the career of Anthony Eden. The latter took over in circumstances which were similar to those which confronted Brown in 2007; he had been kept waiting for too long, had not emerged after a leadership election, and was naturally tempted to secure some kind of 'mandate' from the public. The difference was that Eden succeeded Winston Churchill in the latter stages of the Parliament which had been elected in October 1951, while Blair had hung on for just two years after receiving his (reduced) majority in May 2005.

Brown, in short, was faced with a choice between governing with a Parliament which had been elected when Blair was still regarded as an electoral asset, and calling a 'snap' election whose only rationale was his desire to win a personal endorsement. Ultimately Brown decided against the latter step, but not, apparently, because of distaste for its 'presidential' implications; rather, like Callaghan in 1978 he considered that the polling evidence was inconclusive. However, the important point for the purpose of this chapter is that Brown was very sorely tempted. While he hesitated, party strategists geared up for a campaign which would cash in on his short-lived personal popularity, with posters which advertised the Prime Minister as 'Not flash, just Gordon'. At a time when postmodernism was still fashionable in academic circles, a 'presidential' campaign focusing on the *un*presidential qualities of a party leader looked like life imitating theory.

The advent of leader debates

Brown was acutely aware that he would be the first New Labour leader to face a media-friendly electoral opponent. On the face of it, David Cameron had every reason to run a presidential campaign, since he was more popular than Brown – overwhelmingly so, in the immediate aftermath of the 2009 expenses scandal – and was certainly an electoral asset for the Conservatives. Nevertheless, Cameron was rightly cautious. Although he allowed his image to appear on billboard posters – inviting ridicule from inventive internet users – the 2010 Conservative manifesto bore no trace of his unthreatening visage. This followed the examples of Hague (2001) and Howard (2005), but for less obvious reasons. Presumably it was felt that although Cameron had posed as a 'modernizer' in the Blair mode, he had signally failed to transform his party between 2005 and 2010; indeed, while in 1987 Kinnock could be showcased because he had taken the essential first steps to change Labour, in the circumstances of 2010 Cameron was a leader who had been swept along by events – the financial crisis which began in 2007, and the expenses scandal during which, at best, he showed himself to be more adept than Brown at damage limitation.

In any event, the 2010 general election was bound to be a 'presidential' contest because, at long last, the party leaders could find no plausible pretext for avoiding televised debates. While many commentators complained that the three encounters overshadowed the rest of the 2010 campaign, arguably this was a healthy development: it meant that, instead of judging the relative competence of party leaders through the distorting lens of the press and party-sponsored propaganda, voters could actually judge for themselves. However, the first debate produced the conclusion which the two main parties had been desperate to avoid since they first became aware of electoral volatility: a majority of viewers preferred the leader of the third party, Nick Clegg, to either Cameron or Brown. This was understandable, not simply because Clegg, unlike his rivals, directed his responses towards the camera, but also because he could speak more honestly. After all, the Liberal Democrats had no governmental failures to explain away, and they had not been contaminated by the techniques of spin and deceit which now came naturally to their rivals.

However, the Liberal Democrats were not entirely innocent. Indeed, they had begun to practise presidential politics with a ruthlessness which put their major rivals to shame. In January 2006 the party leader, Charles Kennedy, who had pushed the Lib Dem revival as far as it could go under the first-past-the-post system and had taken a principled stand against the Iraq War, was shoved aside because of a drinking problem which, allegedly, had impaired his performance during the 2005 general election. Whether or not Kennedy's habits really undermined his effectiveness as party leader, his removal was very welcome to those Liberal Democrats who disagreed with his strategy of appealing to disaffected Labour voters; in their view, the party should be vying for the votes of Conservatives who had liked Thatcher's economic policies but recoiled from her 'reactionary' views on social questions. Getting rid of Kennedy was a crucial manoeuvre for Liberal Democrats who wanted their party to swing to the right, but they could not cement their coup until they had disposed of Kennedy's natural successor, Menzies Campbell, who focused on foreign policy rather than domestic matters. Unfortunately for Campbell, in addition to his lack of Thatcherite intoxication he was in his mid-sixties and his best televisual days were behind him. After Brown 'bottled' a possible general election in October 2007 the Liberal Democrats felt that it would be safe to jettison Campbell. In the ensuing leadership contest there could only be one winner – Nick Clegg, who could present himself as a political and physical clone of David Cameron without the baggage of an unpopular party.

The spasm of 'Cleggmania' generated by Britain's first ever televised leaders' debate did not translate into additional seats for the Liberal Democrats; indeed, the party lost five constituencies compared to its performance in 2005 under the allegedly inebriated Charles Kennedy. In part, this was because Cameron polished his performances in the next two televised encounters; in addition, the Tory press (now back to its full 1980s strength, the *Sun* having ditched Brown within hours of his speech to the 2009 Labour conference) performed its usual function, turning its full fire on Clegg until election day. But the disappointing Liberal Democrat result also suggested that the debates were over-hyped in terms of their likely impact on voters. The audience for the first debate might have liked the idea of Clegg becoming Prime Minister, but knew this was very unlikely to happen and that the real contest was between Cameron and Brown. This was reflected in polling for the best person to be Prime Minister, which showed Cameron narrowly ahead of Brown, with Clegg still trailing despite an improvement over the course of the campaign.[57]

If, as seemed quite possible in the days after the 2010 election, Cameron had been unable to assemble a coalition government, his position as Conservative leader would have been precarious, perhaps untenable. As it was, the deal with the Liberal Democrats left him in what should have been a very strong political position. First, despite his below-par performance in the first leader debate, he had been an electoral asset to his party. Second, his public offer of a 'big, open and comprehensive' deal with the Liberal Democrats was pitch-perfect, making it very difficult for his potential partners to play hard to get, let alone to refuse his advances. Thus Cameron could argue that he had dragged his party into a position which made a deal possible, and had then sealed it. Finally, the fact that the leaders of the Conservatives and the Liberal Democrats had been converging in ideological terms since the putsch against Kennedy – Thatcherite in economic matters, unfettered in moral respects by old-fashioned prejudices – meant that this Cabinet would be far more united than any government since at least 1992; and the two parties had received a combined vote share of almost 60 per cent.

The problem for Cameron can be explained by comparison with the electoral record of his supposed exemplar, Tony Blair. After four consecutive election defeats for his party, Blair had carried Labour to a crushing victory in 1997. Cameron, so it seemed to many Tory MPs, had promised to exercise the same magic and bring an end to thirteen years of hurt for his party. Actually he had succeeded ahead of Blair's schedule since the Conservatives had only lost three elections in a row before 2010. But unlike Labour, Cameron's party thought it was unnatural to be out of office for any period of time, let alone thirteen years. Once the euphoria of removing Labour wore off, Conservative members began to reassess Cameron's achievement and found it wanting. Thus while Cameron hoped to utilize the authority of his office and the alliance with the Liberal Democrats to revive his project of Conservative 'modernization', by forcing through legislation on same-sex marriage and maintaining the level of spending on overseas aid, members of his own parliamentary party lost no time in exploiting the obvious issue – 'Europe' – which would cut him down to size.

One of the first pieces of legislation passed by Cameron's coalition was the Fixed-Term Parliaments Act (2011). On the face of it, this measure removed the most potent weapon from any Prime Minister's armoury, by making it impossible to call an election without Parliament's consent (see chapter 1). Henceforth, an election would take place five years after the previous one, unless two-thirds of MPs (not just those present and voting) endorsed a motion to dissolve Parliament, or if a government was defeated by a simple majority in a vote of confidence and no alternative administration could be formed. It was apparent from the outset that the terms of the Act could be circumvented; but it was not passed as a considered measure of constitutional reform. Rather, it was part of the coalition deal, intended to reassure the Liberal Democrats that their Conservative partners would not call an election at a moment which was propitious for them but disastrous for Clegg and co. The government was not very interested in the effect it might have under different circumstances.

Cameron kept to this part of his agreement with the Liberal Democrats, and his coalition duly served its full term. However, in March 2015 he gave an interview in which – accidentally on purpose – he revealed that he would not fight a third general election as Conservative leader. There was a very recent precedent for Cameron's declaration. At the 2004 Labour Party conference Tony Blair had stated that he would serve one more full term as Prime Minister but not lead his party into a fourth general election. Blair knew his popularity was fading and his health was indifferent (Blair, 2010, 508–10). He was deliberately vague about his proposed schedule, but he probably intended to serve for at least three more years, leaving time for a successor (hopefully not Gordon Brown) to bed in before asking the Queen to dissolve Parliament. In 2015 Cameron, by contrast, was much more popular than the Labour leader, Ed Miliband, and had little fear of 'Cleggmania' this time round. His health seemed not to have been affected by his time at No. 10.

At the time of the interview, some commentators and Opposition MPs accused Cameron of making the arrogant assumption that his party would win the forthcoming election. In fact, just like Blair in 2004 Cameron had emphasized the obvious fact that his plan was conditional on his party staying in office. The big difference was the Fixed-Term Parliaments Act, which made a nonsense of his stated aspiration of serving a 'full term'. Under any likely scenario, this meant that he intended to serve for almost five years before handing over the reins to someone who would have to start fighting the election even before she or he could move into Downing Street. Since all Prime Ministers enjoy some kind of honeymoon after taking office, the idea that Opposition parties would lend the necessary support for a 'snap' election any earlier than this was deeply implausible. Thus Cameron can only have meant that he would stand down long before he had served a 'full term'.

Evidently the Prime Minister had not thought things through very carefully, but a man with his extensive public relations training was most unlikely to say anything significant without making *some* kind of calculation. Rather than taking another election win for granted, the only rational reason for revealing his little secret was a fear that the Conservatives might *lose* the election – not because of Labour or the Liberal Democrats, but because of the appeal to grassroots Conservatives of the UKIP leader Nigel Farage, whose populism had already encouraged the defection of two Tory MPs. Farage's fan base extended beyond disillusioned Conservatives, but before the 2015 general election Cameron could only be certain of UKIP's potential to wreak havoc within his own ranks. He was well aware that many habitual supporters of his emphatically *un*modernized party might consider lending a vote to Farage and UKIP, if they had reason to suspect that Cameron would interpret an election win as an invitation to 'go on and on', Thatcher-style, despite his objectionable ambivalence towards 'Europe' and his 'unconservative' acceptance of modern life. In short, whereas before Thatcher it could be argued that party leaders were secondary factors in general elections, owing much of their public approval to long-term identification with their parties, by 2015 it was being assumed in the highest quarters that even people who felt a very strong affiliation to a party could have their loyalty over-ridden by their dislike for a particular leader.

It is unlikely that Cameron's announcement made much difference to the 2015 result, which he regarded as a personal vindication which would help him not just to secure concessions from the EU, but to enhance his credentials when he asked British voters to support 'Remain' in the referendum he had promised back in 2013. Presumably his real game plan was to step down as soon as that vote had been won, since the reaction from the Tory grassroots would have been horrible to behold; if his advocacy had helped 'Remain' to win, there might even have been demands for a vote of no confidence in his leadership. Sensing that the tide would never be more favourable, Cameron decided to get the referendum out of the way as soon as possible after the election. The negotiations with European partners were less fruitful than he had hoped, but he still felt confident of his persuasive powers.

At this point a comparison with the context of Britain's previous 'European' referendum (1975) is helpful. In those days, 'partisan alignment', chiefly based on socio-economic factors, still meant something. However, hard-line members of both of the leading parties had their own reasons for voting against continued EEC membership; Tories because they deplored the infringement of British 'sovereignty', and Labour supporters because they could be persuaded that staying in the EEC would consign the country to the control of a 'capitalist club', as well as constituting a 'betrayal' of the Commonwealth which gave their party its sense of post-imperial mission. Since their core supporters were probably beyond rational persuasion, the party leaders of 1975 (Wilson and Thatcher) signalled that they were in favour of continued membership but decided not to put their reputations on the line, leaving the heavy lifting to other (and eminently expendable) members of their parties – on the Conservative side, Edward Heath, and Roy Jenkins for Labour. In retrospect this co-operation across tribal divisions could have spawned a spectacular political realignment, but at the time the Social Democratic Party (SDP) was not even a gleam in Roy Jenkins' eye. In 1975 the main party leaders could still feel fairly sure that the referendum would not seriously disrupt the existing patterns of party support whenever the next election was held. In those distant days they could also depend on the mainstream media to exaggerate both the benefits of continued membership and the dangers of leaving; and at that time the BBC felt under no particular pressure to report Europhobic sentiments in an 'impartial' way, not least because every newspaper except the Communist *Morning Star* was humming the same pro-European tune.

In 2016, the situation was radically different. The press was heavily biased against 'Remain'; and, since it had to report 'what the papers say' whatever they happened to be saying, the BBC had no choice but to rehearse the anti-European fulminations of the tabloids as if they were credible arguments. Pro-Remain politicians like George Osborne felt that they had no alternative but to respond in kind, presenting 'worst-case' predictions of the impact of 'Brexit' as if they were inevitabilities. The Remain campaigners of 1975 could summon a seemingly inexhaustible stream of celebrities – entertainers and sporting stars – to testify to the benefits of EEC membership, whatever they might really have thought (Garnett, 2007, 44–5). One result of press hostility towards the EU in 2016 was that such 'icons' were far more reticent. Remainers hoped to benefit from the public support of businesspeople, economists and world leaders including the Governor of the Bank of England and President Obama, but these messages failed to 'cut through' to the public, since, in the sneering words of the Brexiteer Michael Gove, 'people in this country have had enough of experts'.

David Cameron had been wounded when his supposed friends Gove and Boris Johnson had joined the 'Leave' campaign. This was a surprising lapse of judgement, since the Prime Minister already had good reason to know that these individuals were never likely to allow their careers to be blighted by an excess of personal loyalty. Presumably Cameron was depressed by their defections because they were an early warning of his own miscalculation. In the 2015 general election, opportunists within the Cabinet had rallied behind Cameron because, on this occasion at least, they were 'all in this together' – they wanted an overall Conservative majority, especially since they knew they could have a stab at the leadership at some point within the next five years. Now Cameron had to face up to the fact that in declaring his intention to stand down at some point in the next five years he had precipitated a prolonged leadership contest, of which the referendum campaign would form an integral and potentially decisive part. People like Gove and Johnson had no need of any 'experts' to tell them that the balance of personal advantage lay with commitment to the 'Leave' campaign, since the final votes in the leadership election would be cast by grassroots Conservatives who would never have been reconciled to a 'Remain' victory, however decisive. As the referendum approached, like Rupert Murdoch in 1997, Gove and Johnson could paraphrase ABBA and expect to feel like they had won even if they lost.

This element of tactical calculation was perhaps the greatest contrast between the referendums of 1975 and 2016, though it attracted little public comment. In the first referendum, the most prominent opponents of continued membership could have been predicted long before the campaign began; Tony Benn, Enoch Powell and Michael

Foot could have done no other, even if their positions were not entirely free from personal considerations. Senior ministers, like Wilson and Callaghan, were certainly not 'Eurofanatics', and had happily played party games with the issue in the past. For that reason, it was difficult to doubt that their position in the 1975 referendum arose from careful considerations of the national interest. In the very different context of 2016 voters could not be confident that *any* of the leading campaigners (apart from Farage) really meant what they said; after all, Cameron himself had flaunted his hostility towards the EU during his bid for the Conservative leadership in 2005. Most voters were confident that the Labour leader, Jeremy Corbyn, was *not* sincere when he delivered half-hearted endorsements of continued EU membership, since his record of Euroscepticism made even Thatcher look like Jacques Delors.

If the referendum campaign provides the most eloquent (if unquantifiable) testimony to a decline in the quality and integrity of leading politicians over the years covered in this book, the preceding discussion suggests some explanations. The leading figures in the 'Remain' campaign, Cameron and Osborne, had both been special advisers. Ranged against them were two journalists – Boris Johnson (*Spectator*, *Daily Telegraph*) and Gove (*The Times*) – and a person (Farage) who had never won a parliamentary seat, despite four attempts beginning at Eastleigh in 1994 when his entrancing personality had attracted less than 2 per cent of the votes. Whatever their abilities, even the most besotted admirer of those five individuals would be hard-pressed to draw a realistic comparison between them and Heath, Thatcher, Wilson, Benn and Powell. Although it might be unfair to dismiss them as fair-weather politicians, there were good reasons to suspect that most of them were more adept at causing crises than curing them. Whatever their innate qualities, they lacked the breadth of experience and seasoned judgement which British voters had come to expect (and indeed taken for granted) in previous generations of politicians.

This deficiency might have been corrected in 2016 by 'elder statespeople', who could confront voters with the enormity of the decision they were being invited to make; but these were conspicuously absent. Between the 1975 referendum and Margaret Thatcher's rise to the premiership, Enoch Powell had written that 'All political lives, unless they are cut off at midstream at some happy juncture, end in failure' (Powell, 1977, 151). However, before 1979, people whose careers had closed under a cloud still seemed capable of winning a respectful hearing in unexpected quarters; for example, when in November 1985 Harold Macmillan compared Thatcher's privatization policy to 'selling off the family silver' he struck a chord with an audience which had never warmed to his prime ministerial catchphrases, and before Edward Heath's death in 2005 many trade unionists had repented of their embittered opposition to his policies on industrial relations. During the 2016 referendum few voters were interested in the utterances of John Major or Tony Blair. Thanks to Black Wednesday and the Iraq War they were utterly discredited, along with almost all of the politicians who had served in their governments, whichever side of the referendum debate they happened to favour. The period between 1992 and 2007, it seemed, had produced a 'lost generation' of politicians who had no lasting achievements to lend credibility to their words, and had opted for lucrative careers as globe-trotting 'keynote' speech-makers at the first opportunity. Instead, the voices from the past which gained some traction were those of the Thatcher years. Lords Heseltine and Lawson were on different sides, the latter no doubt regretting the part which 'Europe' had played in his 1989 resignation from the Thatcher Government. The poison which had been injected into the Conservative Party by Thatcher's enforced departure in 1990 is illustrated by the fact that Lawson had supported Heseltine's leadership bid back in those days when the issue was merely bitterly divisive, rather than toxic. Now these old-timers were at daggers drawn, and their weapons were still sharp.

When Theresa May emerged as party leader and Prime Minister from the all-in Conservative wrestling match triggered by Brexit, it seemed as if a typically 'British' solution had been found. Unlike her high-profile opponents, May boasted the CV of a politician from a bygone age, having been a long-serving local councillor before winning a parliamentary seat. Although no senior minister could be entirely free from self-promoting considerations in the referendum campaign – and the Cameron camp had strongly suspected that May was positioning herself for a leadership bid – she kept a low profile chiefly because she was genuinely torn between 'Leave' and 'Remain'. As such, when more flamboyant leadership rivals effectively baulked their own chances and she emerged as Prime Minister in July 2016, there was reason to hope that she would devote her efforts to finding a way to unite a divided country.

However, as we have seen, May was under the spell of special advisers whose interpretation of 'One Nation Conservatism' excluded anyone who continued to believe in the case for 'Remain' which May herself had supported. Thwarted by Parliament and the courts, May's only recourse was to ask the electorate to replace the current House of Commons with a more compliant body, in direct contradiction of her previous refusal to contemplate a snap election. Bizarrely, when asked during the campaign to recollect the naughtiest thing she had ever done, May confessed that in her childhood she had run through a field of wheat, to the annoyance of the local farmer. For May, personal and political morality were clearly very different things; it did not occur to her that the 'hostile environment' towards immigrants which she had promoted as Home Secretary might have been more culpable than the infliction of superficial damage on a cereal crop.

On Tuesday 18 April 2017, May called a press conference outside No. 10 without previously explaining its purpose. Holding an election now, she told the assembled journalists, would provide the country with 'certainty and security' and prevent her political opponents from 'game-playing' over Brexit. In the world of Theresa May, her own party could not be guilty of playing games, even though the early election was deemed necessary because a contest in June 2020 would not have suited Tory interests. May announced the election as if there was no such thing as the Fixed-Term Parliaments Act. Her judgement in this isolated instance was correct because the Opposition parties capitulated, passing the necessary motion by 522 votes to 13. Just in case, the government had prepared a one-line motion which would have bypassed the terms of the Act, requiring only a simple majority rather than the formal requirement of a two-thirds majority of all MPs.

The scene was set for the most astonishing British general election campaign since the country adopted universal suffrage. Conservative publicity informed voters that local candidates were standing on behalf of Theresa May; the party's name was mentioned, but never highlighted in case it reactivated unhelpful memories. Even Tory ministers were sent an email stressing the importance of maximizing support for 'Theresa May and the Conservatives' (Shipman, 2017, 196). The *Daily Mail*, fresh from its tasteful depiction of senior judges as 'Enemies of the People', adorned its front page with a portrait of May and the headline 'Crush the Saboteurs'. In fact, the newspaper had sabotaged its own cause by selecting a picture of May looking more sinister than 'stable', and using divisive rhetoric which sharply contradicted the Prime Minister's assertion that the country was aching to unite behind her personal 'Brexit' vision.

Even Tory strategists were divided, between those (like the Australian guru Sir Lynton Crosby) who thought that they should secure the biggest possible 'mandate' by focusing on Brexit as well as May, and those (like the special advisers Timothy and Hill) who wanted to look beyond Brexit and exploit the election as a means of winning approval for radical reforms, notably in the funding of adult social care. The mixed messages were certainly unhelpful, but both strategies were scuppered by their common factor – May herself. Under any kind of political system, a 'presidential' campaign is unlikely to prosper when the candidate is a poor communicator. The Prime Minister drew attention to her own weakness in this respect by refusing to take part in any televised leader debate – not exactly the kind of approach expected of someone who is ready and able to 'crush the saboteurs' in opposing parties.

The other points of contention between May's advisers illustrate their failure to appreciate the nature and importance of 'valence voting'. When she asserted that Britons were coming together over Brexit, May was trying to present this as a 'valence' issue – that is, whatever people had thought before the referendum, they were now generally agreed that the national interest lay in the negotiation of satisfactory terms of withdrawal. However, May's insistence on a 'hard' Brexit had ensured that it was still a 'position' issue, on which voters could diverge sharply. If she had adopted a more conciliatory approach during the campaign she could have limited the damage to some extent, but this was far beyond the political skills of the tribal saboteur-slayer. Equally, reform of adult social care was potentially a valence issue – everyone with any knowledge of the subject knew that change was needed. However, Timothy's proposals were controversial, not least among ageing Conservative supporters who thought they would be forced to pay more and have to sell their homes. The threat of a 'dementia tax' provoked a furious backlash, and May had no alternative but to perform an inelegant mid-campaign U-turn.

Once it became clear that May's expected landslide had subsided into a hung Parliament, the Prime Minister stomped through the fields of truth once again, pretending that her party had enjoyed a long and harmonious relationship with the Democratic Unionist Party (DUP), whose qualified parliamentary support she had secured at considerable cost to the British taxpayer, and without thinking of the likely implications for the politics of Northern Ireland. Initially she also failed to express sympathy for Conservative candidates who had lost their seats thanks to the leader-centric strategy. May's hapless performance had ensured too that the Labour Opposition would be left with inadequate leadership; she had made Jeremy Corbyn look like a Prime Minister in waiting even to people outside his 'Momentum' movement. Despite everything, however, if the voters had really been asked to choose a President in 2017 May would have won. She was still preferred as Prime Minister, even after her lamentable response to the post-election Grenfell Tower disaster exposed her inability to exhibit the level of empathy which the British public now demanded from its leaders.[58]

While such findings proved that Labour could never come close to winning a general election under Corbyn, moderates in his party had already tried to unseat him and their chances of success were now even more remote. By contrast, the Conservatives had finished their flirtation with unelectable leaders; Iain Duncan Smith's frequent media appearances after his resignation from the Cabinet in March 2016 were a sufficient reminder of the dark days of 2001–3. May's manoeuvres had kept her in office, but this was not a case of someone surviving in order to fight another day. George Osborne, now editor of the *Evening Standard*, was somewhat indelicate when he referred to May as 'a dead woman walking', but in political terms he was not overstating her situation.[59] Among its other salutary effects, the snap election of 2017 had shown that a Prime Minister without proven or potential electoral appeal holds the position on sufferance.

The Conservatives had clearly blundered in 2017 by basing their campaign on the personal appeal of Theresa May. But what if they had followed the right strategy, but with the wrong leader? After the 2017 debacle many Conservatives eagerly anticipated a re-match with Corbyn's Labour, only this time under a champion who had already twice emerged victorious from 'presidential' contests. By happy coincidence a former Mayor of London was available, and needed little persuasion to answer the party's call in its time of need.

Conclusion: the Johnson premiership

The evidence of the previous chapter suggests that, effectively, Britain now has 'presidential' electoral politics; even the selection of the candidates (aka party leaders) increasingly resembles US primaries, with party supporters able to exercise important influence on payment of a nominal membership fee. As we have seen, this development has been fostered by a number of factors which are impossible to measure independently and are mutually reinforcing, including media practices and demographic changes which have eroded the much-vaunted stability of the British electorate.

All of the roles studied in this book depend crucially on the perceived ability of the Prime Minister to lead her or his party to victory in the next election. The obvious way to illustrate the effect of the electoral role on other functions expected of the Prime Minister is to assess the difficulties experienced by an incumbent who is perceived to be a liability. Whatever the size of the current parliamentary majority, an unpopular Prime Minister will find it more difficult to secure the loyalty of MPs (who in recent decades have shown an increasing propensity to rebel in any circumstances). The task of speaking to the party and the country is much more demanding for a leader who is trailing in opinion polls – Theresa May's conference speech of 2017 would have been an ordeal anyway, without the additional handicaps of a nagging cough, a poorly constructed stage set and an unfriendly prankster

(Seldon and Newell, 2019, 324–9). A popular Prime Minister speaks to and for the country; a struggling premier is forced to *appeal* to it. Loss of authority at home cannot be concealed from other world leaders, undermining credibility in international fora. An apparent vote-loser, like John Major after Black Wednesday, will have to curtail any policy-making ambitions and will find it difficult to maintain discipline among departmental ministers with personal agendas to pursue, let alone to dismiss notorious offenders.

None of this, it might be thought, is either new or surprising: there is bound to be a seepage of support and confidence from any leader who seems wounded beyond recovery. However, the increasing focus on the Prime Minister as an electoral talisman means that *popular* incumbents arguably face even greater pressures and constraints. Once Prime Ministers have lost their electoral gloss, public expectations are lowered to a commensurable extent; but a popular Prime Minister is expected to *succeed* continuously in all the areas covered by this book. Yet 'success' becomes increasingly elusive as the execution of the Prime Minister's various roles turn from 'spin' to substance. Indeed, arguably the more that a Prime Minister and her or his aides create the impression of success, the sharper the contrast will be when political expectations are compared to policy outcomes.

Thus Prime Ministers now face an improbable and inherently self-defeating task, even at the best of times. Domestic developments have made them more *prominent* in politics than ever before. However, this has coincided with a diminution in the ability of all governments – but that of Britain in particular – to insulate themselves from 'abroad'. To a considerable extent this is due to another factor which no Prime Minister could prevent – 'globalization', which has reduced the capacity of governments across the world to exercise 'sovereignty' in the nineteenth-century sense. The impact of globalization has been particularly marked in Britain because of a shift in economic activity from manufacturing industry to the financial sector, leaving it unusually (if not uniquely) susceptible to developments beyond the control of its political institutions.

With hindsight, it is all too easy to argue that successive Prime Ministers could have made their lives easier by reducing public expectations, explaining to voters that the world had changed and pledging to use their best endeavours to help the country respond to new challenges.

Unfortunately this was never realistic in Britain, thanks to the enduring myths arising from its peculiar experience since 1900; a popular press which had no intention of adopting an educative role; and a fiercely adversarial political culture which encouraged Opposition leaders to take advantage of any governmental admission of weakness or failure.

Even if Britain's Prime Ministers would always have been condemned to struggle with unrealistic expectations, they could at least have taken some decisions which moderated the impact of globalization. They could have paid close attention to the emerging domestic economic patterns, preventing (for example) *excessive* dependence on any particular sector; they could have taken steps to maintain the ability of the state to withstand 'exogenous shocks'; they might even have toned down their patriotic rhetoric a bit. Any hope of progress in these respects was dashed at the beginning of our period by Margaret Thatcher, who came to office with a combination of pugilistic nationalism and free-market fervour which convinced her that Britain's problems had been *caused* by modest expectations, which she readily equated with the defeatism of 'moaning minnies'. Thanks to her, Britain led the world in its embrace of the market, emerging from the various upheavals of the 1980s with a bloated financial sector and a shrunken manufacturing base; the state was 'hollowed out' for ideological reasons; and patriotic rhetoric was toned up, particularly after the Falklands, which Thatcher viewed as a vindication of her approach to all political questions. Thatcher also raised adversarial politics to new levels, not just because her views polarized voters as well as parties, but because of the unbridled contempt that she and her media allies showed for her opponents.

Thatcher's successors have failed to repair the consequent economic, political and administrative damage. Indeed, they fall into two categories: those who made no attempt to address her legacy, and those who made matters even worse for themselves by focusing on short-term partisan priorities rather than consulting the national interest. Regrettably, the second category is more heavily populated than the first.

The Prime Minister in theory

When contemplating any political system it is natural to search for the location of power: to identify the institutions where decisions are made with a realistic expectation of promoting specified outcomes.

In 1867 Walter Bagehot exposed the illusion that Parliament's role within the British system could be understood in this sense, showing that the Cabinet was the key decision-making arena. Almost a century later, Richard Crossman argued that the Prime Minister's influence over Cabinet had become so great that it was now more appropriate to speak of prime ministerial government. Both commentators assumed that 'power', in the sense of the ability to take effectual decisions, resided *somewhere* within the British political system. It could hardly be otherwise, since in 1867 Britain administered a worldwide empire, and when Crossman was writing in the early 1960s the state had become a dominant provider of public services as well as a major economic actor.

Since the appearance of Crossman's edition of Bagehot (1963), debate over the Prime Minister's role has proceeded on the same basic assumption. Thus, for example, scholars who reject Michael Foley's idea of 'presidential' government emphasize that Prime Ministers who want to achieve policy objectives depend on the co-operation of institutions and individuals within the 'core executive'. This was a persuasive account of how a government, organized on British lines, might look if it hoped to discharge its decision-making role *effectively*; indeed, governments as a whole, including the Prime Minister, would be more, not less, able to achieve their objectives if the core executive model reflected reality. After all, according to this model, Prime Ministers would appoint ministers because of proven competence and/or substantial public respect. However, insofar as it depended on the idea that institutions and actors possessed independent resources which made them essential participants in the policy-making process, the model was difficult to square with clear evidence that Thatcher's project of reducing the scope of the state had resulted in the 'hollowing out' of Whitehall departments and the erosion of ministerial authority – whether or not the individuals concerned enjoyed the Prime Minister's special favour. The core executive approach suggests that some senior politicians would have to be consulted by the Prime Minister whenever important decisions were at issue. In reality, the diminished status of ministers means that it is even possible for the Prime Minister to take and announce decisions concerning their departments after discussions with unelected special advisers in which responsible politicians take no part.

This is not to say, of course, that such decisions will produce the anticipated results in terms of 'delivery'; and this uncertainty explains why the ability to announce initiatives, whatever their likely fate, has become so prized (and why Prime Ministers tend to cherry-pick the best ones). There has, in short, been a tendency where the Prime Minister is concerned to confuse *power*, in the sense of an ability to effect intentional change, with *prominence*. This confusion is understandable because the Prime Minister's prominence does indeed equate to 'power' over members of the 'Westminster village' and assorted attendants, such as journalists and (particularly) special advisers. But in terms of an ability to direct or even inspire desired practical effects, the Prime Minister is no more powerful than his or her ministers – that is, not powerful at all, compared to holders of the office before 1979.

In other words, the 'core executive' approach overlooked the possibility that the best term to describe the British system of government was not 'prime ministerial' or 'presidential', but *dysfunctional*. This argument is strongly supported by the fact that Anthony King and Ivor Crewe were able to produce a substantial history of governmental blunders between 1979 and the early days of the 2010–15 coalition, while noting that many other examples had been excluded for lack of space. They also reassured their readers that despite their compelling evidence 'the United Kingdom is in many ways a well-governed country. Our political leaders are seldom clowns or buffoons' (King and Crewe, 2013, x, xiv). This would have been more comforting if the authors had not qualified their claims with the words 'in many ways', and 'seldom'.

An honourable ambition?

Thus the life of a British Prime Minister – even the ones who fulfil their main role, and lead their parties to another election victory – is very far from enviable. It is at best a hand-to-mouth (or poll-to-poll) existence – an unceasing attempt to control the few things which the Prime Minister can truly influence in positive ways. In this context, it is unsurprising that Prime Ministers obsess over their performances at PMQs and party conferences, when they can persuade themselves that a little extra effort and inspiration might make a difference to their main electoral role. A cutting retort in the Commons can raise a parliamentary party's morale at the darkest of times, and a rousing speech at the conference can send delegates home with the pleasing thought that the next time they knock on a voter's door they will have something positive to say. However, within days or even hours the good effects can be blown away by a leaked memo, a personal scandal, an incipient backbench rebellion or the unexpected onset of a global economic downturn. The inflated political prominence of the Prime Minister means that such developments always reflect badly on the incumbent. This is (usually) very unfair, placing a ridiculous burden of responsibility on the Prime Minister, who relies ever more heavily on spin doctors to help evade it. No Prime Minister can ever admit to mistakes until they write their memoirs (and even then, sorry turns out to be the hardest word). While Julius Caesar employed a slave to remind him that he was mortal, Prime Ministers have become increasingly dependent on special advisers who make them feel important, less lonely and more lovable. Even Thatcher, who initially chose special advisers in the hope that they would help her to master the range of policy issues facing her government, eventually fell into this psychological trap. Since New Labour, apparently, even the special advisers need (and receive) their own special advisers to massage their egos.

Why, then, do so many politicians still hanker after 'the top job'? It is not difficult to explain why ideologues like Thatcher and Corbyn pursue office; they genuinely want to effect positive change, and their unusual mindsets allow them to imagine that this is possible. At the other extreme, Tony Blair convinced himself that he could make life better for Britons by eschewing ideology and galvanizing government to deliver public services by the most effective means (in practice, for Blair as for all Prime Ministers since 1979, the private sector). However, his confidence that he really could make a difference through 'joined-up government' reflected his lack of previous ministerial experience, and his superficial knowledge of post-war British history. In one of the few comments in his 1976 book on the premiership which have stood the test of time, Harold Wilson wrote that 'Without a sense of history, a prime minister would be blind' (Wilson, 1976, 106). One can only presume that Blair felt he had no lessons to learn from Harold Wilson.

Once he had begun to recognize the difficulties facing any Prime Minister, Blair found his *raison d'être* in popularity, followed a fairly close second by the fringe benefits associated with leadership – access to state secrets, rubbing shoulders with more powerful leaders at international summits, playing tennis with celebrities, etc. None of this equated to real *power* to make life better for British people; but evidently for Blair it was an enjoyable approximation. If Blair just about makes sense in the post-Thatcher context, in turn Blair explains Brown. In 2005 Christopher Foster wrote that the job of Prime Minister had been 'refashioned to suit only people with similar attributes' to Blair (Foster, 2005, 1). Brown could no more escape from the shadow of Blair than Major could block his ears to his ubiquitous 'back-seat driver', Margaret Thatcher. At least in his memoirs Brown enlisted himself in the very exclusive 'do as I say, not what I did' club of Prime Ministers, coming close to owning up to missed opportunities. Whatever he might have done if he, rather than Blair, had succeeded John Smith as Labour leader in 1994, by the time that Brown took office in 2007 he was too steeped in spin to have reversed the post-Thatcher trends. Certainly he would never have steeled himself to reduce his dependence on special advisers and news-managers. A measure of the change in his character wrought by the New Labour years is his conduct in November 2008, when the shadow spokesperson on immigration, Damian Green, was arrested in the course of an inquiry into the leakage of documents which caused acute embarrassment to Brown's government. Brown had been the frequent beneficiary of this kind of thing when he was in Opposition, but apparently was now prepared to see it as worthy of prosecution (Brown, 2017, 240–1). Post-Thatcherite politics had made an estimable individual behave like a self-righteous hypocrite.

But what of Cameron and May, who had the chance (indeed, a good political motive) to react against the corrupting culture of New Labour? It is interesting that, when they took their emotional departures from No. 10, they seemed most affected when they reached the inevitable bit about serving the country they loved. However, in both cases the motivation of public service was warped by allegiance to party, even when this clearly conflicted with the national interest. This kind of 'doublethink' seems deeply reprehensible, but in fact it is compulsory for any prime ministerial aspirant with a highly developed sense of public duty. If the main role of a Prime Minister is to win the support of volatile voters, short-term popularity for their parties and themselves is (almost) everything. Both Cameron and May took decisions which they would never have approved if they had remained as private individuals; yet they contrived to convince themselves that they were doing their best for Britain rather than following their job description and trying (with mixed results) to help their party's electoral chances. Even in his parting speech, Cameron was clearly anxious to make life as easy as possible for his Conservative successor rather than offering any solace to those who thought that the circumstances of 2016 demanded a non-partisan response – even a call for a government of national unity – to the referendum result.

At the time of writing (November 2020) the true significance of May's short-lived 'administration' is in danger of being obscured by the rapid pace of events and a blanket assumption that she was simply not up to the task. So it is worth reiterating that this was a person who previously had held a very significant office for six years, facing up to many tough decisions in a department often regarded as 'unfit for purpose' (see chapter 3). It can be conceded that May was confronted with the most difficult inheritance since Churchill succeeded Chamberlain in 1940. However, for our purposes this makes her subsequent decisions and declarations particularly instructive, since at moments of crisis Prime Ministers with deep knowledge of the British system can be expected to use all the resources at their disposal to produce the least-worst outcome. May's response after July 2016 was to seek personal control over the *political* system with the assistance of her devoted special advisers. The Corbyn factor might have been a decisive obstacle to the idea of enticing Labour and other parties into a 'coalition of the willing', but one suspects that May would always have tried to present the referendum result as an endorsement of her beloved Conservative Party, which had granted the country this unique opportunity to exhibit its capacity for mature deliberation. By opting for a 'hard' Brexit which few parliamentarians wanted, May was trying to cement executive control over the process of withdrawal. She imagined herself as uniquely equipped to speak to, and for, the country; she appointed ministers to senior positions while planning to exclude them from the process of making the crucial decisions; and all of this was done on the assumption that, when the time came, she would achieve the ultimate goal of any Prime Minister by winning an overwhelming electoral endorsement for her party.

Despite all this, May's sense of public duty was palpable and almost painful. The careers of all other Prime Ministers since 1979 were marked by spectacular upward leaps; May's ascent was slow (beginning as a councillor in 1986) and often obstructed. If never quite as 'strong and stable' as she was made out to be, she was undoubtedly and enduringly plucky and persevering. Her miserable fate could easily suggest that the Prime Ministers with the most honourable intentions are the ones who will suffer the most when they feel impelled to seek partisan advantage from a position which should be a rallying point for the whole nation at times of crisis. It is not an attractive prospectus – except, perhaps, for those who have never cared much for the concept of 'the national interest' unless it could be turned to their personal advantage.

'The leadership Britain deserves': Johnson at No. 10

The unpleasant and protracted downfall of Theresa May certainly did not act as a deterrent to would-be successors. The fragmentation of the Parliamentary Conservative Party, in which factions like the all-con-quering European 'Research' Group (ERG) were themselves beginning to splinter, coupled with the various mishaps suffered by leading con-tenders in 2016, encouraged obscure figures to hope that they might win against astronomical odds, like Jeremy Corbyn and Foinavon. The rational calculations which normally govern such affairs gave way to irrational optimism; although the contenders had their own solutions for 'Brexit', it is unlikely that many of them had given much thought to the crushing demands of the job for which they were vying. At one time it even looked possible that the Conservatives might choose the most interesting and able candidate, Rory Stewart, but his pragmatic stance on Brexit was too great a handicap. Within a few months of the leader-ship election Stewart had resigned from Parliament and the party.

It is a cliché of sports psychology that the winning side will be the one which wants it most, and for once this turned out to be true. In the world of politics, Boris Johnson's brief first term as Prime Minister (July–December 2019) could almost be compared to the real-life adventures of the young Winston Churchill. It was a story of audacious gambles and miraculous escapology, in which the hero was the benefi-ciary of good luck as well as his innate cunning. When Theresa May finally stood down, however, Johnson had known that he would only be given the chance to lead his party if his parliamentary colleagues had run out of orthodox options. Even Conservative MPs who doubted that he would stand up to scrutiny in a general election campaign had to accept the fact that ordinary party members found him irresistible. If it turned out that non-committed voters were not equally besotted – and from the outset Johnson's negative approval ratings suggested that this was the case – he enjoyed the inestimable advantage of a main opponent (Corbyn) who was still more unpopular. Even if his adventure ended badly, Johnson's party (as usual) would manage to wriggle free from the wreckage. Such calculations ensured that in each of the five ballots held among MPs 'Boris' was placed first, and by the fourth round he had secured the support of just over half his parliamentary colleagues.

Thus Johnson became the seventh person to hold the office of Prime Minister in the period under review. His elevation came a little later than his preferred timetable, but in many respects he could be counted lucky to have lost the 2016 leadership election. His 2019 victory can be seen as the culmination of a process which began with Thatcher's election forty years previously. Long before the time of writing (November 2020) there were plenty of reasons for thinking that Johnson is a culmination too far, and that his departure from office, whenever that happens, will promote a reassessment of the prime ministerial role. However, in this book we are dealing with the relatively recent past rather than the future.

It was always likely that a Johnson premiership would illustrate the themes examined in this book. However, no one could have predicted a course of events which, within a year, had eclipsed the unending 'Brexit' saga and come close to making Johnson the first Prime Minister to die in office since the equally fertile Lord Palmerston in 1865. A book on the role of the Prime Minister based on those momentous months alone would be very informative. For the present purpose, some of the key developments will be sketched in accordance with the themes explored in previous chapters.

Majority leader

Despite the constitutional chaos which engulfed Britain during Johnson's first government, it could be argued that long-established proprieties were eventually honoured. May resigned because she could not command a majority in the House of Commons for her EU withdrawal agreement, and once it was found that nobody else would fare better, Parliament was dissolved for a general election to break the impasse. However, thanks to the provisions of the Fixed-Term

Parliaments Act there was a considerable delay before Boris Johnson secured the election he craved, during which the House of Commons effectively demonstrated its lack of confidence in his government on numerous occasions – to the point where the case for an election could no longer be resisted by MPs. It was a spectacular example of a Prime Minister profiting from his parliamentary weakness.

Between 1979 and the 2016 referendum, the governments of successive Prime Ministers lost a total of twenty-seven divisions in the House of Commons. May's government managed to lose thirty-three times between the 2017 general election and her resignation little more than two years later. The record of Johnson's first term was even more remarkable; although Parliament was sitting for less than two months, the government was beaten on twelve occasions – more defeats than British governments had suffered between 1979 and the beginning of 'New Labour's' third term in 2005. The only important vote won by the government during Johnson's first term was the one which authorized the general election, thanks not to the Prime Minister's arguments but to the palpable feeling that the public was running out of patience with Parliament.

To the bitter end, May had hoped that she could conjure up a Commons majority for her withdrawal proposals. Johnson, by contrast, acted on the dictum of Churchill's near-contemporary Andrew Bonar Law, who declared in 1913 that 'There are things stronger than parliamentary majorities.' Bonar Law was hinting (unsubtly) that Ulster Protestants might take up arms to resist Irish Home Rule. Johnson's extra-parliamentary weapon was less menacing but more tangible – the result of the 2016 EU referendum. May had tried to translate the Leave victory into a personal mandate, but this was unconvincing since she had cast her own vote on the losing side. Whatever his private thoughts on the subject Johnson could present himself as the embodiment of anti-EU sentiment, with a licence to treat parliamentary resistance as something akin to treachery. Far from trying to build a consensus in the Commons, Johnson alienated even his party's DUP allies – whom he had previously buttered up with pro-Union speeches – by negotiating a withdrawal agreement which they could not countenance; persuaded the Queen to prorogue Parliament to prevent it from reaching an alternative arrangement with the EU; treated the ruling of the Supreme Court that this action was not lawful as no more than a temporary setback; then removed the Conservative whip from twenty-one moderate MPs who had voted to thwart his negotiating tactic of threatening to take Britain out of the EU without a withdrawal deal of any kind.

In the aftermath of the 2019 general election it seemed that Johnson's strong-arm tactics had paid off. However, in chapter 1 it was suggested that Prime Ministers no longer reach that position because they enjoy the confidence of the Commons; rather, their ability to muster majorities for their policies arises from the fact of *being* Prime Minister. Boris Johnson had made no attempt to build a parliamentary reputation, and the events of his first premiership ensured that he would never command the respect of the Commons. This approach seemed to be based on short-term calculations which came naturally to Johnson. But it made his tenure unduly dependent on 'events', which turned against him even before negotiations for post-Brexit trade deals had begun.

Cabinet-maker

Immediately after becoming Prime Minister Johnson conducted a government reshuffle which transgressed all previous understandings of the need to reflect the various interests and policy positions within the governing party. The infatuated *Daily Telegraph* (25 July 2019) hailed the construction of a 'crack' team, but for non-believers a similar-sounding and less complimentary epithet would have sprung to mind. Johnson's determination to cleanse the Cabinet of moderate figures was helped by the pre-emptive resignation of May's Chancellor, Philip Hammond, along with able and pragmatic ministers like David Gauke and David Lidington. Johnson proposed to reward his closest leadership rival, the former 'Remainer' Jeremy Hunt, with a demotion from Foreign Secretary to Defence – an offer which Hunt understandably declined. The few moderates who decided to stay on board quickly reassessed the situation. Amber Rudd, who had supported Remain and served as Home Secretary under May, was a stranger in Johnson's right-wing Cabinet as Secretary of State for Work and Pensions. She lasted two months. In a surreal variant of Geoffrey Howe's 1990 'conflict of loyalties', the Prime Minister's brother, Jo, implied that his own resignation as a junior minister in the Department for Education arose from a (belated) decision to put the national interest ahead of family ties.

Johnson delayed his next moves until after Britain's formal withdrawal from the EU (31 January 2020). In the reshuffle of 13 February, the Prime Minister modified a Remainer-free Cabinet into one in which acceptance of Brexit was not enough. Ministerial competence was not a disadvantage, but neither was proven ineptitude. Genuine personal loyalty was not important either, since it would have been naïve of Johnson to think that any of his senior colleagues were overburdened with that quality. Rather, Johnson wanted a Cabinet which could be controlled.

In a 1975 address to the British Academy, Harold Wilson had said that 'What you cannot afford is a Government of cronies and like-minded people, who can be relied on for their loyalty in Cabinet, but who, for that very reason, cannot deliver a corresponding strength, whether in backbenchers or in popular support in the country' (Wilson, 1976, 31). This was another Wilsonian lesson which Tony Blair did not heed, but Boris Johnson drove a London bus through it. Members of the new Cabinet might not fit the description of 'cronies', but they were certainly like-minded in one crucial respect. Theresa May's ministers had all known that their party's future electoral fortunes – even its continued existence – depended on a successful withdrawal from the EU. After February 2020, almost all of Johnson's colleagues had the additional incentive of having campaigned aggressively for 'Leave'. Although British voters have selective memories, if Brexit went wrong it would be very easy for Labour, the Lib Dems, the SNP et al. to reel off a list of senior Tories who had presented a disastrous policy as if it had been certain to succeed. For these ambitious people, personal credibility was at stake. For once, the slogan 'We're all in this together' really meant something to a Conservative minister.

A survey of Johnson's appointments highlights the tendency for his chosen colleagues to be Brexiteers who, thanks to previous mishaps, were unlikely to threaten his own position. Thus Dominic Raab, who had followed Johnson's example of resigning from May's Cabinet to further his own ambitions but performed abysmally in the leadership contest, was awarded the FCO 'consolation prize'. Meanwhile Jacob Rees-Mogg, who had advertised his fitness for the role of Leader of the House of Commons by lying down on the front bench during an emergency debate on 'Brexit', continued in that role, with a right to attend Cabinet meetings (but not, presumably, in a recumbent position). Rees-Mogg, who would have struck even Gladstone and Disraeli as an anachronism, was another ERG poster boy, whose improbable claims to the party leadership had been scuppered forever by his untimely nap; thus it was safe for Johnson to offer him a comfortable bivouac inside the tent, albeit at a safe distance. Priti Patel, the new Home Secretary, presented almost the starkest possible contrast to Rees-Mogg; it was bizarre that these ministerial colleagues were products of the same century, let alone members of the same party. Highly articulate and energetic, Patel had shown that she was also dangerously impulsive in a brief stint as Secretary of State for International Development (2016–17), truncated by an unwise visit to Israel which had not been cleared officially by the FCO (although apparently she did notify the then Foreign Secretary – Boris Johnson). Whatever Patel's positive qualities, a proven record of reckless decision-making and the circumvention of bureaucratic niceties had not previously been regarded as character traits befitting a Home Secretary.

If Johnson's appointments in February 2020 were open to serious questions, the exclusions were even more telling. Julian Smith, who had been instrumental in negotiating the reinstatement of Northern Ireland's long-suspended devolved institutions, was sacked because Johnson held a grudge against him. But this astonishing decision was barely noticed amidst the furore which followed the ejection of Sajid Javid, Philip Hammond's successor as Chancellor of the Exchequer.

Despite the atmosphere of ill-discipline and ideological excess in Johnson's first term, Javid had given the impression of being a reasonably cool-headed operator. In February 2020 he was invited to stay on as Chancellor – on condition that he dismissed all but one of his special advisers. The idea – first mooted under the coalition government – was that the Prime Minister and the Chancellor should 'share' special advisers to avoid breakdowns in communication. Its revival under Johnson was much more ominous, since it was clearly suspected that Javid would try to keep public spending under at least a semblance of restraint, contrary to the populist designs of No. 10.

This incident was a new instalment in a saga which had lasted almost as long as *The Archers*, but whose story-line had become increasingly fraught since 1979. Under Thatcher, No. 10 and the Treasury had clashed over the best means to control inflation, resulting in the departures of the Chancellor, Lawson and Thatcher's special adviser, Alan Walters. The institutional conflict, suspended in the Major years,

took a new form under Blair and Brown, who did not disagree funda-
mentally over tax and spending but contrived to quarrel over almost
everything else. It was only after Blair left office that serious policy
divisions re-emerged thanks to the worldwide financial crisis. Brown
wanted to reduce its impact by stimulating the economy even if this
entailed a significant departure from post-Thatcherite orthodoxy. The
Prime Minister, who had invited Lady Thatcher to Downing Street in
September 2007, presumably in order to win positive coverage from
right-wing newspapers, had suddenly remembered that she had been
wrong all along. But the Treasury, headed by Alistair Darling, who had
been appointed to do Brown's bidding, refused to comply with the new
thinking, and was seconded by the Bank of England.

The 'austerity' subsequently inflicted by Cameron and Osborne
was highly controversial in some quarters, but not in Downing Street,
where the Treasury's view prevailed. The trouble restarted when
the Cameron–Osborne partnership was broken by Brexit. May took
Gordon Brown's role, urging an end to 'austerity'; but her Chancellor
Philip Hammond reprised Darling's position by following Treasury
advice and digging in his heels. In February 2020 Johnson probably did
not want Javid to resign, but had good reasons for mixed feelings about
a politician who had committed the offence of spelling out his reasons
for voting 'Remain' in a clear-eyed assessment of Britain's post-war
experience.[60] Unlike Dominic Raab, Javid had also performed credibly
in the leadership contest, getting through to the fourth ballot of MPs.
This made him a potential future rival as well as a nuisance. A substitute
for Javid had been warming up just in case – Rishi Sunak, an ardent
Brexiteer with an enthusiasm for 'free ports', whose high-flying hedge-
fund career and marriage to the daughter of a billionaire had excluded
him from the ranks of the 'just about managing'.

Javid's refusal to accept Johnson's terms was presented as the product
of loyalty: he would not hold on to office at the expense of his friends.
This was highly questionable since Javid's advisers would have lost their
government jobs regardless of his decision. Even so, this was much
more than a proxy battle, in which special advisers were merely pawns.
No. 10 clearly felt that these unelected people were of sufficient importance to justify an ultimatum which might bring about the resignation
of a crucial and potentially dangerous minister. For his part, Javid
was willing to risk his political career by resigning, rather than giving

up the right to choose his own advisers. The battle for control of the Treasury, which can be traced back to the 1950s and beyond, had been won by No. 10 in the course of a single interview. No longer would the Prime Minister have to appoint a loyalist as Chancellor and hope that the chosen one would not 'go native'. Javid's successors would have to accept obedience to the will of the Prime Minister as part of their job description. The last bastion of Whitehall had finally been stormed; the Treasury had been 'hollowed out'.

Policy-maker

In forming his post-election Cabinet, Johnson verified a key argument of this book by taking a cavalier approach to the overwhelming majority of appointments. The Treasury was an obvious exception, but the messy elevation of Sunak had been well worth the short-lived media storm it provoked. There was, though, another position which mattered – Minister for the Cabinet Office. This role was allocated to Michael Gove, who had clearly been forgiven for his impersonation of Marcus Brutus, at Johnson's expense, during the 2016 leadership contest. At that time, Gove had disclosed serious doubts about the leadership qualities of his old friend, and announced his own candidacy. After losing heavily to Theresa May, Gove had tried to repair his reputation by refusing to follow the trend of calculated resignations from her Cabinet. On the face of it, these tactics should have deepened Gove's alienation from Johnson, who had taken the contrary course of jumping ship at the most opportune moment. The heart-warming reconciliation between the two bold Brexiteers was a tribute to the influence of another leading Leaver, Dominic Cummings. It also meant that long-running disputes about the role of the Cabinet Office, which had been created to serve the government as a whole, was settled by the February reshuffle. While Johnson was Prime Minister, at least, the Office would be at his service, along with Gove and Cummings.

The rise (and belated fall) of Dominic Cummings invites a consideration of the ability of specific individuals to shape more general developments. We encountered Cummings in the Cameron years, effectively taking control of Gove, his nominal employer, and causing so much disruption that even the easy-going Cameron insisted upon his dismissal. We also noted the presence in Cameron's entourage of a similar 'challenging' individual, Steve Hilton, who soon found himself marginalized and embarked on a new career in the US.

Cummings, by all accounts, was like a turbo-charged version of Hilton – a far more abrasive character, who readily equated failure to accept his ideas with intellectual deficiency. The presence of Hilton and Cummings in influential roles, in a government led by a moderate Conservative like Cameron, showed that the party which once prided itself on 'pragmatism' had become unusually susceptible to individuals who could 'think the unthinkable'. Under New Labour, with its obsessive approach to news management, there had been a fairly clear division of responsibilities between spin doctors, who dealt with the media, and advisers, who contributed unobtrusively (and unsuccessfully) to the policy process. The post-Thatcherite Conservative Party did things differently. While New Labour had been interested in 'delivery' rather than theory, Conservative politicians wanted apparatchiks who could help them win the 'battle of ideas' which they had been fighting (largely in their own heads) since Thatcher's heyday. Like most theorists with a licence to intrude into the world of practice, such figures tended to be contemptuous of more empirical individuals – 'mere' politicians, as well as civil servants.

Thus while New Labour's spin doctors were often 'attack dogs', Conservative functionaries wanted to bark as well as bite: to manipulate the media as well as influencing the decisions of their employers. They were more attuned to the 'alt-right' movement in the US (and to that country's uninhibited style of debate) than to any distinctively British approach to politics. Dominic Cummings was the Platonic ideal of Conservative special advisers – a philosopher-canine, who could mislead the media, trash his enemies, then lead an erudite discourse on the latest fads in behavioural psychology (Shipman, 2016, 36–9). Even so, a Prime Minister who hoped to oversee a functional government would have kept him on a very tight leash, or consulted a vet about the surgical options. Inadvertently, by calling an in/out EU referendum David Cameron, who was well aware of Cummings' unsuitability, gave him the chance to establish a legend as the real driving force of the 'Leave' campaign.

If Cummings had persuaded the wily Michael Gove of his indispensability, 'Boris' would be a pushover. On becoming Prime Minister, Johnson's most important decision by far was to make Cummings his senior special adviser. After the reshuffle of 2020, Margaret Thatcher's claim that 'Advisers advise, ministers decide!' stood in need of still further revision. Now it was the unelected advisers who effectively appointed the ministers; and even then, ministers would not be allowed to rubber-stamp policy decisions without the advance approval of special advisers.

Shortly after the February reshuffle Alastair Campbell launched a wide-ranging critique of the Johnson regime, arguing that its attacks on the civil service were 'part of the Trumpian message that only the leader and his immediate circle have views that count'.[61] Given Campbell's own devoted service to New Labour, this was an extraordinary allegation – like a pot complaining about the colouration of other kitchenware. It was clearly aimed at Cummings, and certainly the latter was borrowing extensively from the New Labour playbook. Campbell's complaint, in essence, was that Cummings was bringing New Labour's modus operandi into contempt by taking its logic to its ultimate conclusions – that is, that even if Blair and Brown had allowed special advisers and spin doctors to become overmighty servants, elected politicians had still been the masters. Even so, it was strangely instructive that Campbell should overlook the family resemblance between the dysfunctionality of the Johnson/Cummings regime and the government of which he had himself been such a crucial component.

Dominic Cummings, of course, could not act entirely alone, and he was not the only unelected figure to loom large in the Johnson government. Other key figures included Edward Lister and Munira Mirza, who had helped Johnson to look effective while he was Mayor of London.[62] But soon after the 2019 election Cummings extended an online invitation to 'weirdos and misfits with odd skills' who might care to join the government machine.[63] Apparently, he wanted to cast his net wider than the Conservative Party membership, despite its abundant stock of individuals who fitted his job description. One successful applicant was forced to resign before he had begun to apply his 'odd skills' to the service of the public, when it emerged that he had exhibited an alarming enthusiasm for the pseudo-science of eugenics.

This unorthodox recruitment drive suggested that Cummings was preparing for a long-term policy programme, in which ministers would be parliamentary facilitators rather than creative influences. The role assigned to Johnson was broadly similar. Notoriously bored by policy detail, he would act as a frontman for the whole operation. This might suggest that, under Johnson/Cummings, even the role of Prime Minister had been 'hollowed out'. More precisely, it was a dramatic clarification of the premier's primary purpose. Developments within Whitehall since 1979 had deprived most other ministers of public recognition as well as policy-making powers. Under the new dispensation, the Prime Minister's ability to effect constructive reform would be unchanged – that is, vanishingly small – but if anything his prominence in electoral politics would be all the greater.

Communicator in Chief and election winner

Johnson did not become Prime Minister because of his ability to command the confidence of the House of Commons; the likelihood that he would be a competent leader of a team; or his proven record as a policy-maker. His single qualification was his ability to communicate, which in turn was expected by his admirers to win votes for the Conservative Party.

More than any of his predecessors, when Johnson spoke to the country he was mainly concerned to talk it up – to speak *for* it (the subject of chapter 5). This had been a constant feature of his speeches during the Brexit campaign, and his appointment as Foreign Secretary in 2016 provided an ideal platform for his patriotic prattle. Thus, for example, in his speech to the Conservative Party conference in 2017 Johnson had ridiculed commentators at home and abroad who found 'reasons to be less than cheerful about this country'. Britain had actually 'become a gigantic cyclotron of talent'. Plagiarizing Churchill, he compared the British people to a lion which would roar once again under Conservative leadership.[64] In the following year he had returned to the backbenches, but still drew a sizeable audience of enthusiasts at a fringe meeting. There was much less about Britain's brilliance this time, since the speech was an unashamed audition for a party leadership which was sure to fall vacant in the near future. Johnson delighted his fans with mocking references to the party's most hated politicians – Jeremy Corbyn and Theresa May – and excoriated the EU and May's Chequers proposals. He did have positive things to say about one politician, though, sneaking in a lavish and selective tribute to his own record as Mayor of London. When he invited his audience to anticipate a 'glorious future', on this occasion he was referring to the prospects of the party under his stewardship, rather than his cyclotronic country.[65]

This style of oratory was not just a product of 'Brexit'; it had been a commonplace of conference speeches since 1979. In this respect, at least, all Prime Ministers since Thatcher (including David Cameron) have been 'populists', not just by acting as 'awkward partners' within the EU for the benefit of the right-wing press but, more significantly, by wilfully distorting Britain's true global status for electoral effect. Since Cameron had run for office on the basis of a misleading account of the financial crisis, there was some poetic justice in his grisly demise after the 2016 referendum (Dorey and Garnett, 2016, 49–81). Brexit just made a re-evaluation of Britain's role even less likely, increasing the vogue for purveyors of eloquent escapism like Johnson. Members of the Conservative Party were particularly susceptible, and persuaded themselves that someone who could raise their morale without asking any awkward questions was likely to win votes at home and possibly even influence other world leaders. Speaking outside No. 10 on the day he became Prime Minister, Johnson showed that he knew what was expected of him, wasting no time on references to the honour that had been bestowed upon him before laying into 'the doubters, the doomsters, the gloomsters'. Now, 'after three years of unfounded self-doubt' – years in which Johnson's own party had been in sole charge of the government – the new Prime Minister claimed that Britain had 'the leadership it deserves'.[66]

However, far from proving to be an electoral talisman, Johnson was used sparingly in a 2019 Tory campaign which was barely an improvement on May's toe-curling effort of 2017. 'Strong and stable' was replaced by Johnson's promise to 'Get Brexit Done' through his 'oven-ready' withdrawal bill. These slogans would not have fared well under forensic questioning, so Johnson did his best to evade it. He did subject himself to two debates with Corbyn – fairly risk-free, given the Labour leader's various vulnerabilities – but sidestepped a confrontation with the BBC's acerbic Andrew Neil and famously hid from another interviewer in an industrial refrigerator (an achievement which Johnson's role model, Churchill, never quite managed). His reluctance to enumerate the children he had fathered did nothing to allay suspicions that, like Dryden's Charles II, he had 'Scatter'd his Maker's image through the land'. Some of Johnson's nineteenth-century forebears might have been equally flummoxed by this question, but Lord Palmerston had never been asked about his private life in a televised interview. None of this mattered in the context of an election which the Conservatives were always likely to win, provided that they avoided fratricide, steered away from promises which might alarm their core voters, and prevented the Prime Minister himself from making too many gaffes.

Meanwhile the right-wing press had learned from its error of 2017, when it had been too confident that the Conservatives would win big to co-ordinate a proficient campaign of vilification against Corbyn. Two years later the *Sun* had decided that Corbyn was 'the most dangerous man ever to run for high office in Britain'; its readers were invited to stave off the 'nightmare' of a Labour government by voting for 'Boris Johnson's Conservatives'. While much of the knocking-copy in the tabloids was culled from yellowing anti-Kinnock clippings, the *Telegraph* had a new argument to offer on polling day; Labour was 'institutionally racist' (an allegation that seemed to horrify newspapers which had once applauded Enoch Powell). On the other side, the presidential flavour was echoed by the *Observer*, whose recommendation to readers after 'a tawdry campaign' was not a vote for a specific party but for 'anyone but Johnson'.[67]

It was no easier in December 2019 than in other elections to calculate the influence of press coverage over individual voting decisions. However, not even the best-informed voter could escape entirely from the media's framing of the contest as a choice between two individuals rather than a range of political parties. The personalization of the campaign was unprecedented in the democratic era, and it was at best highly misleading to draw parallels with earlier elections. Contests between Pitt and Fox, and Disraeli and Gladstone, were personalized because these were individuals who towered over their contemporaries, which not even the most besotted activist could claim of Johnson or Corbyn. In 2019, a majority of voters decided that their negative emotions towards Corbyn were the stronger, resulting in an overall Conservative majority of eighty which, predictably, was presented as a decisive personal endorsement of Johnson. The most striking feature of the result was the Tory advance in seats, mostly in the north of England, which had previously been regarded as Labour heartlands. This marked the final disappearance of social class as a significant (let alone dominant) source of party allegiance – the development, pre-dating Thatcher but becoming more evident in every successive election since 1979, which left the way open for short-term influences such as media coverage and, in particular, positive and negative presentation of party leaders as surrogates for serious evaluations of party 'competence'. If the relative preference for Johnson over Corbyn was not enough, the Conservatives were undoubtedly helped by Nigel Farage's decision not to run candidates from his Brexit Party in Tory-held seats; it was estimated that the concentration of 'Leave' voters in favour of the Conservatives, against divided Opposition parties, doubled the overall Conservative majority.[68]

After a fashion, Johnson had performed the task expected of him. Now he really did command a majority in the House of Commons, he could begin to establish his personal style of government. However, almost immediately there were signs that a comfortable majority was no protection against public expectations. In February 2020 the Prime Minister refused to visit areas which had been seriously affected by flooding. As Alastair Campbell rightly detected, Johnson was determined to exercise some control over the responsibilities of the job he had coveted for so long. The Prime Minister felt (with some justice) that his presence in the afflicted areas would make little material difference – indeed, it might even disrupt ongoing salvage operations. However, Johnson had under-estimated the range of unavoidable obligations which had descended on the Prime Minister since the days of Churchill. Since he had been chosen as Tory leader chiefly because of his reputed morale-boosting powers, his refusal 'to speak to the country' on such occasions looked like an attempt to shirk the only part of his job that he was qualified to perform. When he realized that he would lose popularity if he continued to enjoy the comforts of Chevening and failed to deliver words of sympathy in person, he was greeted with heckling (including a cry of 'Traitor!', along with more crude utterances which he normally heard from the mouth of Dominic Cummings). His response, a series of mumbled clichés and a promise that he would 'get Bewdley done', explained and partly justified his original decision to stay well away.[69]

Campbell's terse verdict, that Johnson's 'Trumpian' tendencies made for 'very bad government', had been anticipated by the opening sentence of a book written during Blair's second term: 'We are badly governed' (Foster, 2005, 1). The new atmosphere in Whitehall suggested that things were going from bad to worse, as the least attractive features of New Labour re-emerged in magnified form. The Permanent

Secretary of the Home Office resigned and instigated a lawsuit against his Secretary of State, Patel, for alleged bullying. Patel, who had already showcased her erratic streak in public statements, was supported by Downing Street in a manner which (whatever the facts in this particular case) suggested that No. 10's favourites would enjoy complete discretion in the way they treated civil servants. Indeed, over the following months it became clear that Johnson was determined to bring an end to the media headhunting which had prevailed in British political life since John Major's 'Back to Basics' speech. This Prime Minister would retain members of his team as long as he wanted them to stay, whatever political or personal offences were charged against them, and whether or not their services were conducive to the national interest.

Pandemic and pandemonium

Even while Johnson was facing the hazards of close contact with angry members of the British public, evidence emerged that a new virus, Covid-19, was being transmitted within the UK rather than just affecting people who had travelled abroad. As the virus spread, Johnson initially followed 'expert' advice – widely attributed to Dominic Cummings – which urged that normal life should continue while the virus ran its course and the (otherwise healthy) population developed 'herd immunity'. On 3 February 2020 Johnson delivered a typically bombastic speech at Greenwich, warning that an over-reaction to the virus would cause unnecessary economic damage and comparing Britain to a 'Superman' figure which would lead the battle to maintain market freedoms in the face of any contagion.[70]

Suddenly alarmed by further advice that his ideological approach would lead to unacceptable levels of fatality, on 19 March Johnson heralded a more active response which would 'send the virus packing'. By the end of the month even he must have realized that such language was inappropriate, as he began to experience symptoms of a disease which could not be combatted by effusions of pseudo-patriotism. A week later he was being treated in the Intensive Care Unit of St Thomas's Hospital. Within a few days of his apparent recovery and return to Downing Street it was announced that he had become a father once again, thanks to a recently kindled relationship – with a former spin doctor and special adviser. Dominic Cummings and his wife also experienced symptoms, and left London to 'self-isolate' with his family near Durham. These movements seemed difficult to reconcile with government guidelines issued in response to the pandemic – rules which Cummings himself had helped to devise. An outing to the picturesque environs of Barnard Castle was explained by Cummings as an attempt to discover whether his eyesight had been impaired by the virus. For a week, Cummings dominated the headlines even of Johnson-worshipping newspapers; even the *Daily Star*, which usually treated politics as if it were a deadly virus, helpfully provided a Cummings mask for anyone who was stopped by police while driving in breach of the official guidelines. The special adviser called a bizarre and unapologetic press conference, held in the Downing Street garden, to flaunt the fact that whether or not 'herd immunity' had worked, Cummings had inoculated himself against any threat of prosecution or dismissal. The venue expressed, with more eloquence than Cummings or even Johnson could have managed, the power-shift which had taken place within Britain's representative democracy; an unelected officer was allowed to display his contempt for the media where once Cameron and Clegg had plighted their political troth. Johnson's peremptory rejection of calls for Cummings' dismissal risked a further diminution of his own authority at this critical time. Within weeks Cummings was making progress with his campaign against what remained of the old civil service ethos. At the end of June Sir Mark Sedwill announced that he would shortly be vacating his positions of Cabinet Secretary, Head of the Civil Service and National Security Adviser. It was a reasonable supposition that, by the end of 2020, none of these titles would be held by a dignitary who felt ambivalent about 'Brexit'.

At the time of writing (November 2020), the full effects of Covid-19 have yet to be registered. The virus presented an unprecedented challenge to governments across the world, and with the benefit of hindsight all of them would have taken different decisions at various times. On becoming Prime Minister, Boris Johnson warned Britain's detractors: 'Do not underestimate our powers of organisation.' He was referring to preparation for Brexit, but the remark was meant to have more general application. In Britain, there had been an attempt in 2007 to gauge the nation's readiness for such a viral pandemic, which had been identified as a 'first-tier' potential threat in the first (2010) report of the National Security Council. But the warnings were not followed up, for reasons which will no doubt be explored by a future inquiry.

As a result of these administrative failures, the Johnson Government was left flat-footed by what quickly turned out to be the greatest national crisis since 1945; the initial decision to let the virus do its worst clearly had been influenced by wishful thinking as well as laissez-faire ideology. When it became clear that inaction was not playing well with the electorate, Johnson learned that, on the whole, it is preferable to have a few competent colleagues in key ministerial positions, just in case something difficult crops up. As it was, his own deployments had left him with a team which might have been adept at infighting within a hollowed-out Conservative Party, but was light on administrative competence or, as it emerged, capacity to benefit from in-work experience. Among the maladroit responses of various ministers, there was a tendency to revert to the New Labour habit of using announcements of good news as if the beneficial results had already taken place. An early symptom of an addiction to over-promising was a wildly exaggerated claim in respect of shipments of protective clothing for health workers. A target was dreamed up for testing front-line staff in the NHS, and when this looked sure to be missed the government tried to move the goalposts rather than making an honest admission that it had failed to introduce testing when this might have saved lives. Even worse, the government continued to insist that it was acting on scientific advice, although its various responses had followed an erratic course which suggested a feverish infusion of politics rather than expertise. Indeed, the fact that a Brexiteer government, in which Gove was a major player, had now decided that 'experts' deserved a hearing after all was in itself ominous; it would be difficult for the health professionals and scientists who lined up at the flag-draped press conferences to step out of the limelight with their credibility intact. When the inevitable inquiries took place these people would make ideal scapegoats, along with a few ministers who could be thrown to the hounds without regret, so long as the vote-winning Prime Minister was untainted by such a spectacular failure. There was certainly little 'expertise' on display in the government's media operation, which continued to work on the assumption that really bad news could and should be buried along with the victims of the virus.

The inadequate ministerial response to the crisis reflected badly on the Prime Minister, since his Cabinet colleagues had been appointed in his name. Up until his illness, Johnson's own contribution had been characterized by bluster and promises rather than effective action; every promising development would be a 'game-changer', which when suitably 'ramped up' or 'turbo-charged' would result in a 'world-beating' achievement. It is not necessarily the case that populists are more proficient at winning cheap applause than meeting administrative challenges – at his worst, during the General Strike of 1926, Winston Churchill displayed a penchant for propaganda to match that of Cummings himself – but that was emphatically true of *this* populist. Once he had been taken to hospital – laid low, it appeared, by his insistence on showing contempt for the virus by shaking hands with its victims – Johnson's media cheerleaders deplored his absence but nothing changed: the previous incompetence continued. Indeed, according to one source the government became even more controlling, with new instructions being issued to ministers with regard to media appearances.[71] Tellingly, the *Daily Telegraph*, which ran this report and in normal times exhibited an obsequious manner towards a Prime Minister who so often graced its pages, quoted a Conservative MP as saying that, 'I'm afraid the Cummings plan of a centralised Government is unravelling on a daily basis.' Presumably this remark referred to the general chaos since the February reshuffle rather than any new evidence of dysfunctionality. It emerged that Johnson had not troubled himself to attend five crucial meetings of the government's key committee on civil emergencies ('Cobra'). The newly faithful Gove tried to insist that Johnson's attendance had not been essential and that he remained fully briefed, but the best way to brief oneself on a rapidly changing emergency is surely to attend a meeting of well-informed people rather than waiting to hear about it afterwards.

Even for the most blinkered English nationalist, the contrasting performances of the Westminster government and the administrations of the devolved nations was too glaring to ignore. This book has not paid much attention to devolution – not least because successive British Prime Ministers have continued to act as if it had never occurred. But the 2020 pandemic made it impossible to ignore the devolution dimension, since the divergence between England and the other nations of the UK suggested the possibility that the governments of Scotland, Wales and even Northern Ireland might respond more successfully to a global crisis because, unlike Westminster and Whitehall, their youthful institutions had not been 'hollowed out' – yet. As Britain was hit by a second 'wave' of the coronavirus in the autumn of 2020, local Mayors – elected individuals whose positions had been promoted by central government in the hope that they would prove more compliant than councils – emerged as a new source of resistance to the discredited denizens of Westminster and Whitehall.

In the 1730s Alexander Pope had written: 'For Forms of government let fools contest; / Whate'er is well administered is best.' Had he been alive in the lockdown of 2020 he would have been forced to acknowledge that some forms of government are so bad that only fools would refuse to contest them. Briefly, Johnson himself was cushioned from criticism, not just because of the serious illness he had suffered but also because it was considered 'bad form' or even unpatriotic to attack a government during a crisis. This attitude was understandably common amongst supporters of Brexit, who presumably would have shown less restraint in their strictures if the Prime Minister had been an equally incompetent 'Remainer'. Apparently, though, many members of the public also felt that this was not the time to rock the boat – a view which could only reflect a more general feeling that Pope was right, and that constitutional coups should not be matters of concern for ordinary voters. This would also explain the widespread public perplexity and indifference during the pre-election tussles over prorogation, and the attendant feeling that Parliament was simply being obstructive to 'Boris'.

Only a constitutional convention composed entirely of 'weirdos and misfits' could convince itself that the current role of the British Prime Minister makes any kind of sense in a liberal democracy. The presidential elements are unmistakable, particularly in terms of the electoral process. One might also argue that the institutions which have begun to put up the most determined resistance to No. 10 – parliamentary select committees, and the courts – are themselves suggestive of US-style checks and balances, and could even lead to a creative constitutional tension between the branches of government. Yet the Prime Minister's lot would still not be a happy one – indeed, it would be even more miserable, acting as a still greater deterrent to people who really deserve to occupy such a prominent position. But in the US, opponents of irresponsible executives can appeal to a codified constitution. In Britain the monarchical analogy seems more apposite than the presidential parallel;

after all, apart from the Cromwellian interlude, the country has never engaged in a serious debate about the best way to cleanse its system of governance from the legacy of 'the Divine Right of Kings', and, though self-evidently less than 'Divine', the Prime Minister is the political legatee of the pre-modern monarchy. When Johnson's life seemed in danger, one *Telegraph* columnist wrote that 'the whole nation felt a cold shiver run down its spine'.[72] This was typical of the veneration shown by hired hacks during the periodic illnesses of George III – and even then it was most unlikely to describe the reaction of 'the whole nation'. Ironically, when George III was free from the illness which made him seem insane, he was more successful than contemporary Prime Ministers in his attempts to reflect the feelings and opinions of his fellow Britons.

In addition, not even enduringly popular US Presidents can indulge in the quasi-monarchical dream of 'going on and on' until nature takes its course, thanks to the two-term limit on their time in office. The lack of similar constitutional provisions in the UK is one reason why, since 1979, a majority of Prime Ministers have been dethroned by their own parties rather than suffering dismissal by the electorate – and why even those (Major and Brown) who were removed from No. 10 Downing Street by the voters spent far too much of their tenure of that historic house worrying (for well-founded reasons) about various attempts to depose them.

New Labour had been a reasonable facsimile of the Hanoverian court, with lower standards of etiquette. In the early days of the Blair Government, Oona King had noted in her diary that 'Watching a Prime Minister walk through a room of MPs is like watching a magnet trail through a dish of paper clips' (King, 2007, 104). She would have noticed a very similar effect when George III hobbled into one of his levees. Of course, US Presidents are not free from monarchical influences; but in this respect at least they owe their inspiration to Britain, the originator of the cult of undeserved celebrity.

Whatever comparisons can be drawn, Johnson's early exploits are a vivid illustration of the fact that the role of the British Prime Minister is now characterized by excessive political *prominence*, rather than *power* in any constructive sense. It is both a symptom, and a significant cause, of a dysfunctional system of government: a serious nuisance which should be abated in the interests of the unfortunate individuals who seek the role of governing a fast-fracturing country.

Notes

1 HC Deb 22 November 1990, vol. 181, cc. 452, 454.
2 https://www.publicwhip.org.uk/mp.php?id=uk.org.publicwhip/member/1806&showall=yes#divisions
3 https://www.theguardian.com/politics/2001/aug/23/uk.euro1
4 https://www.independent.co.uk/voices/letter-who-wields-the-knife-can-win-the-crown-1495144.html
5 https://www.ipsos.com/ipsos-mori/en-uk/political-monitor-satisfaction-ratings-1977-1987
6 https://www.margaretthatcher.org/document/104717
7 https://www.instituteforgovernment.org.uk/sites/default/files/publications/Efficiency%20Unit%20and%20Next%20Steps.pdf
8 https://www.theguardian.com/politics/2005/mar/02/ukcrime.freedomofinformation
9 HC Deb February 2000, vol. 343, cc. 1057–65.
10 https://www.instituteforgovernment.org.uk/ministers-reflect/person/jack-straw/, 15
11 https://www.independent.co.uk/news/uk/politics/john-biffen-s-withering-verdict-on-margaret-thatchers-cabinet-meetings-miserably-disappointing-9035752.html
12 http://www.nicholasjones.org.uk/articles/categories/trade-union-reporting/336-1992-cabinet-records-reveal-government-chaos-and-confusion-over-death-knell-for-coal-industry

13 https://www.theguardian.com/world/1997/oct/26/euro.eu
14 https://www.theguardian.com/politics/2009/jun/04/james-purnell-resigns-gordon-brown-cabinet
15 https://www.ipsos.com/ipsos-mori/en-uk/economy-immigration-and-healthcare-are-britons-top-three-issues-deciding-general-election-vote
16 https://www.dailymail.co.uk/news/article-5929811/MICHAEL-GOVE-GREG-CLARK-say-united-Battle-Britain.html
17 https://www.margaretthatcher.org/document/103764
18 https://www.margaretthatcher.org/document/105032
19 https://www.margaretthatcher.org/document/106941
20 http://www.johnmajorarchive.org.uk/1990-1997/mr-majors-speech-to-conservative-group-for-europe-22-april-1993
21 http://www.johnmajorarchive.org.uk/1991/mr-majors-1991-conservative-party-conference-speech-11-october-1991
22 http://www.ukpol.co.uk/john-major-1992-conservative-party-conference-speech
23 https://www.bbc.co.uk/news/world-us-canada-50752217
24 https://www.theguardian.com/politics/1993/oct/09/conservatives.past
25 https://publications.parliament.uk/pa/cm200102/cmselect/cmpubadm/303/2022810.htm
26 https://www.theguardian.com/politics/2003/mar/21/uk.iraq
27 http://image.guardian.co.uk/sys-files/Politics/documents/2007/06/12/BlairReustersSpeech.pdf
28 For example, https://www.theguardian.com/politics/2007/feb/27/immigrationpolicy.race
29 http://news.bbc.co.uk/1/hi/uk_politics/7010664.stm
30 https://www.youtube.com/watch?v=7iPaiylUYW0
31 https://www.theguardian.com/uk-news/2014/sep/15/david-cameron-emotional-plea-scotland-independence
32 https://www.theguardian.com/politics/2014/sep/19/scottish-referendum-david-cameron-devolution-revolution
33 https://www.gov.uk/government/speeches/eu-referendum-outcome-pm-statement-24-june-2016
34 https://www.independent.co.uk/news/uk/politics/theresa-mays-tory-leadership-launch-statement-full-text-a7111026.html

35 https://www.gov.uk/government/speeches/statement-from-the-n
ew-prime-minister-theresa-may

36 https://www.conservativehome.com/parliament/2016/04/theresa-
mays-speech-on-brexit-full-text.html

37 https://www.independent.co.uk/news/uk/politics/theresa-may-con
ference-speech-article-50-brexit-eu-a7341926.html

38 http://www.ukpol.co.uk/john-major-1994-conservative-party-conf
erence-speech

39 https://www.irishtimes.com/news/politics/state-papers-thatcher-o
pposed-german-reunification-after-collapse-of-berlin-wall-1.411
9052

40 https://www.margaretthatcher.org/document/107789

41 https://www.globalpolicy.org/component/content/article/154/26
026.html

42 https://www.theguardian.com/politics/2015/oct/18/chilcot-pressu
re-leaked-blair-bush-iraq-memo

43 https://publications.parliament.uk/pa/cm200506/cmhansrd/vo06
0719/debtext/60719-1010.htm

44 https://www.theguardian.com/politics/2009/sep/23/barack-obama
-gordon-brown-talks

45 https://www.gov.uk/government/speeches/britain-s-foreign-polic
y-in-a-networked-world--2

46 https://www.politics.co.uk/comment-analysis/2011/09/05/david-
cameron-libya-statement-in-full

47 https://publications.parliament.uk/pa/cm201617/cmselect/cmfaff/
119/11908.htm?utm_source=119&utm_medium=crbullet&utm_ca
mpaign=modulereports

48 https://www.theguardian.com/politics/2015/apr/14/conservative-
party-manifesto-2015-the-full-pdf

49 https://www.brookings.edu/opinions/theresa-mays-india-visit-whe
re-the-rise-of-asia-met-trumpism

50 https://www.brookings.edu/blog/order-from-chaos/2019/06/01/h
ow-trump-undermined-theresa-may

51 https://www.theguardian.com/politics/2013/aug/30/george-osbor
ne-syria-vote

52 https://www.margaretthatcher.org/document/105087

53 https://www.ipsos.com/ipsos-mori/en-uk/most-capable-prime-mi
nister-trends

54 https://www.theguardian.com/media/2002/jun/24/mondaymedia section.politics

55 https://www.theguardian.com/politics/1997/mar/18/past.roygree nslade

56 https://www.theguardian.com/politics/2019/jul/18/john-major-wa s-told-to-impress-murdoch-with-his-confidence-papers-show

57 https://www.ipsos.com/ipsos-mori/en-uk/most-capable-prime-mi nister-trends

58 https://www.ipsos.com/ipsos-mori/en-uk/theresa-mays-leadership -satisfaction-ratings-fall-further-after-general-election

59 https://www.theguardian.com/politics/2017/jun/11/george-osbor ne-says-theresa-may-is-a-dead-woman-walking

60 https://www.sajidjavid.com/eu-referendum

61 https://www.theneweuropean.co.uk/top-stories/why-didn-t-boris-johnson-visit-flood-victims-in-worcester-1-6534372

62 https://www.newstatesman.com/politics/uk/2020/03/whos-charge -inside-no-10-maverick-advisers-running-britain

63 https://www.theguardian.com/politics/2020/jan/02/dominic-cum mings-calls-for-weirdos-and-misfits-for-no-10-jobs

64 http://www.ukpol.co.uk/boris-johnson-2017-speech-at-conservati ve-party-conference

65 https://brexitcentral.com/boris-johnson-speech-conservative-par ty-conference

66 https://www.gov.uk/government/speeches/boris-johnsons-first-sp eech-as-prime-minister-24-july-2019

67 https://www.pressgazette.co.uk/what-the-papers-say-about-the-20 19-general-election

68 https://blogs.lse.ac.uk/politicsandpolicy/ge2019-brexit-party-imp act

69 https://www.theguardian.com/politics/2020/mar/08/boris-johnson -heckled-as-a-traitor-while-visiting-flood-hit-worcestershire

70 https://www.gov.uk/government/speeches/pm-speech-in-greenw ich-3-february-2020

71 https://www.telegraph.co.uk/politics/2020/04/09/system-boris-joh nson-built-unravelling-absence

72 https://www.telegraph.co.uk/politics/2020/04/10/boris-near-death sent-shiver-nations-spine

Bibliography

Allen, Graham (2003), *The Last Prime Minister: Being Honest About the UK Presidency*, 2nd edn (London: Politico's).

Bagehot, Walter (1963), *The English Constitution*, Fontana Library edn (London: Fontana).

Bale, Tim (2016), *The Conservative Party: From Thatcher to Cameron* (Cambridge: Polity).

Bale, Tim, Paul Webb and Monica Poletti (2019), *Footsoldiers: Political Party Membership in the 21st Century* (London: Routledge).

Bartle, John (2006), 'The Labour Government and the Media', in John Bartle and Anthony King (eds.), *Britain at the Polls 2005* (London: Sage).

Biffen, John (2013), *Semi-Detached* (London: Biteback).

Blair, Tony (2010), *A Journey* (London: Hutchinson).

Blick, Andrew, and George Jones (2010), *Premiership: The Development, Nature and Power of the Office of the British Prime Minister* (Exeter: Imprint Academic).

Blick, Andrew, and George Jones (2013), *At Power's Elbow: Aides to the Prime Minister from Robert Walpole to David Cameron* (London: Biteback).

Blunkett, David (2006), *The Blunkett Tapes: My Life in the Bear Pit* (London: Bloomsbury).

Brandreth, Gyles (1999), *Breaking the Code: Westminster Diaries* (London: Weidenfeld & Nicolson).

Brinkley, Douglas (1990), 'Dean Acheson and the "Special Relationship": The West Point Speech of December 1962', *Historical Journal* 33(3), 599–608.

Brown, Archie (2004), *The Myth of the Strong Leader: Political Leadership in the Modern Age* (London: Bodley Head).

Brown, Gordon (2017), *My Life, Our Times* (London: Bodley Head).

Butler, David, and Dennis Kavanagh (1984), *The British General Election of 1983* (London: Macmillan).

Butler, David, and Denis Kavanagh (1992), *The British General Election of 1992* (London: Macmillan).

Butler, David, and Donald Stokes (1974), *Political Change in Britain: The Evolution of Electoral Choice*, 2nd edn (London: Macmillan).

Cameron, David (2019), *For the Record* (London: William Collins).

Campbell, Alastair (2010), *Diaries, Volume One: Prelude to Power, 1994–1997* (London: Hutchinson).

Campbell, Alastair (2011), *Diaries, Volume Three: Power and Responsibility, 1999–2001* (London: Hutchinson).

Campbell, Alistair (2012), *Diaries, Volume Four: The Burden of Power: Countdown to Iraq* (London: Hutchinson).

Campbell, Colin, and Graham Wilson (1995), *The End of Whitehall: Death of a Paradigm?* (Oxford: Blackwell).

Campbell, John (2003), *Margaret Thatcher, Volume Two: The Iron Lady* (London: Jonathan Cape).

Carrington, Lord (1988), *Reflect on Things Past* (London: Collins).

Carter, Byrum (1956), *The Office of Prime Minister* (London: Faber).

Clarke, Ken (2016), *Kind of Blue: A Political Memoir* (London: Macmillan).

Cockerell, Michael (2013), 'Boris Johnson: I'd Love to "Have a Crack at" Being Prime Minister', *Radio Times*, 13 March.

Cockerell, Michael, Peter Hennessy and David Walker (1984), *Sources Close to the Prime Minister* (London: Macmillan).

Cook, Robin (2003), *The Point of Departure* (London: Simon & Schuster).

Consterdine, Erica (2018), *Labour's Immigration Policy: The Making of the Migration State* (London: Palgrave).

Cowley, Philip (2005), *The Rebels: How Blair Mislaid his Majority* (London: Politico's).

Cowley, Philip, and Mark Stuart (2014), 'In the Brown Stuff? Labour Backbench Dissent under Gordon Brown, 2007–10', *Contemporary British History* 28(1).

Crick, Michael (1997), *Heseltine: A Biography*, 2nd edn (London: Penguin).

Crick, Michael (2005), *In Search of Michael Howard* (London: Simon & Schuster).

Crossman, Richard (1972), *Inside View: Three Lectures on Prime Ministerial Government* (London: Jonathan Cape).

Darling, Alistair (2011), *Back from the Brink: 1,000 Days at Number 11* (London: Atlantic).

Denham, Andrew, and Kieron O'Hara (2008), *Democratising Conservative Leadership Selection: From Grey Suits to Grass Roots* (Manchester: Manchester University Press).

Denver, David, and Mark Garnett (2014), *British General Elections since 1964: Diversity, Dealignment and Disillusion* (Oxford: Oxford University Press).

Denver, David, Christopher Carman and Rob Johns (2012), *Elections and Voters in Britain*, 3rd edn (London: Red Globe Press).

Diamond, Patrick (2014), *Governing Britain: Power, Politics and the Prime Minister* (London: I. B. Tauris).

Diamond, Patrick (2018), *The End of Whitehall? Government by Permanent Campaign* (London: Palgrave).

Donoughue, Bernard (1987), *Prime Minister: The Conduct of Policy under Harold Wilson and James Callaghan, 1974–79* (London: Jonathan Cape).

Donoughue, Bernard (2008), *Downing Street Diary, Volume Two: With James Callaghan in No. 10* (London: Jonathan Cape).

Donoughue, Bernard (2016), *Westminster Diary: A Reluctant Minister under Tony Blair* (London: I. B. Tauris).

Dorey, Peter (2014), *Policy-Making in Britain*, 2nd edn (London: Sage).

Dorey, Peter, and Mark Garnett (2016), *The British Coalition Government, 2010–2015: A Marriage of Inconvenience* (London: Palgrave Macmillan).

Dowding, Keith (2012), 'The Prime Ministerialisation of the British Prime Minister', *Parliamentary Affairs* 66(3), 617–35.

Dyson, Stephen (2009), *The Blair Identity: Leadership and Foreign Policy* (Manchester: Manchester University Press).

Efficiency Unit (1987), *Improving Management in Government: The Next Steps* (London: HMSO).

Evans, Geoffrey, and Menon, Anand (2017), *Brexit and British Politics* (Cambridge: Polity).

Foley, Michael (1993), *The Rise of the British Presidency* (Manchester: Manchester University Press).

Foley, Michael (2000), *The British Presidency: Tony Blair and the Politics of Public Leadership* (Manchester: Manchester University Press).

Foster, Christopher (2005), *British Government in Crisis: Or, the Third English Revolution* (Oxford: Hart).

Garnett, Mark (2007), *From Anger to Apathy* (London: Jonathan Cape).

Garnett, Mark, and Ian Aitken (2002), *Splendid! Splendid! The Authorized Biography of Willie Whitelaw* (London: Jonathan Cape).

Garnett, Mark, Simon Mabon and Robert Smith (2017), *British Foreign Policy since 1945* (London: Routledge).

Gilmour, Ian (1969), *The Body Politic* (London: Hutchinson).

Gordon Walker, Patrick (1972), *The Cabinet*, 2nd edn (London: Heinemann).

Gorman, Teresa (1993), *The Bastards: Dirty Tricks and the Challenge to Europe* (London: Pan).

Gowland, David (2016), *Britain and the European Union* (London: Routledge).

Hailsham, Lord (1976), 'Elective Dictatorship: The Richard Dimbleby Lecture', *The Listener*, 21 November.

Harris, John (2004), *The Last Party: Britpop, Blair and the Demise of British Rock* (London: Harper).

Heffernan, Richard (2005), 'Why the Prime Minister Cannot Be a President: Comparing Institutional Imperatives in Britain and America', *Parliamentary Affairs* 58(1), 53–70.

Hennessy, Peter (2000), *The Prime Minister: The Office and its Holders since 1945* (London: Allen Lane).

Heseltine, Michael (2000), *Life in the Jungle* (London: Hodder & Stoughton).

Hogg, Sarah, and Jonathan Hill (1995), *Too Close to Call* (London: Little, Brown).

Hoskyns, John (2000), *Just in Time: Inside the Thatcher Revolution* (London: Aurum Press).

Hurd, Douglas (2003), *Memoirs* (London: Little, Brown).

Ingham, Bernard (2019), *The Slow Downfall of Margaret Thatcher: The Diaries of Bernard Ingham* (London: Biteback).

James, Simon (1997), *British Government: A Reader in Policy-Making* (London: Routledge).

Jenkins, Simon (2006), *Thatcher & Sons: A Revolution in Three Acts* (London: Allen Lane).

Jones, George (1965), 'The Prime Minister's Power', *Parliamentary Affairs* 18(2), 167–85.

Jones, Nicholas (2001), *The Control Freaks: How New Labour Gets its Own Way* (London: Politico's).

Kampfner, John (2004), *Blair's Wars* (London: Simon & Schuster).

King, Anthony (ed.) (1985), *The British Prime Minister*, 2nd edn (Houndmills: Macmillan).

King, Anthony, and Ivor Crewe (2013), *The Blunders of our Governments* (London: Oneworld).

King, Oona (2007), *House Music: The Oona King Diaries* (London: Bloomsbury).

Lamont, Norman (1999), *In Office* (London: Little, Brown).

Laski, Harold (1938), *Parliamentary Government in England: A Commentary* (London: Allen & Unwin).

Laws, David (2016), *Coalition: The Inside Story of the Conservative–Liberal Democrat Coalition Government* (London: Biteback).

Laws, David (2017), *Coalition Diaries, 2012–2015* (London: Biteback).

Lawson, Nigel (1992), *The View from No. 11: Memoirs of a Tory Radical* (London: Bantam).

Lee, Simon (2009), *Boom and Bust: The Politics & Legacy of Gordon Brown* (London: Oneworld).

Mackintosh, John (1962), *The British Cabinet* (London: Stevens & Sons).

Major, John (1999), *The Autobiography* (London: HarperCollins).

Marsh, David, David Richards and Martin Smith (2000), 'Re-assessing the Role of Departmental Cabinet Ministers', *Public Administration* 8(2), 305–26.

Moore, Charles (2016), *Margaret Thatcher, The Authorized Biography, Volume Two: Everything She Wants* (London: Allen Lane).

Moore, Charles (2019), *Margaret Thatcher, The Authorized Biography, Volume Three: Herself Alone* (London: Allen Lane).

Nott, John (2002), *Here Today, Gone Tomorrow: Memoirs of an Errant Politician* (London: Politico's).

Oborne, Peter (2007), *The Triumph of the Political Class* (London: Simon & Schuster).

Oliver, Craig (2016), *Unleashing Demons: The Inside Story of Brexit* (London: Hodder & Stoughton).

Peston, Robert (2005), *Brown's Britain: How Gordon Runs the Show* (London: Short Books).

Powell, Enoch (1977), *Joseph Chamberlain* (London: Thames & Hudson).

Price, Lance (2005), *The Spin Doctor's Diary: Inside Number 10 with New Labour* (London: Hodder & Stoughton).

Price, Lance (2010), *Where Power Lies: Prime Ministers v the Media* (London: Simon & Schuster).

Rawnsley, Andrew (2000), *Servants of the People: The Inside Story of New Labour* (London: Penguin).

Rawnsley, Andrew (2010), *The End of the Party: The Rise and Fall of New Labour* (London: Viking).

Renton, Tim (2004), *Chief Whip: The Role, History and Black Arts of Parliamentary Whipping* (London: Politico's).

Rentoul, John (2001), *Tony Blair* (London: Little, Brown).

Rhodes, R. A. W., and Patrick Dunleavy (eds.) (1993), *Prime Minister, Cabinet and Core Executive* (London: Macmillan).

Rhodes, Rod (1994), 'The Hollowing Out of the State: The Changing Nature of the Public Service in Britain', *Political Quarterly* 65(2), 138–51.

Richards, Steve (2019), *The Prime Ministers: Reflections on Leadership from Wilson to May* (London: Atlantic).

Ridley, Nicolas (1991), *My Style of Government: The Thatcher Years* (London: Hutchinson).

Rose, Richard (2001), *The Prime Minister in a Shrinking World* (Cambridge: Polity).

Seldon, Anthony (1997), *Major: A Political Life* (London: Weidenfeld & Nicolson).

Seldon, Anthony (2004), *Blair* (London: Simon & Schuster).

Seldon, Anthony, with Raymond Newell (2019), *May at 10* (London: Biteback).

Seldon, Anthony, and Peter Snowdon (2015), *Cameron at 10: The Inside Story* (London: William Collins).

Shepherd, Robert (1996), *Enoch Powell: A Biography* (London: Hutchinson).

Shipman, Tim (2016), *All Out War: The Full Story of how Brexit Sank Britain's Political Class* (London: Collins).

Shipman, Tim (2017), *Fall Out: A Year of Political Mayhem* (London: Collins).

Short, Clare (2004), *An Honourable Deception? New Labour, Iraq, and the Misuse of Power* (London: Free Press).

Simms, Brendan (2001), *Unfinest Hour: Britain and the Destruction of Bosnia* (London: Allen Lane).

Smith, Martin (1999), *The Core Executive in Britain* (London: Macmillan).

Straw, Jack (2012), *Last Man Standing: Memoirs of a Political Survivor* (London: Macmillan).

Stuart, Mark (2005), *John Smith: A Life* (London: Politico's).

Tebbit, Norman (1988), *Upwardly Mobile: An Autobiography* (London: Weidenfeld & Nicolson).

Thatcher, Margaret (1993), *The Downing Street Years* (London: HarperCollins).

Thorpe, D. R. (2010), *Supermac: The Life of Harold Macmillan* (London: Chatto & Windus).

Timmins, Nicholas (2012), *Never Again: The Story of the Health and Social Care Act 2012* (London: King's Fund).

Wallace, William (1994), 'Foreign Policy', in Dennis Kavanagh and Anthony Seldon (eds.), *The Major Effect* (London: Macmillan).

Walters, Simon (2001), *Tory Wars: The Conservatives in Crisis* (London: Politico's).

Wilson, Harold (1976), *The Governance of Britain* (London: Weidenfeld & Nicolson).

Young, Hugo (2008), *The Hugo Young Papers* (London: Allen Lane).

Index